TO CHANGE THE IMPOSSIBLE WORLD

Central American Women in Struggle and Resistance

IRMA N GUADARRAMA

ISBN: 9798398562378

TO MY SON, MY DAUGHTER, AND MY SISTER, ANNIE

CONTENTS

Acknowledgments

The individuals I am most grateful for are those I met during my field visits to Central American countries. Though I may vaguely remember their faces and names, their wisdom and experiences have left an indelible mark on my entire being. Through conversations ranging from simple to complicated, I learned so much from these individuals, many of whom I developed friendships with.

However, I must also mention my students at the University of Houston, who were the ones to initially open my eyes to the world of Central America, particularly Guatemala, Honduras, and El Salvador. It was through understanding their struggles that I realized my own ignorance about their histories. This realization occurred two decades ago, and since then, I have embarked on a journey of discovery, exploration, and scholarship. This book is a result of that journey.

Introduction

> *To change the world, one has to change the ways*
> *of making the world, that is, the vision of the world and*
> *the practical operations by which groups*
> *are produced and reproduced.*
> *Pierre Bourdieu[1]*

The iconic images of young combatant females fighting alongside their male counterparts in the insurgent armed conflicts of El Salvador, Nicaragua, and Guatemala in Central America, as well as in the Caribbean island of Cuba, are a testament to the intrigue that have compelled researchers to (re)examine the historical currents of gender inequality. During a crucial period of large-scale violence in the second half of the twentieth century, thousands of women joined the guerilla, as combatants and non-combatants, creating the usual sensation and consternation as expected within an unforeseen phenomenon. However, a gendered armed conflict in the Central American countries was particularly unique because the militant roles of the women ran counter to the traditional wife and mother narratives that were deeply entrenched in each of the countries' dominant patriarchal societies. Certainly, women's accomplishments serve to advance the argument that gender equality can be achieved, at least as they've demonstrated in combat fighting and in heated war-room strategizing. But, as commonly noted, there are many stories behind each image; a historical context laden with facts and figures, analysis and perspectives. In the past, historians' depictions of women's roles in response to the call-for-arms were generally consequential or supportive.

However, the recent works of scholars have yielded a vibrant profile of riveting insights on how women created their own space, as individuals and as a social group. Initially motivated by their ardent convictions that substantive changes must be structural in a society marked by blatant inequalities, revolutionary women progressively adopted a unique perspective as protagonists, confronting and calibrating changes in the injustices and gender biases relevant to their lives. The women's stories are key to understanding their experiences, individually and collectively, specifically on how they navigated through a myriad of obstacles and regressions in their relentless pursuit of democracy.

The discussions included in the topics presented in this book brings into focus several questions, among these are the following: 1) During the armed conflicts and post-conflict periods, who were the women in struggle and resistance and what specific roles did they play? 2) Why is it important to recognize their struggles and challenges in the past and present? 3) Why study the women and what can we learn from their stories, or what implications can we draw from their experiences? The first part of this book's title: 'To Change the Impossible World' is a reference to the motivational factors that compelled so many women to join the guerrillas despite the challenges and barriers, and then, to engage in post-conflict reconstruction. Elaborating on the research and analysis broadly encompassing the work in this book underscores the reality of the women's lives. However, the women's contextual voices particularly stand out because of their common sentiments regarding their integral participation in the armed conflicts and related struggles. These women consistently expressed their sheer desire for a better future for themselves, their families, and their countries, specifically, for the children. What sets the women in the resistance apart from other women seeking justice, such as the Western European and North American feminists, is the fact that the women in the armed conflicts were concerned with issues beyond gender equality. The women envisioned their efforts for the greater good of the public, such as the fight for democratic freedoms, the right to live a life of dignity, and freedom of violence rather than solely for individual or collective benefits. In essence, their struggle embraced a far broader vision of equality, reminiscent of the core Enlightenment values of reason and egalitarian beliefs that fueled the dreams of those who sought change and transformation in our world.[2]

An important goal of this book is to critique the narrative of a history biased toward members of disenfranchised social groups of which women play a major role. Education serves our society in unequal terms, and questions remain integral to whether our institutions have adequately addressed the facts and issues concerning the growing numbers of El Salvadorans, Guatemalans, and Nicaraguans living in the United States diaspora, as well others who are seeking asylum through the U.S. and México border.[3] Many educational programs are steadily attempting to address the most prevalent issues, particularly through the action of dialog, centering on new perspectives and inquisitive insights. The selected themes in this book are intended to increase knowledge and awareness of the need to become actively and conscientiously involved in the current affairs of the United States/Central America. Accordingly, readers are encouraged to assume an advocacy role, and to act upon the injustices in whatever ways that they are manifested.

Central America: The Past is the Present and, in the Future

The history of Central America is inextricably connected to the regions north and south, well beyond the borders of the subcontinent's seven countries. Thus, a foundational knowledge of its history is not only a prerequisite to an overall understanding of its past in relation to its present, but it's also an essential component in the ensuing analytical discussions on imagining its future. The historical accounts of the three countries, El Salvador, Guatemala, and Nicaragua, serve to function as the stage for the specific themes and main subjects in the book.

Before the European conquistadors conquered and colonized the Mesoamerican region of the Americas, from northern region of what is today México to the southern area that includes about half of Costa Rica, the population consisted of widely diverse indigenous groups. Scientists and scholars' works have produced voluminous publications about the history, cultures, and languages, an immense undertaking that has brought to light the phenomenal accomplishments of a civilization dating as far back as fifteen thousand years ago.

In 1523, after the fall of the Aztec Empire, the Spanish army led by Pedro de Alvarado began its expansive expedition into the Central American region.

The state of Chiapas in Mexico was included in the Spanish conquest of Guatemala, Honduras, El Salvador, Nicaragua and most of Costa Rica. In 1522, the Spanish explorer, Gil González, traveled from Panama with his cavalry to ascertain his country's conquest of Nicaragua. The Spanish crown governed the entire region from 1609 until 1821 when the newly established state of Central America gained its independence from Spain (as did México). In 1823, Central America seceded from Mexico and became the Federal Republic of Central America. When the countries – Guatemala, Honduras, Nicaragua, and Costa Rica – became autonomous entities in the course of gaining their independence from Mexico in 1838 (and later, El Salvador in 1841), they terminated their collective federation existence after 230 years. It is debatable whether, as a result of their experiences as a long-time federation, they share similar patterns of post-colonial governance, the emergence of an economy established in structural inequality, and social adherence to the accumulation of wealth by an elite segment of the society.

From the outset, each country was rooted in a historical context of pitting the majority poor against the minority wealthy, which was destined to stir the competing factions into a series of revolts, some of major proportions. It's through the lens of history and critique that I analyze the stories, struggles, and achievements of the women in struggle and resistance.

Democracy Under Threat

Recent development in the study of the erosion of democracy in the Américas has engaged social and political experts in the conundrum of gauging the type or degree of authoritarianism concentrated in the Central American countries.[4] Also known as democratic backsliding, the emergence of competitive authoritarianism has prevailed and expanded in true-fashion pattern in El Salvador, Guatemala, and Nicaragua. In assessing the erosion of democracy in Central America (and globally), an image of conflicting centripetal and centrifugal forces is in full view. The centripetal force, the strong and persistent winds of authoritarianism, seems to manipulate its way into maintaining an authoritative-style of governing while the centrifugal force represents a thinly disguised effort in displaying a democratic façade.

While the three countries in discussion have common underlying characteristics that describe how each has contributed to the weakening of democracy, the scholarship of democracy historians underscore the necessity to resist a broad-stroke analysis in the process. A more effective approach is to study the *why* and *how* democracy has been dramatically reduced and how it's woven into the histories of each country. The historical base at the core of this book, then, has the objective of laying out the fertile ground in which democracy has been systematically dismantled.

An important theme conveyed throughout this book is the role of women in promoting democratic ideals, and that their struggles and resistances are representations of actors-at-war against those that aim to strike down the pillars of democracy. As activists/feminists, their visionary actions demonstrate their implicit understanding of democracy. Their collective stories offer us a closer examination that reveal their unflinching fight for justice that is strongly rooted in human dignity and a desire for the well-being of their families and communities. In so many ways, their actions articulate pathways and imaginations toward progressive change that is inherent in our understanding of democracy. The clarity in their vision for democracy is evident in the image of the rooted tree; a tree that has deep, strong, connected roots versus another that has shallow, weak and fractured ones. Certainly, the well-rooted tree aspires to produce the best future for the next generation. Understanding their worlds, visions, perceptions, struggles, and their willful determination is a map of resistance on how to reverse the negative consequences of a slowly dying democracy.

Book Chapters

Chapters One and Two detail and expand upon some of the crucial historical moments in El Salvador's Civil War. The text represents a structural compilation from the archives of research sources in both English and Spanish. The chapters provide the reader with a broad analytical view of the women's experiences within the context of the 12-year war. The feminine perspective takes center stage in various narrative forms, and although some of the texts are translated from the Spanish language, the focus is on maintaining its original, authentic contextual meaning. These stories are strategically crafted to reveal the struggles and the courage of Salvadoran women, and the extent to which they were willing to sacrifice their lives for the sake of the future of their country. The two chapters include information about women's lives throughout the course of the revolution. The data on female combatant and non-combatant guerrilla members reveal the stories of courage, sacrifice, and bravery that are not substantially well-known outside the corresponding academic circles. Indeed, the researchers whose works I cite in this section and throughout the book deserve a sincere acknowledgement and gratitude for their accomplishments.

Chapter Three, "The Winds of War and Change," features the historical context of Guatemala's 36-year Internal Armed Conflict. Although the women's movement made great strides in championing basic rights for women after the 1954 coup, their efforts were eclipsed by the subsequent dictatorship regimes. It should also be noted that during the post-conflict era, the "traditional" women's movement began to collaborate with the indigenous social movement, thus, re-defining the work of a more *inclusive* women's movement in Guatemala. The focus on the Maya Ixil functions as a way to expound upon the consequences of the war, and to establish the context by which to highlight the women's stories included in Chapter Four, "The Change from Within: Maya Women's 'Journey of Hope'." The Guatemalan Armed Conflict inflicted torturous pain and suffering amongst innocent, unarmed civilians, and the Maya women were particularly targeted. Understandably, the details on the horrors of war may be difficult to digest, or disturbing. However, it's an important historical aspect that adds authenticity to the women's stories. Rather than discuss the revolution in comparison to El Salvador, Chapter Four explores the lives of Mayan women for whom tragedy was a near-death experience, and then, through a long, arduous journey, how the women were able to renew their lives in completely different terms.

Chapters Five, "Nicaragua, Our Beautiful Country: From a Liberating Revolution to a Repressive State," chronicles the highlights of the phenomenal story of the country's victorious war against the four-decades long, Somoza dictatorship, and the subsequent tragic consequences that the Nicaraguans are living today. Women played a dominant role as revolutionaries, and in the post-revolution era continued to make considerable advances toward equality. However, their struggles were stymied as quickly as they advanced, and although, their specific actions seem all but defeated, their voices emerge with a resounding declaration that they have yet to declare victory. Chapter Six describes the women's battles in present-day Nicaragua under the dictatorship of Daniel Ortega and his wife and vice-president, Rosario Murillo. The women's narratives serve as a focal point to showcase their work and progress, and to describe the multitude of difficulties they struggle against in the context of a repressive, authoritative government.

Relevant Research Issues

The chapters in this book conform to the usual practice of using research data that consist of a wide-range of information bases compiled and organized to produce specific outcomes. Historical context is in the background but women's stories are in the foreground. The historical content included on each country is selected deliberately to highlight the impact, directly or indirectly, on women's lives. As a whole, the women's stories, then, create the underlying current throughout the book. The fact-finding research undertaken in the preparation of this book was purposely unrestricted; the archival research sources are varied and include interview data, publications such as books and journal articles, as well as newspaper periodicals, and multi-media materials such as documentary videos and films. The digital age tools have been invaluable in providing the means by which to collect data and information in countries where repressive governments have stifled the freedom of the expression. English and Spanish sources are equally represented, if not in quantity then, in quality. Some of the Spanish language material included translations into English, however, in some cases it was necessary to produce my own translations.

One of many challenges in the task of collecting historical, accurate information on the women that participated in the guerrilla is the lack of a single source for the depository of the data. For example, in Nicaragua, a total of guerrilla members, men and women, range from 15,000 to 18,000.[5] However, the Nicaraguan Revolution was a grassroots phenomenon that included the participation of 250,000 to 300,000 civilians.[6] Many sources agreed upon the fact that the number of women in guerrilla increased as the armed conflicts progressed. Post-war or conflict demobilization data collected by external sources such as the United Nations offered yet another view. A general consensus, then, is that women combatants in the Nicaraguan Revolution (FSLN – Sandinista Front of National Liberation) consisted of 25 to 30 percent of the total number, about 5,000 or so. The Salvadoran armed conflict had a slightly lesser amount, about 4,400 or 30 percent of the total (around 15,000), although one of the guerrilla organizations, the ERP – Ejército Revolucionario del Pueblo, had as many as 40 percent female combatants.[7] The Guatemalan armed conflict documents have the most inconsistent data base, perhaps due to the longevity of the war (36 years) and the high attrition rates among the women combatants. Guatemala's united guerrilla, the URNG (Unidad Revolucionaria Nacional Guatemalteca), developed in the early 80s, included four different guerrillas. Of the overall total of around 6,000 participants serving as combatants, approximately 1,440 women or 25 percent served during the 1978-80 period of the war.[8]

Another important research topic is oral history as source of credibility. The women's stories in this volume are genuine and authentic. I relied on first-hand or historically verified sources published by social scientists, such as anthropologists, sociologists, and historians. In addition to the work of scholars in the areas of gender studies, the primary sources came from writers that based their information on personal experiences. Indeed, collecting, analyzing, and interpreting authentic narratives about traumatic events that the subjects personally experienced should be examined with a critical eye and filtered through the contextual lens of unprecedented moments of enormous upheaval. Historian David Carey points out that interviewees' past accounts of events, as difficult and heart-rendering as they were, often attach *meaning* to experience, and that by remembering the events, a process of reconstruction is at play.[9] Thus, their narratives are imbued with some imagination, omissions, and embellishments. There is also the importance of *dignity* in the manner by which the interviewee refused to speak. Or shared only certain parts of their stories because they felt shame, for themselves and their families. *Silence* as a coping strategy was used by women who endured horrendous torture by the state military forces. Thus, in every instance of fact-finding and interpretation, the intent was to use only the most reliable sources and to treat the women's responses with respect and dignity.

The Challenges of Historical Imaginations

Every historical period has its defining moment(s). The women whose stories are featured herein followed their own guiding principles based on specific challenges wrought by a period of peak cold war against a background of centuries-old states of oppression. Historical accounts of women involved in conflict in other contexts and timeframes reveal how circumstance plays a pivotal role in their lives. For example, the political scenario that led to the Spanish Civil War of 1936, with two extremes, opposing positions and several factions in between, created a space for women to embrace an alternative vision of social life based on anarchism. The Mujeres Libres, organized in 1934, fashioned the lives of women as emancipated participants in a society where power relations between men and women were less divergent and more on an even keel. Although the organization's raison d'être was firmly rooted in the women's causes, the members rejected the economic model of the feminist identity expounded upon by their contemporary European counterpart. As author Martha Ackelsberg explains, the Mujeres Libres distinguished themselves from their contemporaries, rejecting the feminist label and by focusing on the establishment of anarchist reform strategies that specifically address the poor, disenfranchised women.[9]

In another example, the Cuban women who joined the military during the country's revolutionary war (1956-58), were personally ushered into the force by Fidel Castro. Castro availed himself of their popular involvement and utilized the army's resources to demonstrate what some may argue, a propagandistic display of the revolution's support for women. Indeed, the Cuban military afforded women in the Mariana Grajales Women's Platoon and other similar units, the opportunities to prove their combat and military tactical skills, thereby scaling the hierarchy to become integral associates of Cuba's prized armed forces.[11] However, the majority of women for whom emancipation meant equal rights for their social group beyond the illuminating roles in the military were unable to successfully develop a feminist agenda outside the parameters of the (restrictive) socialist government. As in the cases of the female combatants in the armed conflicts in Central America, Cuban women played an essential role in the revolutionary process from its initial phases. But despite their efforts, the feminists' or women's rights advocates' working agenda became an arduous task that evolved into an on-going process despite the revolution's rhetoric that consistently pushed the vision that both women and men could be liberated on equal footing.[12]

As illustrated in the abovementioned examples of the Spanish Civil War and the Cuban Revolution, historiographies with feminist themes rely on relevant theory and analytical tools to examine critical questions. Importantly, the historical facts juxtaposed against the periphery and center of the thematic strands of feminism bring into the discussion the focus on the rich, contextual meanings of each topic. Thus, the historical content in this book, laden with facts of detailed historical importance, has the objective of providing the reader with the broad contextual base that is necessary to create a fullness of understanding to the extent possible. Noteworthy is the acknowledgement of intersectionality in its role in identifying feminist struggles where women's voices are intricately combined with what they perceive as the social, economic, cultural, and political factors; where their voices of resistance are situated within powerful misogynist institutions in which centuries-old predatory cultures have systematically continued to silence them.[13]

The historical content and analysis in each of the chapters on El Salvador, Guatemala, and Nicaragua are examined within a broad and diverse feminist theoretical scope. Imbedded in the women's stories of experiences that include repression, torture, violence, and death are connections with heteropatriarchy, the ultimate masculine domination and its toxic reiterations. Women who suffered sexual violence were victims of this toxic hypermasculinity adopted by predators that conform to a society that emboldens males to aggressively assault women based on the illusion of superiority. Questions that emerge from these factual provocations point to a line of inquiry, such as, who were the women? (a well-described portrait); Where are they? (location includes geographic and physical descriptions, date and time); What is the political, social, cultural, economic context? (as individuals and as part of a group or collective); What are the details of the event(s)? (specific to the actual events, all with what happened before and after); What were the consequences? (as a result of the event or incident what happened to the women).

To Change the Impossible World is a historical account of conflict, strife and change in three Central American countries, and by foregrounding the struggles and resistance of women the reader invariably becomes a participant in the process of examining the genealogy of power for which women have been particularly impacted. Specific theoretical underpinnings on power and knowledge expounded by French philosopher, Michel Foucault, have served to substantiate the claims by feminist who persistently seek to document how male dominated power has systematically led to negative consequences for women. Foucauldian feminism inherently accepts the genealogical approach that identifies and describes in ascending order the power bases of domination, linking or connecting variables that reveal different modes of re-analysis.[14] When applied in a historical context, the genealogical analysis aims to yield insight into how the mechanisms of power are reproduced through domination and privilege, as well as in extended and multiplied forms, thereby creating interconnections. An important task in understanding the manifestations of power is identifying and separating the interlocking components and following their footprints from their points of inception. Thus, historical narratives of the kind presented in this book serve the purpose of facilitating in this process, and in determining how resistance coexists with power. According to Foucauldian feminists, the act(s) of resistance is not radical or revolutionary, rather a continuum of strategic acts that represent possibilities for eventual change.[15]

In present-day Guatemala, El Salvador, and Nicaragua, women exercise diverse forms of feminisms where representations of multiple subjectivities exist.[16] Women utilize the concept of "difference" as a tool to strengthen their acts of resistance, whether as a collective or as individuals.

The study of history offers social scientists the tools by which to understand and interpret events at different points of time. A comprehensive historical view is prerequisite to developing crucial perspectives that facilitate our understanding of the change process and its implications for solving current and future problems. However, a framework for the study of historical events that have transpired within periods of enormous instability, complexity, and chaos presents unique and difficult challenges, even in light of the extraordinary efforts by scholars and activists alike.

Recent emergent thought on the methodological frameworks in the social science research fields includes scholarship focused on an interdisciplinarity approach. In his theoretical interpretation of the sociolinguistics of superdiversity, Jan Blommaert explains that *complexity* is at the core of superdiversity. This includes a construct of "superdiverse spaces," which consist of dynamic interplays. Therefore, methodological tools compatible with superdiversity are best utilized to question the underlying assumptions about how societies function and change at the micro and macro-levels.[17] The mixed methodology toolkit includes essential deep and slow ethnographic immersion that examines the different points of a polycentric center and its ever-changing composition. The results of this approach would defy a singular, linear conclusion.[18] Instead, the outcome is likely to yield a landscape of simultaneous occurrences consisting of an array of unique and varied histories of people, places, and their activities. Thus, by applying notions of Blommaert's research methodology, a close examination of the historical narratives presented in this book would produce multiple and layered "chronicles of complexity." These chronicles would consist of observable patterns that can be readily explained, as well as features or structures with underlying unpredictability and/or instability.[19] This type of investigation creates an urgency to view the present with a critical eye on the past, and to ask relevant questions about what is actually happening now. It recognizes the present as a moment-in-history within a context that is complex and chaotic. The challenge is not only to discover the truth in plain sight but to observe and document the data that are invisible and/or buried within. Although social scientists may follow an academic protocol, activists/feminists may adopt a perspective that is more suitable for the task at hand. Instead of asking a formatted question such as *"Is the world so impossible that it cannot be changed?"*, they may be more inclined to act deliberately and confidently *to change the world, one way or another.*

Chapter One

Women, the Heart and Soul of the Civil War

> *First let me tell you, a woman is never more equal*
> *to a man than behind a .45 pistol.*
> Re-quoted in Jane S. Jaquette,
> "Women in Revolutionary Movements
> in Latin America"[1]

El Salvador experienced a dark period of history when two factions, the FMLN guerrilla (Farabundo Martí Front for National Liberation) and the Salvadoran military, engaged in a brutal combat for twelve years (1980-1992). The civil war caused widespread devastation in a country already struggling with a debilitating economy, resulting in the loss of approximately 75,000 civilian lives and tens of thousands of soldiers. The UN report of the Commission on the Truth for El Salvador, "From Madness to Hope: The 12-Year War in El Salvador," describes some of the cases of brutal repression and suffering that occurred during the conflict. The data presented in the report are a testament to the most horrendous and unspeakable tragedies: 22,000 human rights violations were documented with 60 percent of them being extrajudicial killings, 25 percent disappearances, 20 percent were torture. Approximately 85 percent of civilian killings were attributed to state agents such as the military and death squads, while the FMLN was responsible for 5 percent. Furthermore, the war in El Salvador resulted in the displacement of approximately one million people, many of whom were survivors of massacres similar to the scorched earth tactics employed by the Guatemalan military during the genocidal era of the late 70s and early 80s.[2]

The El Salvador Armed Conflict, the 36-year Internal Armed Conflict in Guatemala (1960-1996), and the Nicaraguan Revolution (1978-79), collectively resulted in a regional catastrophe of war following the Cuban

Revolution (1953-59). While both the Cuban and the Nicaraguan wars meet the criteria as transformative revolutions, Nicaragua's success was cut short by the outbreak of the Contra War (1981-1990).[3] The armed conflicts in Guatemala and El Salvador came to an end in a dismal manner, which prevented them from negotiating in a truly revolutionary fashion. This was a time of upheaval when other regions of Latin America were also plagued by violent conflicts that resulted in the deaths of thousands of civilians, and countless numbers of extreme cases of human rights violations.[4]

The United States' Dominant Role

One of the most notable and well-researched aspects of these violent conflicts is the significant influence exerted by the United States, which is recognized as the world's most powerful military force. From the presidency of Dwight Eisenhower (1953-1961) through Ronald Reagan (1981-1989), the United States played a dominant role in Central America as the primary defense against the perceived threat of the Soviet Union as a nuclear power. Out of fear that the "rebel" forces were aligned with the "communist bloc" during the Cold War, the United States provided significant support to strengthen the military capabilities of the state governments. This effectively prevented the guerrillas from gaining power. Following Nicaragua's victory in 1979, the United States continued to support the anti-Sandinista Contras in their efforts to regain control of the government. Each of the three state governments – El Salvador, Guatemala, and Nicaragua – possessed a vast arsenal of superior-grade military equipment for ground, naval, and air assaults. The military aid provided to these governments during the periods of armed conflict amounted to billions of dollars, an extraordinary sum, particularly during the Reagan presidency. The cost of combating the insurgency included funding for counterinsurgency efforts in each country, the militarization of Honduras, and the support for maintaining the state repression. The overwhelming support highlighted the interventionist role of the United States and greatly contributed to the state governments' ability to counter attack the insurgencies, resulting in the staggering death toll among guerrilla combatants and non-combatant civilians.[5]

Forty years later, the remnants of war remain deeply ingrained in Salvadoran society. Social and economic problems related to inequality continue to hinder efforts to improve the quality of life for the majority of people. If history serves to develop an understanding of how events shaped the outcomes, then, in the case of El Salvador as a starting point, it is the period during which people's collective memories played a significant role in deciding their future.

The 1970s, the Pivotal Years

In the early 1970s, Chinda (Gumercinda "Chinda" Zamora), a middle-aged woman, married and mother of nine children, worked as a labor union organizer and midwife in the areas around the rural communities of La Ceiba and Las Vueltas. She relates her story about one of her encounters with a National Guard soldier to Joaquín Chávez, author of the book, *Poets and Prophets of the Resistance.*[6] At the time, Chinda was on the "blacklist" as a dangerous militant because of her work with the labor union. The Guard was stationed throughout the neighboring areas, on orders to conduct surveillance and threaten residents, and if the soldiers deemed necessary, they would detain, torture and even execute those that were suspected of being radicals or subversives. Chinda lived in a secluded area in the mountain to escape persecution but would return to the villages at night. Chinda used her midwife identity to disguise her labor union activities. On her walk home one night, she was stopped by Guardsman who proceeded to interrogate her – what was her business and why was she walking so late at night? Chinda opened up her secretive bag full of herbs and ointments and explained that she was on duty as a midwife. The Guardsman seemed satisfied and then asked her if she knew a woman by the name of Chinda Zamora. Chinda replied that she did know the woman, but she hadn't seen her lately. Chinda was able to avoid capture this time, however, she was eventually arrested and imprisoned a few years later.

Chinda was by the state's standards a very dangerous woman. She was one of the three lead organizers behind the *Union Trabajadores Campesinos (UTC)* in Chalatenango, a department or province in northeastern El

Salvador, along with Facundo Guardado, José Santos Martínez, and Justo Mejía. Their efforts led to an unprecedented peasant movement whose militant members engaged in all aspects of the revolutionary efforts. Chinda stood beside the powerful union members, and eventually the entire union joined the major armed organization, the FMLN – Farabundo Martí National Liberation.

Revolts, Electoral Fraud, and Coup d'état Waves

As a young girl, Chinda lived in and around the rural communities of La Ceiba and Las Vueltas, which are located in a region covered with rolling hills amid the two summits of Cerro Picacho and Cerro El Infiernillo. This area is known as the volcano corridor of the Chalatenango province. Families subsisted in planting and harvesting corn, beans, and sorghum, and cash crops such as coffee and sugar. In 1931, the U.S. Great Depression impacted the coffee industry, and the consequences were devastating for families like Chinda's. Her parents were contemporaries of Agustín Farabundo Martí, the labor union leader whose reputation for his rebellious and tenaciousness had won over the support of thousands of campesinos. The rallying cry among the peasants was the same then as it was during Chinda's leadership with the UTC labor union. Far from being extravagant or unreasonable, the demands were basic like decent wages and working conditions, and use of vacated land, all necessary for sustaining a meager subsistence. However, after sixty years since the inception of the Central American Congress of Workers organization in 1911, and the perseverance of leaders such as Martí and others, Chinda's labor union demands become more radical and astute. They called for the restructuring of the capitalist society, politics, and political economy. They demanded justice including higher living wages, improved working conditions, access to clean water, and an end to the abuses perpetrated by landowners.

Martí's rebelliousness and courage were etched in the memory book of Chinda's family and friends. An entire generation came to know Martí as a folk hero, the legendary leader that represented the hearts and minds of struggling, hard-working peasants that for the first time began to consider a revolution. However, before Martí there was Anastasio Aquino, in 1832, who had led a year-long revolt with 3,000 campesinos in protest against gross injustices committed against mostly indigenous farmers. Aquino's status as a cacique offered him an unprecedented voice among the powerful elite and wealthy oligarchs who took advantage of the hard-working peasanty to further their wealth and prestige. The existence of slavery to which indigenous people had been relegated since colonial times was further exacerbated by the usurpation of the ancestral lands, which left poor peasants landless. The wealthy oligarchs, who owned of the indigo monocrop economy, justified their actions by falsely claiming that their profits were used for the betterment of the entire country. The vast profits were used to fund infrastructure projects, but these were solely for personal gain, with no consideration for the welfare of the Salvadoran people. The rebellion culminated in the capture and execution of Aquino, who was brutally killed as a warning to other rebels who dared to speak out. Like Martí, Aquino was considered a hero, and Chinda's parents and grandparents recall his bravery as one of their leaders. His violent death by decapitation symbolized a fight to the bitter end, a true revolutionary spirit.

Agustín (or Augustín in English) Farabundo Martí was born in 1893. Despite living in a community of hard-working, impoverished campesinos, his family was relatively better off due to his father's status as a moderate landowner. Interestingly, Martí's father had adopted the surname of Martí from Cuba's renowned writer and one of the founders of the communist party, José Julián Martí Pérez. Farabundo Martí, nicknamed "el negro," attended university before expelled due to legal issues. He gained valuable insights into the struggles of exploited campesinos by living and working among peasants and obreros in México and Guatemala. Upon returning to El Salvador, he became a labor union organizer. In 1928, then-President Quiñones Molina recognized Martí's activism and exiled him to Nicaragua. During his year in Nicaragua, Martí collaborated with Augusto César Sandino, whom he had previously met in México during the insurgency efforts to overthrow the powerful, U.S.-backed conservative faction of the Nicaraguan government. Martí was a committed Marxist and leader of the Socorro Rojo Internacional, while Sandino, who was two years his senior, was primarily focused on nationalist ideals. Both men dedicated their lives to fighting for the rights and freedoms of the working poor, and their names became synonymous with heroism and hope.[7] The leaders of the Salvadoran and Nicaraguan revolutions named their guerrilla organizations, respectively, the Farabundo Martí Front for Liberation (FMLN) and the Sandinista Front of National Liberation (FSLN), respectively, as a way to honor their heroes, and popularize their movement of armed insurgence.

'*La matanza*,' which translates to "the killing," refers to the mass assassinations of thousands of individuals labeled as "communists" on January 22, 1932, by the state military. However, in reality, the victims were mostly poorly armed peasants and university students who were protesting as part of a campaign to institute labor reform. Martí was not part of the group because he had been captured several days before the uprisings and was unable to send a communiqué to the protestors to inform them of the military's intentions. The protestors were gunned down with machine guns, and not just them, entire towns were targeted as well. The most destructive and incisive massacres occurred in El Canelo and Nahuilzalco. The operation aimed to annihilate "communists," but less than 10 percent of those killed were actually participating in the communist party.[8] Extrajudicial executions continued for weeks, and Martí was assassinated on February 1st. The official count of deaths is unknown, mostly because the crime was so despicable, and the military and the wealthy elite scrambled to hide the truth. Some historians claim that at least 12,000 people were killed, others estimate that 40,000 lost their lives.[9]

The events that occurred before, during and after the "matanza" are well-documented history due to the tragic nature of the events and their long-term consequences. A year before the "matanza," President Romero's successor, Arturo Araujo was inaugurated, and General Maximiliano Hernández Martínez was his Vice President. Araujo, a wealthy landowner, aimed to govern with an equipoise between the working class and the wealthy elite, but the oligarchy insisted on their own hierarchical governance. Araujo's selection of General Martínez as VP was a strategy to assuage their discontent. Within nine months, the oligarchy's support for the military grew exponentially, leading to the eventual ousting of President Araujo, and VP General Martínez took control of the government. The coup d'état was cautiously accepted by Martí and the organized protestors and supporters, but with a military official at the helm, they realized that their demands would never be heard. President Martínez proclaimed that "free elections" would take place in early January (1932), but his deception became obvious when he refused to certify the winners of the elections of the Communist Party of El Salvador (PCS) candidates. There was little doubt that the military and the wealthy elite had formed an unbreakable bond of power after the "matanza."

The tragic events of 1932 marked a compelling chapter in a history marred by extreme violence. At that point in history, revolution was not a viable solution for people struggling to feed their families, but signs indicated massive revolt was imminent. First, despite their differences, the military and the wealthy oligarchs recognized their inimitable strength when they combined forces against their common "enemy." Their actions led to an incremental state of authoritative, fascist rule. There were eight coup d'états within a five-decade period (1931-1980). Coups became the military's instrument of choice to install new leadership that matched their power and dominance. Salvadoran voters became increasingly frustrated with frequent election fraud.[10] Secondly, killing unarmed, innocent civilians was of no consequence to either the military or the wealthy elite. The massacres were intentionally planned to "cast a wide net" in order to kill a few guerrilla fighters, and "scorched earth" tactics were meant to unabashedly increase the deaths of civilians for their own distorted purposes. Thirdly, the cumulative effect of the massacres could arguably be described as genocidal.[11] The military excessively extended its destructive maneuvers to entire indigenous communities, resulting not only in catastrophic deaths but also in creating a culture of fear and silence among the survivors. The emotional pain and trauma were a constant part of the victims' suffering, and erasing the memories also meant reshaping native identity, language, and customs. The 1932 "matanza" triggered a hatred for "everything indigenous," and the systemic racism had the effect of slowly but eventually causing the death of language and culture. As in most cases of cultural contact, there is arguably a certain amount of endogenous language loss and a decline in the use of customs among indigenous people. However, it is well-known among social scientists and linguists that the intended eradication of language and culture is a tragic consequence of colonialization.[12] Additionally, the appalling horror and affliction wrought by the "matanza" had a collective impact on the Nahuat-speakers, and what linguist call "language death" clearly exemplifies what happened to their language and culture.[13] Moreover, in the intent to "kill off the Indians," the perpetrators opened up pathways to planting the seeds for a revolution. The immense and extreme poverty, persistent exploitation of the workers, huge economic gap between the oligarchs who lived in luxury, and the peasantry that struggled every day and demanded nothing more than the opportunity to live a dignified life created the perfect storm for a call to action. The accumulation of factors had an effect on the fomentation of a major rebellion that ultimately led to the *revolution*.[14]

***

I was a woman who was never afraid, a quote from Gumercinda "Chinda" Zamora.[15] Chinda learned not to be afraid. Throughout her life she witnessed the brutal killings and mutilations of so many innocent people. Her clandestine lifestyle was due to the military repression that had steadily increased since the "matanza" forty years ago. In the summer of 1974, an organized group of peasants rebelled against the government's refusal to support their negotiations for leasing land to cultivate corn and beans. This rebellion, known as the first *La Cayetana Massacre*, resulted in the group's leader being shot and killed by the soldiers. Four months later, National Guardsmen descended on the small town of La Cayetana in the San Vicente Department and began killing the unarmed civilians. The guardsmen captured the group behind the land occupation protest and corralled each member into a local church. The guardsmen proceeded to torture the men ordering them to lie down, face down and naked while the soldiers stomped on their backs. Six laborers were shot dead and their mutilated corpses were scattered in the streets. The *Cayetano Massacre* sent shock waves throughout the labor organizing community because it was the first massacre that

21

involved an entire community.[16] Now, more than ever, the solidarity amongst campesinos was strengthened, and by joining the UTC (Union de Trabajadores Campesinos) they recognized their strength in numbers.

Chinda suffered a profound and tragic loss when her dear friend, co-founder of the UTC, and brother-in-law, Justo Mejía was brutally tortured and assassinated on November 9, 1977. Mejía was captured by the paramilitaries in San Fernando, near Chalatenango. The torture he endured was an inexplicable horror; he was badly beaten, and his eyes were gouged and bleeding. The men forced him to walk until he collapsed and died. As they buried his body, they falsely accused him of being a thief in front of the crowd of onlookers. Two weeks later his body was exhumed and prepared for a proper funeral in his hometown of La Ceiba. Thousands of people, including families, friends, acquaintances, and activists from Chalatenango and beyond, attended the funeral to offer their respects, and to honor the man who was best known as a caring, dedicated teacher. Chinda remembers him in this remark: "He was such a helpful [colaborativo] and wise [alcanzativo] man. Nobody told him what to do. He knew the work that needed to be done. He came to my house often and said, I have a task [una tarea]. God willing, we will be able to complete it."[17] Eight months later, in August, 1978, the paramilitaries led another massacre in the area, known as *La Ceiba Massacre*, which resulted in the killings of six children and two women, all relatives of Justo Mejía.

The Paramilitary's Evolving Role

By the end of the 1970s, the Salvadorans felt the extreme intensity of the repression. The paramilitaries had increased in size and their brutality was overwhelming. Chinda lived among communities where families were torn apart due to their allegiances to either the state paramilitary or the revolution. Up to 150,000 campesinos joined the Nationalist Democratic Organization (ORDEN), the military's rural component of El Salvador's counterinsurgency unit. These individuals were provided with US-made military uniforms and equipment, including automatic rifles, and their training was based on guerrilla warfare imported from the Green Berets.

These tactics were known for their extreme measures to eliminate individuals labeled as dangerous and armed communists.

The ALPRO and the Salvadoran Security Forces

ORDEN, a significant paramilitary unit, was established in 1963 under the leadership of General Médrano, who was in charge of the National Guard and the Armed Forces High Command.[18] The United States provided special funding for this unit as part of the Alliance for Progress (ALPRO), a regional initiative launched by the Kennedy administration to counter the Soviet Union during the Cold War. El Salvador received substantial funding aid from the US, which was intended for modernizing and restructuring the economy, as well as for implementing labor and education reforms.[19] However, the ALPRO support also included the development of a counterinsurgency apparatus as a contingency, which the military/oligarch government of El Salvador used to create a US-style, world class military institution. The United States State Department, including the CIA, had a direct influence on its development by providing specialized training, military equipment, and funds to maintain its operations. It was part of the Salvadoran Armed Forces, a complex, broad network of military units and intelligence agencies. The intelligence branch was the Salvadoran National Agency (ANSESAL), which collected personal data on individuals deemed as subversive or blacklisted as communist leaders. The Security Forces included the National Guard, Treasury Police, National Police, and the Customs Police, which carried out the abductions, tortures, and assassinations. Initially, these actions were carried out with cautious deliberation, but eventually they evolved into the infamous "death squads."[20]

The death squads' murderous activities were sustained largely by the wealthy oligarch families and military personnel, representing the extreme far-right political faction. Their targets varied, but they clearly sought to eliminate the nascent leadership amongst the religious and lay members of organizations such as the Christian Based Communities.[21] With every tool of warfare at their disposal, and together with guerrilla warfare battalions such as Atlacatl, the death squad machine committed the most brutal, heinous, and extreme violence against non-combatant civilians and entire communities and towns.[22] The Salvadoran government failed to implement the agrarian, labor, and education reforms as declared and agreed upon by the ALPRO. Even more concerning is the fact that death squads continued to terrorize Salvadorans after the Peace Accords of 1992. Their targets expanded to include gang members, without substantial evidence of crimes committed; some were killed as part of a "social cleansing" mission.[23]

The question remains on why the Salvadoran government agreed to the ALPRO terms. Was their primary intent to benefit from the United States' generous support and funding, while denying culpability or responsibility for any wrongdoing?

Guerrilla Organizations and the Farabundo Martí Front for National Liberation (FMNL)

As Chinda and other UTC leaders worked indefatigably as organizers in Chalatenango, guerrilla groups began to emerge in response to the intense military repression. Salvador Cayetano Carpio, a former communist party leader, studied "the revolution" in the Soviet Union for a couple of years and later, in 1970, founded the Popular Forces of Liberation (FPL). The FPL guerrilla eventually recruited 1,500 to 2,000 troops, and enjoyed the support of tens of thousands of campesinos in the Chalatenango Department.[24] Carpio, also known by his nom de guerre, Marcial, believed in the North Vietnam revolutionary model of a prolonged war with camp bases established in the guerrillas' mountainous strongholds, while other guerrilla organizations preferred the alliance with the Cuban revolution (1953-1959).[25] Between 1979 and 1981, during a crucial moment of dire need and in order to counter the forceful and powerful attacks by the US-backed Salvadoran forces, the Farabundo Martí Front for National Liberation (FMNL), established an alliance with the Democratic Revolutionary Front (FDR), the umbrella of a broad network of organizations, as well as Cuba, the Nicaraguan Sandinistas, and México. The FMLN also harnessed the support of the European community. The integration of the existing five guerrilla organizations into the FMLN completed the consolidation process.

On January 10, 1981, the FMNL-FDR launched its initial offense from its military stronghold in the Department of Chalatenango. The five guerrilla organizations united in solidarity were: The Popular Forces of Liberation (FPL), Revolutionary Popular Army (ERP), Salvadoran Communist Party (PCS), National Resistance (RN), and Party of the Salvadoran Revolution (PRTC).[26]

Chinda was among the thousands who believed in revolutionary change. And, although Chinda did not use any armed weapons, she was nevertheless arrested, detained and interrogated by the security forces for alleged subversive behavior. However, the next generation of women took bolder steps in their participation as revolutionaries.

The Genesis of the Gendered Guerrilla Movement

As early as 1962, a few Salvadoran women were integrated into the "feminine column" of the guerrilla organization, the United Front of Revolutionary Action (FUAR), coordinated by Schafik Handal and Castellanos Figueroa.[27] FUAR was the first of its kind to promote an armed revolution after the 1932 massacre. From 1951 to 1964, the leadership of the Salvadoran Communist Party created networks in the rural communities that worked in harvesting coffee in the western regions, and in the cotton plantations in the eastern region. However, when the campesinos attempted to set up unions, their efforts were swiftly deterred by paramilitary troops. As a result, many chose to join FUAR, which generated a couple of thousand followers within a two-year period However, the leadership was split over whether the group should take up an armed insurrection. Marcial (Carpio) criticized the leaders for creating a scenario that he claimed would fail because a revolution requires much more than one guerrilla organization.[28] FUAR did not evolve as the leaders planned, but the decision to grow a revolution from the New Left had planted the seeds of determination.

At the heart of the Salvadoran Civil War, was the phenomenal social movement that brought together thousands of people from almost every corner of the country. Shayne's assertion that "revolutions are made successfully by social movements above and beyond the parameters of guerrilla movements" sheds light on what the research findings have established.[29] Indeed, the long-standing, dire deficiencies in the social and economic conditions in a country governed by the super wealthy and a military obsessed with power created a ripe revolutionary climate, where just about anyone could become motivated to participate. The leaders that emerged from the New Left movement were profoundly critical of the injustices perpetrated against the campesino families that consistently experienced land insecurity and the essential basics for a dignified life. The economic hardships pushed some women to urban migration, especially single women with children. The new leaders rejected the constant lies of politicians that mostly represented the wealthy elite and the military bourgeoisie, and the numerous electoral frauds, and the utter absence of basic democratic freedoms. As the gut-wrenching war dragged on for years and with brutal intensity, the calamitous killings of thousands of innocent people deeply everyone. While the communist ideals of Marxism and Leninism initially formed the guerrilla organization framework, the ideas and thoughts emanating from internal consciousness-raising processes eventually gave way to the transformed people's revolution.

Student Activism and University Reform

Many student activists that turned insurrectionists, became actively involved through the University of Salvador (UES), the country's national (public) institution. Following the 1918 reforms at the University of Cordoba in Argentina, many Latin American universities, including those in Central America, sought to follow a similar path of democratization of the academic curriculum, essentially creating an autonomous university. In 1963, the UES's rector, Fabio Castillo, a proponent of educational reform who later served as Minister of Education in 1976, administered a four-year plan that included the substantial improvements of the quality of the university curriculum. As a result, the student enrollment increased exponentially, with the added availability of scholarships for students who needed them.[30] The 1960s era of reform was a unique moment in the university's history.

Thousands of students, many of whom would not have had the opportunity to attend, were not only learning about democratic ideals, but practicing democracy within their autonomous learning environment. However, within a decade, the Salvadoran government's repressive and indifferent nature led to a brutal retaliation, which ultimately overturned many of the university's democratic advances.

The October 1960 (Double) Coup d'Etat

Following the overthrow of President Lemus in a coup d'état in October 1960, the Governmental Civic-Military Junta used its transitional power to pre-establish conditions for the next government. Among the proposed guidelines were the renewed emphasis on the democratic process of holding free and completely open elections, as well as the development of a stronger social program aimed at suppressing illiteracy and raising educational levels of all students. The aforementioned ideals, along with others of similar nature, were immediately met with skepticism by the military leaders. They perceived the presence of civilians, such as Fabio Castillo, a Cuban Revolution supporter, among the junta members as a threat.[31] As predicted, in just three months (by year's end in 1960), the military officers in San Salvador staged a revolt that resulted in the removal of the current junta and the installation of a military junta led by Col. Rivera. The assertion was that a military intervention was necessary to maintain a control of communists and supporters of the Cuban revolution. The rhetoric was clearly aimed at bolstering their defenses out of self-interest, while also maintaining an alliance with the United States.

A Groundswell of Support

In November 1960, against the background of the military revolt led by Col. Rivera and the junta, a new political party emerged. This party was closely associated with Catholic Action, an international movement that advocated for "Social Christianity." The Christian Democratic Party (PDC), known as the Partido Democrático Cristiano, was founded by three broad groups. The first group consisted of Salvadoran students who were part of the

University's Catholic Action branch, known as the Acción Católico Universidad or ACUS. The second group was made up of Catholic intellectuals who had distanced themselves from the "old conservative guard" of the Catholic Church. Finally, the Confederation of Latin American Christian Trade Unions (CLASC) formed the third group.[32] The Catholic Action movement represented a radically unique, positive and progressive vision of a social reality that differed from the dominant conservativism espoused by the Catholic Church for decades. The Christian Democratic Party's broadly-based composition of students, Catholic intellectuals, priests, teachers, and middle-class non-communist populace posed a threat to the military and the wealthy elite, as well to members of the Communist Party (PCS). As a major political party, the PDC accomplished the remarkable feat of creating an inclusive appeal that was rarely seen in the country's history. Students that adhered to the Catholic Action principles actively engaged in the PDC to promote an agenda for *a nonviolent social revolution in El Salvador.*

In 1972, the Christian Democratic Party (PDC) joined forces with two other political parties (MNR and UDN) to support José Napoleón Duarte, a popular San Salvador mayor in his bid for president. Following the election, a fiery argument erupted over the counting of votes. Despite Duarte and his opponent, the right-wing favorite, Col. Molina, both claiming victory, the National Assembly ruled that they would take charge of the election. However, despite Col. Molina being declared the winner by the Assembly, a revolt ensued led by a group of rebel soldiers led by Col. Mejía broke out two days later. Col. Mejía claimed a short-lived victory by declaring that the San Salvador capitol city's military guard was supporting him. In fact, he grossly miscalculated the aggression by the Salvadoran government's military force. Following a violent battle, Col. Mejía ultimately abandoned the coup d'état, and Duarte was exiled, as were Mejía and his collaborators.[33]

The 'New Left' Student Movement of the 1960s

The Salvadoran president, Col. Molina, targeted the University of El Salvador (UES), claiming the students were Marxist and as such, revolutionary and subversive. However, what Molina interpreted as subversive rebellion was actually a part of the New Left movement led by students worldwide. They were protesting in solidarity with each other and calling for revolutionary reforms. During the1960's, the era of television and radio, the New Left student movements created repetitive shock waves as people watched and listened to the violent confrontations between police and student protesters in México, Spain, North Vietnam, and France. Student activists in Latin American countries such as Chile, Uruguay, and Brazil brazenly touted their New Left revolutionary rebellion. The Salvadoran university student activists were enrolled in a specific degree program known as General Studies, which allowed them to form a cohesive group with common views about the New Left and a revolution.[34]

President Molina responded to the students' activism in the typical repressive manner, which caused dismay and horror among the student body. He ordered government troops into the university campus to control all student protests. After a year, the troops were finally withdrawn. However, two years later, in September 1975, more than 2,000 UES students marched peacefully from the university to the downtown Plaza Libertad. They were met with military-style gunfire by the National Guard, resulting in the deaths of thirty-seven students and the disappearance of dozens more.[35] The UES students were specifically protesting the government's decision to spend an exorbitant amount (30 million USD) on hosting the Miss Universe Pageant. However, as a result of the massacre, discussions about the initial reasons for the protest faded, and more and more student voices clamored for an armed insurrection.[36]

Both Col. Molina's fraudulent election and crackdown on university students served as fuel for activism that quickly escalated towards an armed insurrection. The unintended radicalization of students had severe consequences, as the Salvadoran government responded with even more repressive and deadly tactics.

***

Radicalization in the Rural Community Schools: A Collective Vision

In rural towns and communities, the Archdiocese of San Salvador sponsored the *Escuelas Radiofónicas* (1960s - 1970s)*,* a grassroots educational network of volunteer teachers/community leaders that taught daily literacy classes to adults. The attendees, called "radio students" were taught daily classes while specialized subject teachers taught the primary children. During the same period, the Salvadoran Catholic Church developed "Peasant Universities," or "Centers for the Promotion of Peasants," with the aim of graduating hundreds of students from nine rural areas. For example, in Chalatenango, from 1967 to 1977, a total of 15,000 students had attended. The proliferation of grassroots networks led to the emergence of numerous social organizations, providing people with access to education. For many, this was their first experience in a classroom. A collective vision had taken root, with education seen as the key to effecting greater societal change, a belief that the populace readily embraced. This quote, by the priest, Martin Barahona, in charge of a school in Chalatenango, expresses the popular sentiment: "There will never be a deep change in the country's structure until we devote ourselves to educate in all aspects our men from the countryside."[37]

Schools served as the primary socialization hubs for the communities during the educational change processes. Literacy campaigns were a significant part of these efforts, engaging hundreds of volunteers as teachers. Many women from diverse backgrounds joined the literacy and political movement, including Lil Milagro Ramírez, a member of *El Grupo (the Group)*, the predecessor of the guerrilla organization, ERP (Ejército Revolucionario del Pueblo).

Lil Milagro Ramírez was among a handful of female university students at UES (University of El Salvador) that founded *La Masacuata* (Nahuat for deer-serpent), a group of socially conscious, Social Christian activists and poets. *La Masacuata* eventually evolved into *El Grupo* in 1969. *El Grupo,* which served as the precursor to the Ejército Revolucionario del Pueblo (ERP) guerrilla organization, was founded in 1972. During the same period,

Cayetano Carpio and others founded the FPL guerrilla (Fuerzas Populares de Liberación).

Lil Ramírez' personal story is not well-known, and there is conflicting information regarding her date of birth, with some sources indicating 1945 and others 1946. However, it is believed that she was assassinated by the Salvadoran military in 1979, after being detained and tortured since she was captured in 1976. While Ramírez was not known as a "feminist" she was described as an intelligent poet, and a loyal member to the revolutionary movement. She was also the "traditional" woman that cooked welcomed meals for her fellow comrades, or the consoling mother that offered compassion and understanding.[38]

Ramírez and her colleagues in *El Grupo* were pioneers in promoting an armed insurrection and forging alliances with the burgeoning groups of activists in the countryside. She personally experienced state repression during her participation in the 1968 ANDES (teacher union) strike. She helped her fellow comrades to safety during the violent milieu when the military opened fire at the crowd. Several were killed. She wrote the following letter to her father before she went into hiding:

> *Do you remember we were there during the first ANDES strike? I was one of the most committed to that struggle and my feelings of frustration and impotence began to take shape when I saw the helpless people who were asking for justice and got repression and death in response. I will never forget the morning when we took the dead bodies of the workers killed by the Guard to the cemetery ... those were the first times that I reflected on this country and its political conditions ... at that point I thought we had to find another way.*[39]

The events that compelled the urban and the rural alliances toward coalescence were constructed by three transformative scenarios that occurred during the same time period. First, as described above, the success of the Christian Democratic Party with its Social Christianity emphasis and the support of the Catholic Action demonstrated that the Salvadoran people from widely diverse segments of the population were eager to collectively participate in the establishment of a democracy, without the threat of the power regime enforced by the military and the wealthy elite. Secondly, the renewed identity of the Catholic Church created an unprecedented opportunity for the poor and marginalized populace to become fully integrated into the democratic process, and be able to participate in shaping their own and their children's future. And thirdly, the adoption of *Paulo Freire's* philosophy and method for teaching literacy, especially to adults, was highly compatible with the delivery of homilies promoted by liberation theologians, combining learning to read and write with an understanding of self in society and becoming liberated from oppression. These ideas and their origins are discussed in the following paragraphs.

A Major Political Event of the Century

The Second Vatican Council of 1962 and the Second Episcopal Conference of 1965, were considered major political events of the century and its consequences could not have been greater than in all of Latin America, including of course, Central America.[40]

The proclamations in the Second Vatican Council documents of 1962 described the Church in a very different historical perspective. It declared that the Church's role is not only spiritual but contextual since it belongs within the community. The Church exists in a communal environment and the sacrament of baptism deems every member as "equal." At the Second Episcopal Conference in Medellín, Bogotá in 1965, the bishops took a bolder step and asserted the actions that were at the core of their proclamations. These included defending the rights of the oppressed, promoting grassroots organizations, and denouncing the unjust actions of the world powers that work against the self-determination of the weaker nations."[41]

The extraordinary transformation of the Church must have seemed ultra-revolutionary to many Salvadorans that were already contemplating the need for drastic change in their society. But, of course, those that were rigorously opposed to the Church's new role were the conservative military and oligarch sectors that perceived the change not only as antithetical to their religious beliefs, but as a threat to their power as an authoritative regime. Although the Church had consistently worked against the incorporation of secular ideologies such as socialism or communism in the 1930s and 1940s, the Second Vatican Council chose not to condemn communism, but instead stood firmly in favor of the critics of capitalism abuses. In 1979, Archbishop Romero expressed his sentiments concerning the disunity that existed among Catholics in Latin America: "I believe that the path to unity lies in a 'preferential option for the poor.' ...we found Jesus Christ among the poor and there was no problem... ."[42]

In the late 1960s, Lil Milagro Ramírez participated as a volunteer teacher of adult literacy classes in Cojutepeque, a city just East of the capitol city of San Salvador. At the time, the Ejército Revolucionario del Pueblo (ERP) had yet to be formalized. As a member of *El Grupo*, she was keenly aware like everyone else that the education of the masses was a prerequisite to a successful revolution. The collaboration with the campesinos in the formation of a combined urban/rural front guerrilla was an imperative undertaking by the student activist. With extremely high illiteracy rates among the campesinos, an effective educational process had to address the urgency to educate as many people as possible within a limited time frame, and at the same time to help them construct a meaningful knowledge base that allows for critical thinking and the building of self-confidence. Furthermore, in order to carry out this campaign, volunteers had to undergo extensive training on a wide scale.

The renewed identity and function of the Catholic Church was vigorously accepted by the poor and marginalized populations in the rural areas of the country. Within a few years starting in 1968, Christian Base Communities, known as CEBs, were organized and developed through the pastoral work of religious clergy. Dozens of CEBs cropped up in several areas, across various departments. The initial team usually consisted of a priest and a nun, but once they began their work, community members joined the task force and took on leadership roles. Education was at the center of their mission. The *Bible* was at the forefront of every lesson, but oral discussions on pressing issues or problems dominated the mostly illiterate groups of adults. Certain messages resonated more than others; amongst these was the meaning of "liberation," not the kind of being liberated at the time of death, but the liberation that anyone can achieve (with God's blessing) during a lifetime. Liberation is within reach if one is willing to struggle for it.[43]

The literacy projects that Lil Ramírez and other student activists engaged in were part of an extension of the pastoral mission sponsored by the Church. They joined the Center of Social Studies and Popular Promotion (CESPROP), founded by a sociologist, Father Juan Ramón Vega and Catholic students. They were trained on how to help adults become literate using the pedagogy popularized by Brazilian Paulo Freire that integrates consciousness-raising (conscientização) with literacy development. The pedagogy is student-centered, beginning with an understanding of their reality. Through "problematizing" and didactical conversations, the learners acquire a different perspective on how the power structures result in inequality. Most importantly, the *how* and *why* they are victims of long-standing and debilitating poverty. The learners continuously generate familiar words and expressions as they learn to read and write. Gradually they build meaningful frameworks for literacy development. Rather than a dispenser of information, the teacher assumes the role of facilitator and observer, challenging learners to think critically and independently.

Ramírez and dozens of other university and high school students associated with Catholic Action were highly active in CESPROP. Many of their peers also became activists, and a few even joined the armed insurrection later on. The government authorities became suspicious of their work, and in some municipalities, the Catholic Schools was prohibited from teaching particular songs to their students.[44]

The Teacher's Revolution (and Casualties)

While the children of the wealthy elite and military hierarchy enjoyed pricey educational schooling such as private schools in San Salvador, the United States, or Europe, the majority of children, many of whom lived in extreme poverty, attended state-run schools in deplorable conditions. Newly graduated teachers from public universities were assigned to these schools, unless they had some connection with a high-ranking military official or were affiliated with the correct political party. The Salvadoran government's low regard for the teachers' services was evident in their low-paying salaries (about $80. per month), without benefits. A few teachers took issue with the government's ineptitude and decided that the best option was to organize themselves. Within a two-year period, the teachers had formed their own organization, becoming the first autonomous teacher union in El Salvador's history.[45]

The Asociación Nacional de Educadores Salvadoreños or ANDES, was officially recognized on June 21, 1965. The teacher's organization drew from its collective strength of fourteen thousand primary school teachers to demand that the government protect their legal rights and improve their working conditions with decent salaries and medical care. Beyond the essential stipulations that addressed their working conditions, the ANDES members established proposed curricular changes which were specific to working with children and their families in marginalized contexts. Their proposal called for specific instructional approaches, such as Paulo Freire's *liberation pedagogy*, the teaching of critical thinking skills, a renewed focus on El Salvador's history, and on the construction and establishment of a democratic society.

The government's lack of an adequate response compelled the ANDES members to deliberate their next steps with bold strategies. In ANDES' first confrontation with the government of President Sánchez Hernández in 1968, nearly four hundred teachers, mostly from the Department of Chalatenango, participated in a two-month strike as they camped outside the Ministry of Education building in the country's capital. The message inherent in their narrative was a call for dignity: "la dignificación del magisterio."[46] The government's concessions were woefully inadequate, and ANDES organized a larger strike in 1971. Thousands of teachers, students, and supporters protested in the capital and throughout the country. Military, security forces, and ORDEN (paramilitary) forces attacked the demonstrators at various locations, including Chalatenango, Santa Ana, and Chalchuapa. Many suffered mild and severe injuries, while at least one university student, an engineer, and two university professors were killed, including a Mexican professor, Luis Quezada, who had survived the 1968 Tlatelolco massacre in México.[47]

Among the leaders and future president of ANDES was teacher, *Mélida Anaya Montes*. Appalled at the disastrous and egregious assaults on teachers, and speaking on behalf of herself and ANDES, Anaya Montes declared that their only option was to counter the repressive forces with violence since words were not sufficient or powerful against a viciously armed regime.[48] Many teachers joined the guerrilla as did Anaya Montes, who eventually became a high ranking member of the guerrilla, Fuerzas Populares de Liberación (FPL), while others chose a path of stability by becoming affiliated with the national political party PCN (the Partido de Concilación Nacional).[49]

The Church's Revolution (and its Casualties)

By the late 1960s, the repressive forces of the Salvadoran military had affected thousands of non-combatants, but the targets were primarily students, teachers, labor and social movement leaders, and even government officials. The memory of thousands killed in the 1932 "la matanza" still haunted those who had been most affected such as family members or close friends. The people killed by the Salvadoran regime were deemed the subversives, the "internal enemies." However, the shock value was elevated to new heights when members of the clergy were assaulted and killed, as if they were "enemies" too, and were no longer protected by their religious affiliation.

The first targeted priest was Father José Inocencio Alas who was abducted by ORDEN (or similar paramilitary force) shortly after he had given a speech at the Agrarian Reform Congress in 1970. Fr. Alas was a member of clergy that had strong connections with the campesinos in rural areas. He fully supported agrarian reform, and consistently pressed the government to bring much needed aid to the families. The archdiocese' radio station, YSAX, had broadcasted his abduction around the clock, and listeners were asked to pray for Father Alas. To everyone's relief, their prayers were answered and Fr. Alas was found, injured but alive.[50] He had been left for dead on a mountain cliff south of San Salvador.

Father Nicolas Rodríguez' dismembered body was found days after his abduction by the National Guard on January, 1972. Incredulously, the Catholic Church accepted the military's explanation that Rodríguez had been killed by unknown assailants.

Father Rutilio Grande's assassination was particularly impactful because of his work with the CEBs and his relationship with the Archbishop Oscar Romero. Upon his arrival to San Salvador as the newly elected Archbishop, Romero was welcomed and briefed by Fr. Grande. Just three weeks later, Fr. Grande and another priest, Fr. Alfonso Navarro, were assassinated while traveling with other parishioners to celebrate Mass in a nearby town. Archbishop Romero recognized how Fr. Grande had been instrumental in organizing and developing thirty-seven CEBs and training 326 catechists in the community of Aguilares, in the department of San Salvador. Within an eight-month period, the community had created their own grassroots leadership, mobilizing laborers to join with the Christian Federation of Salvadoran Campesinos (FECCAS) in 1973. The organized group had considerable success in May, 1973, when workers at the Aguilares' La Cabaña Sugar Mill set up a peaceful six-hour strike, demanding the promised salary increases that had been previously negotiated but then turned down by the management. Although the strikers were able to recoup some of their lost earnings but short of the salary increases, the strike was nevertheless considered a success. The infuriated oligarchs and their government supporters attributed the development of the labor organization and its outcome to the work of Fr. Grande and his grassroots leadership, despite the fact that he and all clergy members worked within the confines of a strictly pastoral agenda. The Aguilares example, along with other similar developments, attained an historical commendation throughout Latin

America for its collaboration with the Church, touting its evangelizing efforts' direct influence on the community and grassroots organizations.

The persecution of priests and laity continued. Between 1977 to 1981 eleven priests were assassinated and at least sixty priests were exiled, some forcefully. What was once considered the assassination or even the mistreatment of a priest as an anomaly, was now a systematic, deliberate strategy perpetrated by the military and powerful elite.

The 1980 assassinations and attempts on religious clergy were particularly impactful and tragic. In January, 1980, two Mexican nuns were abducted and taken to the National Guard barracks. They were released several hours later, only after Archbishop Romero had intervened and demanded their release. In June, a Salvadoran nun was severely beaten with a machete, receiving blows and cuts to her face and neck.[51] Then, in March, 1980, the unthinkable and tragic assassination of Archbishop Oscar Romero while saying Mass sent the entire country into total disarray. While he was considered a representation of the "internal enemy" by the ruling Salvadoran regime, Archbishop Romero had deepened his connection with the Salvadoran people, especially the marginalized masses afflicted with poverty and social injustices. His sympathizers clung to his every word. His Sunday sermons broadcasted on YSAX were rarely missed since everyone was tuned in.[52]

When four American "churchwomen" were reportedly raped and murdered on December 2, 1980, the international community expressed horror and disbelief that this could possibly happen to the women who were in the country to fulfill their missionary duties. The case was investigated because family members of the women insisted, and although the government tried to cover-up the crime, the findings revealed that the military was involved in the planning and execution of the murders. The Commission on the Truth report concluded that Maryknoll Sisters Ita Ford and Maura Clark were returning from Nicaragua to return to Chalatenango, and Ursuline Sister Dorothy Kazel and lay missioner Jean Donavan, both staying in La Libertad, went to the airport to pick them up. After the four women drove away from the airport, they were stopped by Sergeant Colindres Alemán and four

National Guard members. They forced the women to an isolated area, where they were raped and shot execution-style. The next day they were buried in shallow graves in a nearby municipality and their vehicle was torched. A day later, the U.S. ambassador discovered the graves and ordered their bodies exhumed and taken to San Salvador.[53] Needless to say, the religious community was particularly saddened but angered over the murders of the four women. But the U.S. government was not sympathetic according to Raymond Bonner, who quoted Ambassador Jean Kirkpatrick upon learning of the women's heinous murders: "They weren't just nuns. They were political activists on behalf of the Frente."[54]

Inquiries surrounding the women's murders yielded no evidence that they were in any way involved with the insurrectionists. Background information on the women reveals their dedication to their social work as missionaries.

Sister Maura John Clarke (1931   1980)

Sister Maura was 19 years old when she joined the Maryknoll Order. After graduation from the Teachers College and teaching in the Bronx for five years, Sr. Maura was assigned to Nicaragua on a mission to help people in the aftermath of the 1972 earthquake. She left in 1976, and after an absence of three years, she returned to Nicaragua. After Sr. Carla's death she decided to join Sr. Ita in her ministry in El Salvador. The two sisters had attended a regional meeting in Nicaragua, and upon returning to El Salvador they were met at the airport in San Salvador by Sr. Dorothy Kazel and Jean Donovan.

Jean Donovan (1953 – 1980)

Jean Donovan was 26 years old when she traveled to La Libertad, El Salvador (1979) to work as a Caritas Coordinator, in the distribution of food for the needy. Her passion for working as a humanitarian was noteworthy since she gave up her well-paid, accountant job in Cleveland to dedicate her life to helping others. One of her dreams, along with Sr. Dorothy Kazel, was to open up an orphanage/clinic to care for the children victimized by the war.

Sister Ita Ford   (1940-1980)

Sister Ita Ford was 21 years old when she joined the Maryknoll community in 1961. Sr. Ita worked in Chile from 1973 to 1980, then, responded to Archbishop Romero's call to serve in El Salvador. She arrived in El Salvador in 1980 shortly after his assassination, and worked with the Emergency Refugee Committee in Chalatenango with her colleague, Sr. Carla Piette. In a tragic accident, Sr. Carla Piette died in August, and four months later, Sr. Ita was killed.

Sister Dorothy Kazel   (1939 – 1980)

Sister Dorothy Kazel joined the Ursuline Sisters Order in 1960 in Cleveland, Ohio, where she was born. In 1974, she joined the Cleveland Diocese's mission team in El Salvador where she participated in the development of CEBs (Christian Base Communities).

***

The eventual convictions of at least some of the perpetrators, and the international attention on El Salvador's human rights violations did not deter the military from committing more assaults against the religious clergy. A case in point was the execution style murders of six Jesuit priests, their housekeeper and her daughter by the Atlactl battalion in 1989.[55] One of the priests, Fr. Ignacio Ellacuria, had been an advocate for social justice; his voice particularly significant since the assassination of Archbishop Romero in 1980.[56]

The Catholic Church's transformation during the critical period of the revolution throughout El Salvador impacted the lives of the entire population. Faced with the stark inequalities wrought by abject poverty and opulent wealth, the Church fittingly decided to work alongside the people who most needed their help. *Liberation Theology* and its core message of advocating for change on behalf of the parish and its parishioners, was subject to a wide array of opinions. Although the message of justifiable use of violence was not explicit in *Liberation Theology*, it was nevertheless part of the messaging inherent in the fight for liberation. Author Gustavo Gutiérrez discusses the Liberationist's responsibility to support the revolutionary efforts of Christians "in spirit at least if not in action."[57] His book, *A Theology of Liberation*, published in 1971, introduced diverse and controversial topics that at the very least, highlighted the challenge of the Church's renewed identity. For the revolutionaries seeking to fight in the frontlines, the call to action was a call to an armed insurrection.

'The Other Matanzas' – Massacres in the Countryside and More Human Rights Violations

The United Nations report (2001) details pernicious assaults on non-combatant civilians, highlighting the patterns of human rights violations for which the Salvadoran military regime was deemed largely responsible. However, it should be pointed out that without the immense and consistent support by the United States government, the Salvadoran military would not have had the means to commit the military actions on such a massive and destructive scale.

President Reagan perceived El Salvador as critical to the security interests of the United States. In his first year as president (1981-82), his administration allotted $82 million to El Salvador, almost five times what the country had received from the United States in a thirty-year period (1946-1979). From 1980 to 1982, the Salvadoran government received $354 million, and between 1984-85, another $312 million. President Reagan understood to some extent the inhumane reign of terror that the military regime inflicted upon its non-combatant civilians. Despite promises from the Salvadoran government to halt human rights violations, Reagan insisted on demonstrable proof before certifying the allocation of additional aid. In 1982, Salvadoran President Magaña's assurances on land reform progress satisfied President Reagan. However, after the six-month certificate was signed and the aid was distributed, the Salvadoran government continued to commit the violations. After the fourth certification was issued to the Salvadoran government, and it was discovered that the claims were once again false, it became clear to the United States that the certification process was a complete farce. Despite this, President Reagan insisted that the United States continue its military support to El Salvador. In a joint session of Congress in 1983, President Reagan praised the Salvadoran government for "making every effort to guarantee democracy, free labor unions, freedom of religion, and a free press..."[58]

During the first six months after the inauguration of President Reagan, 7,152 Salvadorans were killed, over half were unarmed peasants, some of them abducted from their homes and killed.[59]

The former president approved the allocation of billions of dollars as aid to the Salvadoran government to defeat the guerrilla forces.[60] The U.S. government provided El Salvador with the best, world-class military equipment and training, but to the great dismay of many, the resources were used for the worst reasons. A case in point is the massacre in El Mozote, a rural community in the department of Morazón, where up to a thousand non-combatant civilians, entire families and their extended members were murdered between December 11-13, 1981.[61]

Despite the aid, the Salvadoran government could not declare a clear victory, greatly frustrating the Reagan administration.[62] The Salvadoran armed forces increased from 10,000 to 1979 to 24,000 in 1982 to 56,000 in 1987. And although the FMLN insurgency had the capability of defeating the Salvadoran military, the United States' intervening arm prohibited this possibility through its enormous support that enabled El Salvador to sustain a war indefinitely.

The Tragedy of the Honduran Partnership with the United States

The Table 1.1, "Massacres During the Salvadoran Civil War," includes the information on assaults perpetrated against non-combatant civilians by both the Salvadoran and the Honduran military forces. Most of this information is available in documents such as in the report, "From Hope to Madness." However, some of the assassinations included in Table 1.1 list were not well-documented and disseminated. Specifically, under the "River Massacres," the data reveal how civilians caught in the crossfires of the Salvadoran military forces attempted to flee to the Honduran border, and upon crossing the river that delineates the boundary, were attacked by Honduran military troops. The Honduran government played a supportive role in the Salvadoran Civil War because of the aid received from the United States. Raymond Bonner writes about top secret information shared with the National Security Council on 1983, which revealed CIA operatives in Honduras, including patrols into El Salvador for the purpose of destroying guerrilla bases.[62] The Reagan administration supported the Honduran military in 1983 with $31.3 million along with a substantial amount of military hardware such as helicopters, counterinsurgency planes, mortars, howitzers, communications equipment, and patrol boats. Bonner describes the United States' intervening role in Honduras as the case of transforming a "banana republic" dominated by the United Fruit Company into a military base developed by the United States and ruled by Ambassador Negroponte and the Honduran Minister of Defense, General Gustavo Alvarez."[63] Mercenaries were bankrolled to perform military services such as piloting planes to ferry soldiers to their posts. Clandestine jails with torture chambers were set up in Honduras to "give Honduras the ugly face of El Salvador."

The revolutionaries who initially hesitated to join an armed insurrection became angry and embittered over the atrocities committed by the Salvadoran government forces. The killings, massacres, disappearances, and assassinations unleashed by the repressive regime, provided a compelling reason to become a soldier of war. As the violence escalated, women were increasingly likely to participate in the armed conflict.

Table 1.1 Massacres During the Salvadoran Civil War

Massacre	Location	Fatalities	Description
March 1981	El Junquillo, Morazán	At least 55 mostly women and children, few men – killed execution style	Military operation consisting of Cacaopera civil defense and soldiers attacked the inhabitants on night of

			March 11th, killing each in execution style, raping some of the females, even the little girls. Then, they burned their homes and stole their food. They had full knowledge that the guerrillas were not present in the area.
December 1981	El Mozote, Morazán; and five surrounding villages/towns	In El Mozote 200 killed execution style; investigations led authorities to conclude that in all around 1,000 civilians were assassinated.	Atlacatl Battalion entered El Mozote on Dec. 11th. Men were tortured and executed, then, the women, then children. In the next two days, the military continued killing civilians in nearby areas: La Joya, La Ranchería, Los Toriles, Jocote Amarillo, Cerro Pando.
River Massacres May 1980	Chalatenango on Sumpul River border	300-600 civilians	About 250 Honduran soldiers stood guard on their side of Sumpul River; when hundreds of civilians attempted to flee across the river to Honduras, Salvadoran soldiers shot and killed 600 civilians; Honduran soldiers, collaborating with Salvadoran government pushed the civilians back to El Salvador.
March 1981	Department of Cabañas	20-30 killed; 189 reported missing	4,500-5,000 campesinos forced to

	bordering Lempa River with Honduras.		flee their homes and cross the Lempa River to Honduras for safety. Air assaults by U.S. helicopter gunships targeted the civilians during their flight.
October 1981	Same area as above.	147 killed, including 44 children.	Civilians attempting to cross the river to safety.
November 1981	Same area as above – Department of Cabañas bordering Lempa River with Hondurans.	50-100 civilians killed.	Another counter-insurgency operation by the Salvadoran military kept 1,000 civilians under attack for 13 days.
May 1982	Eastern Chalatenango, Sumpul River	(Unreliable data, unable to provide an approximation.)	Belloso Battalion unit of Salvadoran military fired at civilians crossing the Sumpul River as they fled toward Honduras for safety.
August 1982	El Calabozo, San Vicente, alongside the Amatitán River	Over 200 men, women and children	In a military operation meant to hunt down guerrilla members, some 6,000 Salvadoran troops swept through an area inhabited by civilians. The families, fleeing from the military, tried to hide in El Calabozo but were discovered by the Atlacatl Battalion and taken prisoners. They were assassinated.
Around the Countryside	Throughout Chalatenango Department	Hundreds of civilians	In military operation using scorched-earth tactic, soldiers kill

May 1982			habitants and burn their homes and destroy their crops.
January 1982	Nueva Trinidad and Chalatenango	150 civilians killed	Government forces in land and air military operations sought to regain control of populated areas where the guerrilla was stationed.
August 1982	San Vicente	300-400 civilians killed	Military operation in a campaign for pacification purposes.
February 1983	Las Hojas - Department of Sonsonate	16 non-combatant civilians killed execution style	Salvadoran military unit, Jaguar Battalion and a civil defense unit sought members of Las Hojas cooperative of the National Indigenous Association, who were beaten, bound, executed.
1982-1984	Throughout the Country; Guazapa received the most intense attacks.	Various deaths due to bombardments, mostly indiscriminate attacks on towns where guerrillas presumably were hiding.	Consistent, regular bombardments on civilians, including air attacks by U.S. A-37 jets, Huey helicopters, Cessna spotter planes.
July 1984	Cerron Grande, Chalatenango	68 members of the Christian Base Community, including 27 children.	In a 3-day operation, Atlacatl Battalion and other military units used land and air power to attack and kill civilians, where presumably guerrillas were hiding.

Stepping into the Revolutionary Role

The women's voices featured in this work are drawn from the research of scholars who have personally witnessed the testimonies of former female guerrilla members. Without their rigorous and dogged investigations, historical accounts of this and other similar conflicts would undoubtedly be incomplete and biased. Our understanding of the contributions made by women and the impact of their work on their own lives and the lives of others would be limited without their efforts.

Researchers generally find that women joined the guerrillas because it was a way to achieve social justice, and fulfill their duty based on their principled beliefs. They believed that their actions would contribute to creating a society that serves everyone, especially the historically marginalized people. There were other reasons, of course, such as to be with family members or to escape the repression. However, the women's testimonies exclude any notion that their gender was a reason for participating.[64] Prior to and during the Salvadoran war, women's issues were often viewed through the lens of broader societal needs and struggles, and the concept of "feminism" did not seem as a key to achieving equality. It was only in the post-war 1990s that women developed a collective vision of gender equality and successfully introduced a social and political discourse centered around feminism.

One can argue that the majority of all women living in the embattled zones throughout the country were part of the twelve-year civil war. The revolution was the bonding agent, however, the extent to which women participated, and under what circumstances were decisions made by the individual woman.[65] The underage children had less leverage in the decision-making, especially if their entire family joined.

***

Organizing the Women in the Guerrilla

Researchers Vásquez, Ibáñez, and Murguialdy worked out a scheme by which to organize the former guerrilla female members that they interviewed.[66] They identified five groups as the following:

1. The young revolutionaries from urban sites. These women were under twenty years old when they enlisted in the guerrilla fronts, living in the clandestine camp sites.

2. The young revolutionaries from rural sites. Like the women from the urban areas, they were under twenty years old when they joined the guerrilla front.

3. The adult revolutionaries from urban sites. The women in this group were from urban sites. They were over twenty years old when they enlisted and they had one or more children.

4. "Comandos urbanos." These revolutionary women participated in the urban commands in the capital city of San Salvador.

5. Collaborators of the guerrillas. These revolutionary women collaborated with the FMLN in control zones. They lived normal lives as citizens but carried out guerrilla activities in secret.

Kampwirth describes the former guerrilla women that she interviewed as having had substantial contact or had participated in relevant organizations which she labels as "pre-existing organizations." These include the social/educational organizations sponsored by the Catholic Church, where the revolutionaries' aspirations were developed and nurtured. At the public university, the Salvador University Catholic Action and the Catholic Student Youth organizations spearheaded some of the major groups that served to educate revolutionaries, including the women. [67] These groups consisted of the Christian Democrat Party (Partido Democrático Cristiano, PDC) – 1960; Committee of Representatives of General Studies (CRAC) – 1967; and the People's Revolutionary Movements of the 1960s and 70s.[68]

At key moments, these women became convinced that joining an armed insurrection was the right choice, and they actively participated in these organizations. If there's a pattern in this decision-making process it's that each decision was complex and personal. Kampwirth's research reveals that young women made very difficult choices, and many opted to put aside their ambitious personal goals to fulfill what they regarded as their "calling." Kampwirth's extensive interviews with former female revolutionaries in El Salvador and Nicaragua focused on social and educational backgrounds.[69] The Salvadoran (urban) guerrilla women tended to have more educational experiences than their male counterparts, and although many originated from the rural areas of the country, they preferred to migrate to the urban areas. Educational opportunities played a major role on whether the females had attended school, and the women had greater access to school in urban centers.

However, as they took on tasks they never imagined before, some women discovered new pathways towards a better future. For example, they developed new skills such as grassroots organizing, advocating for human rights on a national and international level, leadership development, and grant writing. Some women even became feminists and proudly spoke out for women's rights, calling an end to the injustices long perpetuated by patriarchal systems and judicial practices that hindered the advancement of women.

The Table 1.2 lists the guerrilla organizations, and the approximate year that each one was formalized; the organization(s) that were closely aligned with the guerrilla that served as its armed body; and the approximate numbers of women in each organization. The data also include some information about the roles that the women held. Due to the irregularities in the original data base, the information is based on approximations.

Table 1.2 FMLN 1980 (Farabundo Martí National Liberation Front) and FDR (Democratic Revolutionary Front)

Guerrilla (Year Founded)	Major Organization w/ Guerrilla	*No. of females
FPL – Fuerzas Populares de Liberación, 1970	BPR - Bloque Popular	696 (Had

	Revolucionario; (1975) FTC – Federación de Trabajadores del Campo	most political cadres.)
PRS -Partido de la Revolución Salvadoreña (Armed Forces: Ejército Revolucionario del Pueblo – ERP, 1972) RN – Resistencia Nacional (Armed Forces: Fuerzas Armadas de Resistencia Nacional - FARN, 1975)	LP-28 – Ligas Populares Febrero 28 FAPU (1974) – Frente de Acción Popular Unificada	754 1,549 (Had the highest number of women in the ranks.)
PRTC – Partido Revolucionario de los Trabajadores Centroamericanos, 1976	MLP – Movimiento de Liberación Popular	1,056 (Had the lowest number of women in the ranks.)
PCS – Partido Comunista Salvadoreño (Armed Forces: Fuerzas Armadas de Liberación – FAL, 1979)	UDN – Union Democrática Nacionalista	334

Source: 1992 – 1993 United Nations Observer Mission in El Salvador (ONUSAL); data reveal that 30 – 40 percent were female. (Note: this is not a comprehensive list.) *The numbers changed during the course of the war. Total number of FMLN members in 1984, 10,000; in 1994: 15,000; Grand Total number of female members: 4,402; Ages: 90 percent between ages 14 and 40; Demobilization data: 8,552 total were processed: 2,485 females (29.1 percent)

The Lacuna in the Chronicles of the Revolution

The alliances between the urban sector (the New Left) and the peasant movements in the rural regional areas of Chalatenango, San Vicente, and Morazán formed the extraordinary strength of the insurgency. If it constituted the "backbone" of the movement as posited by Chávez, then the women's roles were at the heart and soul of the revolution.[70] Several sources have documented that at the least 30 percent of the total members in the guerrilla were women. However, the exact numbers of women that participated as combatants compared to non-combatant brigadistas, or members of the rearguard, working in various combatant and non-combatant roles is next to impossible to discern.

Women's roles in the guerrilla evolved from a "liberation" ideology rather than a "revolutionary" structure.[71] Front and center of the much touted "liberating vision" was the goal of creating an alternative society that constituted the proposed Revolutionary Democratic Government (GDR, Gobierno Democrático Revolucionario). However, liberation was a national concept inclusive of the entire family. The consensus among the population was that the struggle for liberation included the eradication of hunger and illiteracy, the development of basic economic structures such as decent housing, access to clean or potable water, and the establishment of a democratically-run government. The grassroots organizations that civilians had developed and maintained for decades were integral to the organizing efforts and practices of the communities in the control zones of the FMLN. In the task of "normalizing civic life," women played a central role in administering these social and economic needs, as described by María Caminos:

> *There are literacy campaigns and clothes-making. There are councils of elders who know all about popular and traditional medicines and who are teaching university-education doctors how to cure certain illnesses. This is one example of how the revolution recovers the values of its people. A 'glass of milk' campaign intends to give every child under*

seven one glass of milk per day – something that has never been done in El Salvador.[72]

Guazapa: The Stronghold

The constant bombardments from A-37 planes and Huey helicopters that enveloped the small town of Guazapa forced the inhabitants into a constant state of absolute survival. Guazapa, in the department of El Salvador, just twenty miles north of the capital, was targeted by the Salvadoran military between 1983 to 1985 because it was considered a guerrilla-controlled zone. Journalist Raymond Bonner vividly recalls the events of spring of 1983 when the elite U.S.-trained Atlacatl Batallion terrorized the Guazapa Volcano area, killing residents and destroying everything in its path. The remains of people unearthed from shallow graves revealed the atrocities committed by the troops. Men, women and children had been executed with guns and machetes. The bare adobe walls were covered with graffiti scribblings by the troops, congratulating themselves for their anniversary work.[73]

In the same way as other guerrilla-controlled zones, Guazapa inhabitants organized their communities in the most practical and efficient manner. The FPL guerrilla commanders encouraged a structured organizational plan in Chalatenango, which facilitated the development of a Local Popular Power (PPL) where residents created their own local government. In San Vicente, Cuscatlán, and Usulután, the PRTC organization encouraged a well-structured local revolutionary government that included a 'self-defense' section that helped the residents employ emergency security measures.[74] In Guazapa, men and women campesinos formed collectives and cooperatives that led to greater assurances that everyone had the basic essentials, at least as much as possible.[75]

The cattle cooperative provided milk for the vulnerable members of the community. The agricultural cooperative addressed food insecurity. Civil disputes were managed by an elected commission. Literacy classes were organized and children attended school regularly. Medical care became available, and alcohol and illegal drugs were banned. Women created novel inroads in their involvement. In 1981, an all-female battalion was organized in Guazapa. There were support roles such as doctors, medics, nurses, cooks, radio operators, and farmers, but women were also combatants. Women assumed tasks and leadership roles that had never been previously available to them. It was 'liberating' to a certain extent, compared to their past experiences. However, their struggle for equality within the context of a deeply-entrenched, traditional patriarchal society was ironically, an uphill battle.

Despite the efforts of the women in the guerrilla to convince the commanders to uphold and promote gender equality, their pleas were in vain. The guerrilla organizations were primarily focused on the revolution agenda, and women were encouraged to participate simply to increase their numbers.

Women in the Rural Areas: To Join or Not to Join

In Ilja Luciak's research, the twenty-two Salvadoran women interviewed shared their personal stories, which reflect profound sadness and even tragic circumstances that compelled them to weigh the decision on whether or not to join the guerrilla.[76] The Table 1.3 below: "Women's Stories on Joining the Guerrillas" lists the women and brief excerpts or descriptions of their (selected) stories. Many women were beyond their combatant years, having had children who served in the guerrilla and killed in combat. They chose to participate in the rearguard, as cooks, for examples. Some women felt they had no choice because they were driven by the threat of being killed by the government forces. Others like Rosa, Mirta, and Vasilia were young enough to participate in the frontlines as combatants, medics, or radio operators. Whatever their circumstances in sorting out their decisions, the women shared a life of great suffering and an inescapable feeling that their lives would never be the same again.

Table 1.3 Women's Stories on Joining the Guerrillas in the Rural Areas -1970s-1980s

Location/Name	Reasons for Joining

San José Las Flores, Chalatenango	
Doña Avelina	Having lost her husband and young son while they were fleeing from their home as government military soldiers attacked them, and after four brothers and four nephews were killed in the war, Doña Avelina joined the guerrilla as a cook to help out the troops.
Doña Antonia	Doña Antonia joined the guerrilla because of the repression – and she had no land. Many women in the guerilla believed that after the war they would be granted the right to own land.
Doña Amparo	Doña Amparo joined because she wanted change: *"The people didn't have jobs, and organized we could effect change."*
Doña Cecilia	(The war gave the women few choices.) *"We had no other alternative than this one."*
Doña Carmen	*"I joined out of fear that the armed forces were in the area persecuting people. Many people died. This made one afraid."*
Doña Rosa	Doña Rosa joined the guerrilla movement at the age of seven. She felt it was her obligation: *"Since my father joined, so did I. If my father had been part of ORDEN (a right-wing paramilitary organization), I also would have been part of it."*
Doña Mirta	Doña Mirta joined *"to follow my brothers. There were three of them, and all died in the war."*
Doña Raquel	Doña Raquel joined, she *"was part of a massive incorporation. They said it would be only for three months but it became more."* (Sometimes entire villages were integrated into the guerrilla.)
Doña Abigail	*"Well, they told us that if we didn't go voluntarily, they would take us along by force. So, I joined voluntarily."*
Doña María	*"We organized because the FMLN told us to. We*

	didn't know why. They told us that those who did not join – who knows what would become of them. At best, they would be killed by one group or the other."
Doña Reyna	Doña Reyna worked as a cook in the guerrilla. She was very ill and by joining the guerrilla she was able to get healthcare. *"I was only bones. I joined, and I cured myself."*
Meanguera, Morazán	
Doña Lucía	*"The party [FMLN] told us that they were joining forces to improve the situation and that if we won, there would be a government with the participation of all, and there would be equality."*
Doña Purificación	Doña Purificación wanted to *"help and support the muchachos in their just war.*
Doña Dora	Doña Dora wanted to help the guerrillas. She cooked and fed the FMLN fighters starting in 1979 and continued to serve throughout the war.
Doña Bartola	Doña Bartola joined to escape the army's repression, particularly *"the massacres and bombardments that happened in the community."*
Doña Miriam	*"The army killed my family, and they threw bombs. One of them fell on my house, and I was left with nothing. They burned everything."*
Doña Angela	Doña Angela joined because she was afraid and, *"because they forced us."*
San Esteban Catarina, San Vicente	
Doña Flora	*"We were recruited by force. And yes, my husband stayed with the FMLN and he was killed."*
Doña Felicita	Doña Felicita joined *"because there was so much suffering and because they killed my two brothers in cold blood – they hanged them."*
Doña Romilia	Doña Romilia joined *"because they were fighting for us - the poor – and to escape the poverty, but*

		things got worse."
Doña Fidelina		(cooked for the guerilla troops for 13 years) – *"I loved my people, and this is the only reason for me. There was no clothing nor money or anything, only love for my people."*
Doña Vasilia		Doña Vasilia was a combatant in the guerrilla forces. She joined in 1977 at the age of 12, *"because I wanted to fight and because of my mother who had been killed by the army."*

***

Young Women in the Urban Sites Join the Guerrilla

Karen Kampwirth's research on former female guerrilla members reveals a particular pattern of lived experiences that she believes predisposed them to become involved in the armed struggle.[77] In her book (1996), Kampwirth conducted in-depth interviews with thirty-five women who had joined the guerrilla, and most of the women's names are listed as pseudonyms.

The table below, "Women's Stories on Joining the Guerrillas," lists four women whose lives illustrate the specific background experiences that Kampwirth features in her work.

The Interviews

Sonia Aguinada was raised by her grandmother who was politically involved, and would take little Sonia with her to political events.[78] In her late teens, Sonia became actively involved in organizations such as the Young Communists and eventually, joined the Ejército Revolucionario del Pueblo (ERP) guerrilla organization. *Bianca* was also in her late teens when she joined the guerrilla underground. As a high school student, she had been a member of the Revolutionary Brigade. *Ana Guadalupe Martínez* became politicized while participating in the student movement at her university. She

56

was a medical student for four years and then, made the decision to join the guerrilla organization for humanitarian reasons. She was one of the few women in the guerrilla to achieve rank, and in post-war politics was elected to the Legislative Assembly. Finally, *Gloria* was deeply affected by the assassination of Archbishop Oscar Romero. She was a university student when she decided to join the guerrilla organization.

Initially, a few young women joined the guerrilla. But the numbers steadily increased as the struggle escalated and women began to find their niche in the guerrilla organization. As previously mentioned, by the end of the war, a third of the total number of guerrilla members were women.

Table 1.4 Women's Stories on Joining the Guerrilla

Name	*Description*
Soñia Aguinada	Soñia attributes active involvement in the guerrilla to her grandmother's influence. Her grandmother "raised her" from the time she was an infant since her mother was sixteen when she was born and her father passed away before her birth As a little girl she participated in demonstrations with her grandmother who was a founding member of the Communist Party's Women's Fraternity (Fraternidad de Mujeres). Her grandmother, who read the daily newspapers, knew what was happening in the country's politics, and related to Soñia her experiences and knowledge about the 1932 Matanza, Farabundo Martí and Communist Party founder, Miguel Marmol. One of her uncles, a union activist, was killed in 1968; she continued to demonstrate alongside her grandmother in support of the teacher's union, and she joined the Young Communist's Organization (Juventud Comunista) at the age of thirteen. Soñia joined the ERP guerrilla organization when she was seventeen years old. This was a momentous decision that caused a rift between her and her family. The 1972 electoral fraud that cost (candidate) José Napoleón Duarte the presidency greatly affected her decision to join the guerrilla.

Bianca	At nineteen years old, Bianca was active in the Revolutionary Brigade of High School Students (Brigada Revolucionaria de Estudiantes de Secundaria), and when her parents found out, they were extremely concerned. At the time, death squads were terrorizing communities, instilling fear in families. Bianca's parents pressured Bianca to leave the organization, but instead, Bianca left home and joined an urban guerrilla cell, and engaging in dangerous activities such as "distributing literature and making bombs." She eventually became a combatant. (Kampwirth p. 62)
Ana Guadalupe Martínez	Ana was born in an agricultural community on her grandparent's farm. She was the oldest daughter of four children; her father was a retired military officer. The family moved to the city of Santa Ana so that the children could attend high school and college. While in high school, Ana learned about the teacher's strike because one of her teachers was part of it. Going on strike to protest inequality or unfairness was the first lesson that Ana learned on the meaning of engagement in the democratic process. While her parents discouraged her to participate in the teachers' strike, her aunt's involvement in the Teacher's Union exemplified the kind of engagement that Ana wanted to follow. In1969, she began her studies in medicine at the University of El Salvador. She participated in various demonstrations as part of the university student movement, and then, began to participate in the ERP guerrilla organization activities. After four years of medical school, Ana decided to pursue a path of humanitarianism, to help others like her mother had encourage her to do so. She went underground and became dedicated to the revolutionary struggle in the ERP. Fast forward several years and Martínez eventually achieved the rank of second in command in the guerrilla, and then, in the post-war era she was elected to the Legislative Assembly.
Gloria	Gloria was eleven years old when Archbishop Romero was assassinated in 1980. His murder profoundly affected her and her family. It was a tragedy that she could not forget and years later,

<table>
<tr><td></td><td>as a college student, Gloria went underground and became an active ERP guerrilla member in late 1980s.</td></tr>
</table>

***

La Montaña' Social and Political Experiment

Life in the guerrilla encampments was incredibly dangerous, to say the least. In addition to the violent assaults from the state military, the constant maneuvering through the mountainous terrain presented many environmental hazards. A large percentage of the guerrilla organizations included young men and women. Kampwirth suggests that at least one fourth of the women were students at the time they joined, and that, on average, women were more educated than men.[79] Although the diversity amongst the groups was staggering, the revolutionary agenda required the same standards of performance for everyone. Women actively engaged in novel activities where they could excel, and those with formal schooling had a greater advantage over those who had not attended school or were poorly educated. Thus, the women who emerged in the ranks were generally better educated. While the guerrilla commanding units tried to promote the message of "equality" between men and women, in reality, women experienced the similar discrimination and *machista* attitudes that were prevalent in the greater Salvadoran society.

Numerous reports from related research indicate that women in the guerrilla movement faced discrimination, yet there were no complaints specifically related to gender-based mistreatment.[80] However, interview data show that some women rejected the notion that discriminatory practices were based on gender. Even ranking females within the guerrilla dismissed women's concerns about gender-based discrimination. Women who persisted in filing complaints were reprimanded and sometimes re-assigned. Clearly, the women had not yet reached a level of consciousness that allowed them to analyze how the discrimination they experienced was rooted in their gender.

Kampwirth recounts how women's organizations inside the guerrilla promoted female empowerment, leading to unexpected yet positive outcomes for the women, despite creating tensions among the male comrades. The story was told by Yamilet, one of Kampwirth's interviewees.[81] Yamilet was integrated in one of the guerrillas and recalls that one of the male commanders suggested that women form their own organization as a way to reduce the stress levels caused by strained relationships between men and women. Eventually, the women learned to use their collective strength to acquire certain products specifically for them, such as sanitary napkins and woman's underwear. They gradually gained self-confidence and in one case, the women were so bold as to call out one of the commanding officers that habitually used his privilege to "use" women for his pleasure. The commander who had initially pushed for the formation of a gender-based organization accused the women of using this group against "them" and subsequently ordered its dismantling. Women used their experiences in "la montaña" (encampments in the mountains) to understand about sexual harassment and other ways that discriminate against them, and how they could remedy their situation. But their gender-based agenda was sidelined as the guerrilla organizations became more militarized and vertically hierarchical, especially right before the military final offensive in 1989. There was a prevailing belief that the situation would improve *after* the revolution, and women would be able to stay the course and pursue their feminist agenda. Nevertheless, the revolution was an important portal of opportunity, transforming the lives of women as they advanced novel ideas, creating a political and social space for feminist thought and action. In hindsight, the feminist leaders were key to creating a foundation for the evolution of feminism, which later became one of the most significant development for women.

The Road Toward Feminism – One Step at a Time

The war raged for years until the Peace Accords, signed on January 16, 1992, marked an end to the violent confrontations, even so, sporadic killings, assassinations, and kidnappings continued. The struggle was particularly laborious for women who believed that the liberation process was far from over. The women that took initial steps to organize themselves around issues and concerns sought to accomplish goals that were relevant to all

Salvadorans, not specifically addressing gender issues. One example is CO-MADRES, an organization founded by women who had lost a relative, presumably a victim of the repression, and most likely killed, disappeared, or incarcerated by the state. This organization, founded in 1977, continued to be active after the war. Many other groups were formed for particular purposes and functions, and by mapping out the trajectories of these within a time frame, we can draw certain conclusions about how feminist organizations evolved, despite the obstacles and hurdles that impeded their progress.

The Table 1.5 is based on the research archives that Lynn Stephen and others have analyzed, from the First Wave of Salvadoran women's movement (1957 to early 1970s) to the Second Wave (1975-1992).[82] During the First Wave, the *Women's Fraternity* was active from 1957 to 1969. The organization boasted a membership of 1,500 women, mostly market vendors, professionals, teachers, and nurses. The women organizations active in the 1960s to early 70s focused on issues that were of interest to labor and professional sectors.

Stephen's list of organizations is divided into three phases: *First Phase, (1975-1985)*; *Second Phase (1985-1989)*; and *Third Phase (1990-1992)*. The First Phase organizations continued in the similar vein as those in the First Wave, except that in the mid-1980s, the focus turned toward issues related to women survivors of the war such as economics, human rights, health, and literacy.

In the *Second Phase*, starting in 1985, the organizations featured two important characteristics. In the first instance, there's an expansion in the scope of the organizational goals and objectives. In 1986, CONAMUS (Coordinadora Nacional de Mujeres Salvadoreñas) delivered on the creation of a clearinghouse, setting up a broadly-based information center that includes a variety of women's groups. Secondly, the emergence of an organization that exclusively addresses the interests and issues of indigenous women marked the beginning of a new approach to feminism. The women behind these organizations worked in conjunction with feminist groups from other countries in Latin America and Europe, and gradually, a confluence of ideas and thoughts evolved and were incorporated into the organizations' missions and goals. A series of international conferences were instrumental in bringing women together to share ideas and advance creative ways for achieving their goals. For example, in 1985, the United Nation's Women's Conference was held in Nairobi; three Latin American and Caribbean Feminists ENCUENTROS were held - in Bogotá, Colombia (1981); in Lima, Peru (1983); and Bertioga, Brazil (1985).[83] Women like Norma Guirola de Herrera, a founder of IMU (Institute for Research, Training, and Development of Women) were well-versed on feminist theory and philosophy, and their work contributed to the foundation of a burgeoning feminist movement. Norma Guirola was assassinated in 1989; her family and supporters, feeling indignant over the killing, were even more determined to carry out her work. In 1991, they founded CEMUJER (Centro de Estudios de la Mujer "Norma Virginia Guirola de Herrera") to offer training and grassroots organizing assistance to women's groups.

Finally, the emergence of CONAMUS played an important role in the opening of the first women's shelter in the country in 1989, which was perceived as a formidable accomplishment that addressed the social and legal aspects of gender-based violence.

The *Third Phase* (1990-1992) in Lynn Stephen's research was a critical period of development, characterized by the influence of strong feminist waves and movements throughout the United States, Europe, and even in Latin America. As more women became involved, their voices and self-confidence gained strength. Women became empowered and demanded change, but they also attracted rebuke from a broad range of critics. Salvadoran social attitudes toward women hardly changed after 1989, and the most vocal anti-feminist critics came from the dominant conservative and traditional sectors of a patriarchal and homophobic society. Women leaders that became feminists received the brunt of the backlash, but were undeterred in their determination to institute changes. The language and messaging were focused on the groups' tenets of feminism. The CEF (Centro de Estudios Feministas – Center for Feminist Studies) proudly focused on "feminist" issues and themes; MAM (Movimiento de Mujeres "Mélida Anaya Montes" – Mélida Anaya Montes Women's Movement) named after the leader of the powerful teacher's union in the late 60s and 70s and later a ranking member of the FPL guerrilla organization, and adopted the term, "feminist autonomy"; and in 1992, the Colectivo Lésbico Feminista Salvadoreña de la Media Luna – Half-Moon Salvadoran Lesbian Feminist Collective was organized as the first self-proclaimed lesbian organization in the country.

Table 1.5 Second Wave Phases

First Phase 1975 -1985	*Description*
CO-MADRES - 1977, Comité de Madres de Reos y Desaparecidos Politicos de El Salvador Monseñor Romero	Grassroots organization, founded in 1977 in response to extreme levels of repression and in defense of human rights. CO-MADRES was one of two organizations that remained active throughout the war and beyond.
AMES – 1979, Asociación de Mujeres de El Salvador	Its work was directed toward market vendors, maids, and urban slum dwellers. Emerged from FPL; was greatly affected by deaths of Anaya Montes and Carpio.
CUMS – 1980s, Comité Unitario de Mujeres	Founded by Salvadoran women exiled in Costa Rica.
ASMUSA – 1983, Salvadoran Women's Association	Organizations that focused on issues related to women: economics, survival in the war, human rights, health and nutrition, literacy, and housing. ORMUSA remained active after the other two were dismantled in the 1990s.
FMS – 1984, Federación de Mujeres	Same as ASMUSA.
ORMUSA – 1985, Organización de Mujeres Salvadoreñas	Organization of Salvadoran Women.
Second Phase 1985 - 1989	*Description*
CONAMUS – 1986 Coordinadora Nacional de	Originally set up as a clearinghouse for other organizations, it opened up the country's first

Mujeres Salvadoreñas	women's shelter in 1989.
IMU – 1986, Institute for Research, Training, and Development of Women – Instituto para la Investigación, Capacitación, y Desarrollo de la Mujer	IMU facilitated the development of grassroots organization in the areas of communications, legal rights, and education. Its founder was Norma Virginia Guirola de Herrera, a well-known pioneer on feminism (assassinated in 1989).
AMIS – 1986, Association of Salvadoran Indigenous Women – Asociación de Mujeres Indígenas Salvadoreñas	First organization of its kind to address the concerns and issues of indigenous women in El Salvador.
COM – 1989, Coordinación de Organismos de Mujeres	First national coordinating organization of its kind that included five women's organizations.
Third Phase 1990 – 1992	*Description*
CEF – 1990, Centro de Estudios Feministas – Center for Feminist Studies	CEF was focused on the dissemination of feminist-oriented materials.
DIGNAS – 1990, Mujeres por la Dignidad y la Vida – Women for Dignity and Life	The organization was founded by members of the National Resistance (Resistencia Nacional – RN) as part of a strategy to broaden their support for women and to be able to receive international funding. RN was one of the five political parties/guerrilla organizations (FARN) that constituted FMLN and had the highest number of women in the ranks. In 1992, DIGNAS broke away from their affiliation with the RN and became an autonomous organization.
CEMUJER – 1991, Center for Women's Studies – Centro de Estudios de la Mujer "Norma Virginia Guirola de Herrera"	Founded with a feminist agenda that provided technical assistance to women in the form of legal aid, and on training in grassroots organizing.
IMC – 1991 Iniciativa de	Theme-based feminist agenda.

Mujeres Cristianas – Christian Women's Initiative	
MUES – 1991, Mujeres Universitarias de El Salvador – Salvadoran University Women	Theme-based feminist agenda.
CMPDI -1991Concertación de Mujeres por la Paz, la Dignidad, y la Igualdad – Women's Coalition for Peace, Dignity, and Equality	Originally formed in association with the RN, the CMPDI became an organization that welcomed groups seeking an identity independent of their political party affiliation. It focused on coalition-building efforts. It served as an umbrella for 24 organizations.
MAM – 1992, Movimiento de Mujeres "Mélida Anaya Montes" – Mélida Anaya Montes Women's Movement	The founders (Lorena Peña and others) maintain that MAM is an autonomous organization even though Mélida Anaya Montes was a ranking member in the FPL guerrilla organization. They adopted the term, "feminist autonomy."
CLFSML – 1992, Colectivo Lésbico Feminista Salvadoreña de la Media Luna – Half-Moon Salvadoran Lesbian Feminist Collective	El Salvador's first self-proclaimed lesbian organization.

***

Las Dignas Organization: 'Nosotras, las mujeres' (We, the Women)

Mujeres por la Dignidad y la Vida or *Las Dignas* was formally introduced at a summit, *El Encuentro de Mujeres por la Dignidad y la Vida* on July 14, 1990.[84] It was at the end of the twelve-year civil war and a female ranking member of the FMLN guerilla organization, Resistencia Nacional (RN), proposed the idea of a woman's organization to bolster the guerrilla's political party appeal, and even attract international funding. A group of former combatants including Morena Herrera, started their organizing efforts with the immense networks of the RN's Concertación de Mujeres coalition that included 24 women organizations. These were organizations in departments controlled by the RN, mostly in rural and semi-rural areas of Cuscatlán, Cabañas, La Libertad, Santa Ana, and San Miguel.[85] The initial charge was to unite the women, but remain well enough independent to initiate original and focused agendas. The women leaders, accustomed to combat in the front lines soon realized that to take on such a responsibility they would need to follow the "militant's bible" and stay loyal to the principles of the 'revolution,' adhere to the rigors of discipline, concretize the information to carry out the mission in exact terms, practice the ultimate sacrifice, and fight to the death. However, instead, they discovered that by applying the principles of feminism for which they ascribed, their lives would be utterly transformed. As feminists they learned to think critically, to analyze their experiences against a feminist theory in order to understand the inequality and hierarchical relationships between men and women. They realized how the political institutions subordinate women, and about the power relations that perpetuate inequality. Through confronting their past political practices, they opened up opportunities for the creation of a new reality that was more horizontal and democratic.

The following statement from Gloria Castañeda de Zamora exemplifies the incredible journey of discovery, at least for some of the women:

> *When I first heard the word feminism, it was like speaking about the devil. I didn't know what it was about, but they had told me that it was bad.... Now we have been learning that there are different currents of feminism and that feminism is simply the revindication of women... It's still very hard for us women to have the ability to speak openly about ourselves. It's a process. There are still a lot of individual interest, political interests, party interests....* [86]

A historical account of the first decade of *Las Dignas* chronicles the difficulties in the process of uniting a very diverse group of women at a national level. One of the first challenges the group encountered was the decision to break away from the Resistencia Nacional, the guerrilla organization, and become an autonomous body. Without the organizational and financial support of the RN, *Las Dignas* had to find a new identity and support base.[87] Not all women wanted to join *Las Dignas* unless they would receive something in return. The different sectors, urban and rural, each had their own unique situations and specific needs. It was an enormous challenge and almost impossible to conquer. But, the group persisted in working with the women; at every turn of events, *Las Dignas* re-grouped and tried yet another approach. They came to the realization that a "strategic" approach to addressing issues and problems was insufficient. The circumstances of women who were struggling with poverty and lacked sufficient literacy skills, for example, necessitated a "practical" approach that enabled women to work and learn simultaneously. The following quote eloquently describes their self-discovery and the pathway toward empowerment: *"Y empezamos a re-descubrir el mundo, a leerlo y verlo de otra manera, a ver las otras mujeres, a vernos nosotras...*[88] Eventually, *Las Dignas* decided against the division of strategic vs. practical, and instead opted for the creation of a wide-ranging platform where women could organize and take on their own projects.

Concluding Remarks

Despite the end of the war, a wide array of issues and problems related to extreme poverty and other social factors continued to persist.[89] After the war, the poverty rates decreased slightly from 65 percent in 1992 to 59 percent in 1998; extreme poverty fell from 34 percent to 26 percent. Adult literacy and life expectancy rates remained the same or worse than before the war. During the same time period, rural farmers or campesinos experienced declining wages, and the price for agricultural goods declined, increasing poverty levels. Between 1994 and 1995, the crime rate soared to 138 per 100,000, exceeding the rate at the height of the war, which was 55.3 per 100,000. Undoubtedly, these and many others served as obstacles in the work of *Las Dignas* during their initial ten years. However, the organization developed a practical plan based on their specific criteria to address these. Their plan encompassed a global vision, connecting with both the international and local communities of feminists, and building on grassroots organizing and development. Their ideas and recommendations were (and still are) inclusive of all women, and of all ages. The platform that they developed and disseminated as a result of the series of coalition-sponsored events and debates in the "Mujeres '94," (leading up to the 1994 elections), included issues that overlapped with the United Nations Beijing Platform for Action of 1994-95.[90]

In 1979, the United Nations General Assembly adopted *CEDAW* (The Convention on the Elimination of all Forms of Discrimination against Women) with specific guidelines that focus on action plans to end discrimination against women.[91] Its framework includes the definition of discrimination against women as "any distinction, exclusion or restriction made on the basis of sex." Additionally, its major work includes the development of assessment protocols to monitor a country's progress in following the adoption of the Convention's articles. The most recent periodic report (2017) submitted by the Committee on the Elimination of Discrimination against Women to El Salvador ("Concluding Observations on the Combined Eighth and Ninth Periodic Reports of El Salvador") elaborates on the progress and achievements of the Salvadoran administration, as well as some of the most pressing areas of need. The document specifies the acceptability of the action plans that the government has committed to develop and implement, e.g., areas in institutional and legal framework, as well as access to justice. The report considers recommendations of major importance, such as the following: 1) the need to provide women who were victims of the armed conflict with reparation measures; 2) to improve the quality and speed by which to investigate and prosecute acts of harassment, discrimination, violence, and assassination of female human rights defenders, and offer remedies and reparation to the victims; 3) to allocate sufficient resources to the implementation of policies and action plans to ensure a violence-free life for women; 4) to improve an action plan to prevent and combat trafficking and sexual exploitation of women and girls, particularly in gang-related situations; and 5) to improve efforts to eradicate illiteracy, especially among women and girls in rural areas.

Salvadoran women who seek abortion *care can only* do so through clandestine circumstances, and are often exposed to unsafe procedures. Women are at great risk of suffering blotched abortion procedures, and if they seek emergency care, the hospital staff is required by law to report the women to the authorities. Women are prosecuted and imprisoned if found guilty of having an abortion or even a miscarriage if the judge is convinced that an "abortion" was committed. It is the absolute criminalization of abortion and is perceived to be extraordinarily unjust for Salvadoran women.[92] Clearly, the Salvadoran authorities reject the charge that criminalizing abortion is discriminating against women. Regardless of whether it is acknowledged as a violation of human rights, women are consistently denied justice.

Feminists have a deep understanding of the politics of injustices. In their estimation, the revolution has yet to yield the results that women believed in from the moment they decided to fight in the civil war.

Chapter Two

Their Memories, Words, and Courage: A Journey Toward Healing

> *"... making the pain visible,*
> *what the war had made invisible"*
> *Las Dignas*

Post-conflict El Salvador marked a new chapter of immeasurable suffering and chaos. Despite the *Peace Accords of 1992* and efforts to demobilize and reintegrate into civil society, the women who had participated in the guerrillas were left behind. As a social group they received the least benefits in war reparation and compensation, and suffered from deteriorating health consequences.[1]

Las Dignas recognized the need to address the mental health issues that burdened women who had experienced the profound trauma of losing a loved one and the resulting psychological impact. They developed a program of support groups, allowing women to begin the healing process by "making the pain visible, what the war had made invisible" (*hicimos visible el dolor invisible de la guerra*).[2] Initially, the participating women hesitated to even attempt to recall their painful lived experiences during the war. The healing process was gradual as the women created their own narratives to help them release the emotional pressure. The mountains where they had spent so much time enduring the torturous explosions of war, evolved into a metaphorical symbol of "Mother Earth" protecting and nourishing their struggle: *"las montañas nutrientes de la lucha, no fueron entes abstractos, fuimos mujeres, las mujeres montaña, las montañas con recuerdos de mujer"* (...we were women, women-mountains, the mountains with the memories of women).[3] The mental health program (*programa de salud mental*) achieved considerable success in its first few years. Not all of the participating women adopted the feminist ideals embedded in *Las Dignas'* philosophy. However, it was evident that the riveting stories of these women were essential to our understanding of how the revolution impacted them. Norma Vásquez, Cristina Ibáñez, and Clara Murguialdy (and Morena Herrera) organized the research project and published their work, titled *Mujeres-Montaña: Vivencias de Guerrilleras y Colaboradoras del FMLN.*[4]

The women's stories included in the *Mujeres-Montaña* are organized by themes. In the following section are twelve stories (selected) from the publication to illustrate a sample of the collection. The stories are written in the original Spanish language. However, following the excerpt, a translation is provided to facilitate the English language reader.

Selected Stories from Mujeres-Montaña: Vivencias de Guerrilleras y Colaboradoras del FMLN

1. Gloria Castañeda, Resistencia Nacional – (RN).

Spanish

No quedaba ningún chance de reflexionar, era la euforia, un contagio, un ir haciendo y hacienda acciones y no pensar, simplemente te dejas ir y vives ese instante con gran fuerza y te entregas a él sin medir consecuencias. Dejábamos a los hijos en cualquier lado, entrenábamos de noche, hacíamos cualquier cosa, no había limites ni condiciones en la entrega, queríamos hacer cuantas cosas se pudiera, no importaba qué ni cómo. La reflexión vino cuando ya estábamos bien zampadas y no había camino de regreso.

English Translation

We got caught up in the euphoria, a contagion, to take immediate action without considering the consequences. We would leave our children with family or friends. We would train at night. There were no limits. We wanted to do everything we could. It didn't matter how. When we realized what was happening, there was no point of return.

2. Margarita Villafranco, Partido Revolucionario de los Trabajadores Centroamericanos – (PRTC).

Spanish

A mi me reclutó una compañera muy buena y me entró con el discurso de que teníamos que sacar al imperialismo yanqui de El Salvador, me comenzó a generar conciencia antimperialista y clasista y me atrajo; también por mi conciencia religiosa yo era muy sensible al aspecto del sufrimiento humano.

English Translation

My girlfriend who recruited me told me that we had to get rid of the empiricist yanqui. I reflected upon my conscious against imperialism and inequality. And insofar as my religious consciousness I thought logically about the aspect of human suffering.

3. Silvia, orphaned at a very young age; enlisted in the guerrilla at age 18.

Spanish

Yo desde muy jovencita estaba en grupos de la iglesia y ahí estudiábamos, hacíamos muchos cursos de lo que llamábamos realidad del país y me acuerdo que Monseñor Romero nos explicaba cómo teníamos que vivir la Biblia en la vida real. Así aprendíamos, los pasajes de las Sagradas Escrituras los aplicábamos a la realidad y entonces era que entendíamos de política. Fue por medio de la Iglesia que decido meterme en la vida política y cuando me incorporo plenamente al partido, todas las reflexiones que habíamos hecho en ese grupo me ayudaban a entender lo que se decía. Era más bonito y la gente entendía más si le hablabas de la palabra de Dios y de cómo estábamos cumpliendo con la lucha sus mandatos.

English Translation

When I was growing up, I participated in church sponsored youth groups. I had many classes where we discussed the reality in our country. I remember Monseñor Romero explaining to us that we had to live the Bible, in real life. That's how we learned, by applying the sacred scriptures to reality and that's how we understood politics. It was through the church that I decided to enter into politics. And when I became part of the political party everything we had discussed in that group helped me better understand the political discussions. It was beautiful the way people understood when we talked about the Word of God and how we were accomplishing the mandates.

4. Milagros, enlisted at age 24 through her church.

Spanish

Había unos seminaristas en la parroquia que nos hablaban de las injusticias y los problemas que había en la sociedad, de los niños que no asimilaban en la escuela porque estaban mal alimentados….Nos decían que en América Latina estaban ocurriendo grandes cambios, hablaban del Che Guevara y de la revolución cubana, decían que en El Salvador se podría dar una situación igual porque había mucha injusticia y desempleo, porque no había respeto a las personas. Me invitaron a participar en seminarios con el enfoque de la Iglesia y después dijeron que en el país se iba a dar un cambio social, que era para construir una nueva sociedad y un nuevo hombre con un pensamiento diferente y me dijeron que era importante que yo participara en ese proceso.

English Translation

There were some catechists in our parish that would talk to us about the injustices and problems in our society that children could participate in school because they were malnourished. They would tell us that Latin America was going through some big changes; about Che Guevara and the Cuban Revolution, that the same could occur in El Salvador because of so many injustices and unemployment and the lack of respect for the life every human being. I was invited to discuss the role of the church and then, I was told that there would be a social change in our country so we would be able to construct a new society, the New Man with a different perspective. And they told me it was important for me to participate.

5. Lorena, a medic, enlisted at age 27.

Spanish

Mi mamá, como muchas mujeres de esa época pese a que eran muy tradicionales, se metía en cuestiones políticas. De ella fue que escuché que teníamos que estudiar y prepararnos, pero no para ganar dinero solamente sino para ayudar a la gente que no tenía nada. Los ricos siempre pueden comparar salud o lo que quieran, nos decia, pero los pobres son los que necesitan y no tienen cómo.

English Translation

Even though my mother was very traditional like so many others during her era, she was nevertheless interested in politics. She told us that we had to study and prepare ourselves not only so we can maintain ourselves but so we can help the people that don't have anything. The rich can buy healthcare or whatever they want, but the poor are the ones in need and they don't have the means.

6. Alejandra, se incorporó a le edad de 14, y a los 21 años como combatante.

Spanish

Nos incorporamos porque mis papas se metieron en eso, como ellos se metieron también nosotros. Yo tenía 9 años. Mi mamá daba catequesis y decían que ella era guerrillera, que la iban a matar y entonces ya no vivíamos tranquilos porque ella estaba con ese miedo. Primero murió mi papa, después en un operativo mataron a mi mamá. Yo vine a San Salvador porque me mandaron a reunirme con mis hermanas y para que diera testimonio de lo que habían hecho en ese operativo, pero ese no era mi lugar. Al fin en el '86 dije me volvía a la zona y me fui.

English Translation

We got involved because of our parents, and just like them we got involved. I was nine years and my mother taught catechism. They said she was a guerillera [revolutionary] and she was going to get killed. Then, we lived in fear just like my mother. First, my father died. Then, in a military operation they killed my mother. I came to San Salvador because I was told to reunite with my sisters and that I should give testimony about my role in that military operation. But that wasn't my place. Finally, I left at the end of 1986; I returned to the zone.

7. Elvira, se incorporó en un frente guerrillero a los 18 años 1989.

Spanish

Lo que pasa es que la vida de ellas giraba alrededor de la guerrilla y la guerra y vivían una situación tremenda porque la gente no hallaba ni siquiera cómo mantener a sus hijos, entonces las muchachas, niñas de 10 o 12 años, en vez de estar aguantando hambre en su casa, o tal vez ya ni casa tenían, se iban a los campamentos donde por lo menos tenían la comida asegurada y los zapatos y su vestido y ahí estaban seguras aunque les tocara trabajar un poquito.

English Translation

Some little girls as young a twelve years-old joined the guerrilla refugee camps out of necessity. They came from very poor homes where a parent or both parents were gone. The lack of food was a dominant problem. At least in the refugee camps the young girls had food, a pair of shoes, and clothes, even if they had daily chores.

8. Rosario, joined the student movement in 1985 and eventually served as part of the guerrilla's urban command.

Spanish

Cuando me incorporé a la lucha ya había pasado por un proceso de cambios enmi manera de pensar y veía las diferencias entre los ricos y los pobres, entre los trabajadores y los que no trabajan; luego, la repelladita que me dieron en la iglesia me ayudó bastante. Me incorporé de manera consciente y creo que si no lo hubiera hecho no me lo hubiera perdonado en toda la vida.

Era distinto el caso de otras que se incorporaron porque sus papas os sus hermanos ya lo habían hecho porque vivían en el frente o en el refugio y ahí las reclutaron, quizás con 12 o 15 años. Ellas se comportaban distinto a quienes habíamos entrado por conciencia … nos dolía mucho cuando malgastaban las cosas que les mandábamos desde aquí, pero uno pensaba qué se les puede pedir a esas cipotas que en realidad su vida ha sido la guerra….

English Translation

By the time Rosario had joined the struggle her way of thinking and perceiving had changed dramatically, which she acknowledges was due to the influence by the church. She understood inequality that existed between the poor and the wealthy. She alone experienced a level of consciousness that transformed totally and if she hadn't she would not have forgiven herself. Rosario joined as a result of conscious-raising unlike the young girls who sought shelter in the refugee camps because their older siblings and/or parents had joined out of necessity.

9. Elizabeth enlisted at age 18 and spent eight years in the camp; she never attended school but learned to read and write while in the guerrilla.

Spanish

¿Por qué me animé a participar? Bueno, ellos nos daban bastante charlas, nos decían que esto iba a cambiar, que ya no íbamos a estar sumergidos por los yanquis, a nosotros nos hacían ver eso y dijimos, 'vamos a morir o a vivir mejor', porque esa era la consigna, además nos decían que eso iba a durar un día o lo más una semana y que después podíamos regresar a seguir estudiando y que la educación iba a ser mejor, gratis. Bueno, nos presentaban un montón de oportunidades y yo me la creí, mi familia también.

English Translation

Why did I decide to participate? Well, we had many discussions and they told us that we would not succumb to the yanquis; we would ask ourselves: are we going to die and live better? And, they would tell us that it [revolution] would last a day or a week and afterwards we could return and continue our studies. And our education would be better and free. Well, they presented at lot of opportunities and I believed them and so did my family.

10. Esther, age 27, began as a collaborator with the guerrilla when she found out her husband had deceived her.

Spanish

A mi, lo que hacía que siguiera participando es que nos decían que ya no iba a existir el guaro (licor), que lo iban a tratar de erradicar un poco, porque en mi comunidad a cada paso se encontraban las ventas de guaro y no se podía vivir con los hombres bolos (borrachos). Yo por eso trabajé con muchas ganas, éramos cinco los que ellos pusieron de directivas, pero solo las dos mujeres nos mantuvimos.

English Translation

For me the reason I continued to participate was because they told us that they would eradicate the guaro (liquor) because in my community you can find a liquor store in every block and no one can live with drunk men. That's why I worked so hard.

11. Ana, collaborator in the rearguard front for 14 years; six of her children died during the war.

Spanish

Usted sabe que uno por los hijos da la vida así que cuando ellos me dijeron 'mama, nosotros no queremos morir con los brazos cruzados ni masacrados, nosotros nos vamos a la lucha y al lado de usted se queda el pueblo,' yo me di a la tarea de ir a los campamentos a moler. Como mis hijos estaban en diferentes organizaciones, yo me iba un mes donde el campamento del ERP y otro al de las FPL y luego al de la RN. Mi corazón de madre no entendía de divisiones.'

English Translation

You know that when children are your life, when they tell you Mama, we don't want to die with our arms crossed, or in a massacre. We are going to fight and by our side are the people; I decided to work in the guerrilla camps to grind corn and since my children were in guerrilla camps, I would go to the ERP camp, the FPL camp, and then, the RN. As a mother my heart could not distinguish between the divisions.

12. Alma was active in the guerrilla for 14 years and was a combatant for a time until her partner was killed after which she joined the communication division.

Spanish

Yo quise especializarme en el manejo de armas y aprender el arte militar, ese era mi objetivo, pero no me dejaron, me pusieron en comunicaciones. Yo estaba convencida de que podía ser una buena combatiente, de que podía llegar a ser jefa de un pelotón, pero me cuentearon sobre la importancia estratégica de las comunicaciones y no me quedó más remedio que pasar 10 años en eso.

English Translation

I wanted to specialize in the use of weapons and learn the military arts. That was my objective. But they didn't let me. I was assigned to communications. I was convinced that I could become an effective combatant and eventually achieve the rank of squad leader. But they pointed out the important strategy of communications and I didn't have any other option so I stayed there for ten years.

Female Child Soldiers Narratives

Narratives about female child combatants depict the harrowing experiences of young girls who joined guerrilla groups as children. Their life experiences are marked by the kind of unbearable suffering that few adults could possibly endure, yet as children they had to face the consequences. The war took away a part of their lives that can never be regained. If women were among the groups that suffered the extreme consequences of war in scale and depth, then female child soldiers were doubly victimized. Despite this, research reveals that in the post-conflict era, the needs and rights of child soldiers were largely ignored.[5]

According to Beth Verhey's research, a follow-up survey (completed by UCA/UNICEF) includes the data on the ages of the young recruits in both the FLMN and the FAES (Salvadoran Armed Forces). The median age for FLMN children recruits is 12 years old, while the FAES reported a median age of 15.8 years. The majority of the children in FMLN guerrilla were in the "less than 10 years-old and between 10 and 14 years old" brackets, which adds up to 93.4 percent. The majority of the children in the FAES were "15 years or older." Both armed forces recruited children but the FMLN had the younger ages. About 92 percent in the FMLN group reported that they joined voluntarily, compared to the FAES group's responses that only 47 percent joined on their own volition. Considering all age groups in both armed forces, 60 percent of the children that joined were between 7 and 13 years old. Reportedly, the FMLN had more female soldiers, all ages, than the FAES.

Selected Stories From Alan Henríquez Chávez' Thesis, "De la locura y a la esperanza truncada: memorias de desarme, desmovilización y reinserción de excombatientes en El Salvador posconflicto." [6]

Griselda_1

When I didn't have my family anymore, a friend of my mother, Albertina said, I'm going to take her with me. But- I thought she was taking me to her house, but she brought me here, for the war. She dropped me off here in Las Vueltas, with the guerrilla. I was ten. I was introduced to the comandante who told me: you're very young but here you will stop growing up. It was around 1987 or 88 and I was here. What was sad for me was that I had to attend this school for 6 months. It was so hard going to that school because we would practice all day long, and then also at night. The exercise was very heavy. It got to the point where I couldn't bend down to go to the bathroom because I was sore all over. After we finished school in 6 months we had to decide what job we wanted: to cook, to help as a brigadista or a combatant. But since I've never been to school I couldn't sign up to be a radio operator or a medic, so I was either a cook or a combatant. And I don't like to cook because those poor cooks would walk around with pots on their heads. So, that's why I decided to become a combatant.

Griselda_2

The first time I was in combat to prove myself according to them, they would order us to go fight. No more than five of us and I remember that time when I stood by a tree and started to cry. I said, here I'm going to do it, here they're going to kill me. What should I do? And one of my compañeros told me either you fight or they kill you. He pushed me down to the ground and that's where I started to feel brave. Time went by. And when I was twelve I started to fight because at 12 years old you are a combatant. When I was twelve we spent days in this little mountain, here in the frontline, looking out all day long. The 'posta' we called it. And one day I stepped on a mine. It felt as though something had exploded like I had flown away up in the air. But I acted quickly and I stood up and I couldn't see any of my compañeros. Then, I saw them come out from hiding in the tall grass, they thought the soldiers had attacked us. They just kept looking at me.

They had to carry me for eight days, then, we came up against the Atlactl battalion and they decided they couldn't carry me anymore; that they would be killed. So, they found a tunnel nearby and left me there for four days. They left me a bottle of water. After four days I heard my compañeros returning. One of them said that they would probably need to bury me in the tunnel. But then, they saw that I was still alive and were very surprised. They said, she's alive, she's alive! But my wounds were like molded cheese with little worms coming out. It was full of worms. They cleaned up my wounds and I felt better after two months,. Then, I went back to the front lines but when they ordered me back to the little mountain I started to tremble. I just couldn't go back. I was afraid I would step on another mine. They got mad at me because I wouldn't go there. I was twelve at the time.

Griselda_3

When I was 13 my friends would tell me "look now you're really pretty and it's time that you find a boyfriend to get together because maybe here we're going to die. You don't know if you'll be alive the next morning. When I had my period for the first time I was 13 yrs. old. I didn't know what it was. Then, they explained it to me but I didn't know until then. Well, that happened and then I had a boyfriend who was the father of my daughter and I was with him. Then, my period stopped and I thought maybe it was supposed to come once a year. Then I found out I was going to have a child. I was happy because I felt that I wouldn't be alone anymore. I was pregnant, I didn't know how many months. I didn't know anything. I would still go on patrols with him, fighting even though I was pregnant. He was happy but when I was seven months pregnant he was killed. I had left to go stay at Los Ranchos cabañas. I was seven months pregnant when he was killed. And eight days later, my daughter was born.

Digna_1

I enlisted not because I wanted to, well I did but because I had to. We started to organize ourselves in 1979 because my sisters were killed in 1980. So I was eleven years old when they killed my sisters, After that my father started to organize and I went with him. I was in the guerrilla because I was twelve but afterward I started going with the father of my two daughters. He was a combatant. We were all there with him, then I returned to Chalatenango with him. Then, I was fully enlisted in the guerrilla. I didn't enlist to fight as a combatant, I joined to work with the militias, preparing their food. My husband organized the militias. It was dangerous because we were with the troops. I helped out taking care of the wounded soldiers because there was a hospital in a tunnel where we could all hide from the aerial bombardment. When they wounded the compañeros I would cover their mouths because they were screaming with pain.

Digna_2

I was a medic. I saw that my compañeros needed the help. Perhaps, God gave me the strength and I learned how to give injections to heal. I would treat the wounded because there were so many accidents here and I 'm not afraid to treat the wounds. But I don't like to be in hospitals. I don't like it.

It's that I suffered because I was a medic in the front lines. But I also worked in communications for several years. But then I went back to being a medic, that's always been my main function. But I was a combatant first, but then I saw how someone needed help. So being a medic was the most for me. Being a combatant is fine also because you're defending but maybe being a medic is the most important job because you're saving a lot of people's lives. Also a radio operator because if you're treating a wounded compañero you can use the radio to call for help. The two jobs are the most important because you're saving lives. But being a combatant is important too. Maybe the best work I did was when I laid down beside a wounded compañero with bullets flying all around us. But maybe God gave me the strength because I was not afraid. What motivated me to stay in the guerrilla, I think like I said, I saw how they killed two of my sisters all at once. I was eleven. And maybe that gave me the strength because its incredible to see that they're killing your family and there's nothing you can do at the time. Maybe that's it. I didn't feel hatred but I felt so badly because they killed my family. And almost killed me. But maybe that's what motivated me to keep fighting.

***

A Closer Look at the Women and Their Testimonies

Thousands of women participated in the civil war yet we know only a fraction of their stories. Thankfully, some of the women have documented and published their stories, sharing their individual testimonies with a wider audience. This section provides brief background summaries of some of the women.

Ana Guadalupe Martinez Menéndez served as ranking member of the Ejército Revolucionario del Pueblo (ERP) guerrilla organization. She became involved in politics while a student at the University of El Salvador and after the electoral fraud of 1972, joined the ERP. She was captured by the Salvadoran military in 1976 and spent nine months in clandestine prison, enduring painful, humiliating torture. She chronicles this experience in her book, *Las cárceles clandestinas*. She was released in a prisoner exchange between the military and the guerrilla. She rejoined the ERP in 1978, and toward the end of the war, travelled throughout Europe on a mission to inform others about the Salvadoran war. After the war, Martínez returned to her medical practice and also, was elected to the National Assembly with the Partido Demócrata Cristiano (PDC). You can listen to an interview conducted by Jean Krasno (translation provided). (Also, Karen Kampwirth interviewed Ana Guadalupe, included in this volume.) The brief interview is available *by* Jean Krasno.[7] Another book written by Martínez is in English, *A Woman from the Liberation Front Testifies.*[8]

Nidia Díaz, whose birth name was María Marta Valladares, was studying Psychology at the University of El Salvador in 1975 when she joined the Partido Revolucionario de los Trabajadores Centroamericanos (PTRC) guerrilla organization. She had participated in the social movements opposing the military government, and was influenced by the Partido Demócrata Cristiano (political party). As a commander, she directed guerrilla units between 1981-85 in San Vicente and San Miguel departments. She was captured by the Salvadoran forces in April, 1985 and detained and tortured for six months. In her testimony concerning her detention and torture, she recalls the presence of CIA agent Félix Rodríguez (also known as Max Gómez). This information is also documented in the work by researcher/author Ilya Luciak.[9] The matter of CIA agent Félix Rodríguez and his conduct deserves at the very least public scrutiny. Rodríguez took into possession a piece of clothing from Nidia Díaz who at the time was a prisoner in the torture chamber; he took her brassiere and displayed it in this home, as if to display a trophy. In an interview published in 2012, Díaz was asked about the civil war, whether it produced the expected outcomes. Díaz responded in the affirmative, saying "we dismantled the dictatorship." Yet, the country is presently teetering on the verge of a dictatorship under the presidency of Nayib Bukele, much to the dismay of those that lived through the horrors of the 1980's war.[10]

Lorena Guadalupe Peña Mendoza enlisted in the Fuerzas Populares de Liberación (FPL) guerrilla organization at the age of 17. She became a ranking member of the FPL and directed two fronts between 1980 and 1990.

Lorena, whose nom de guerre was "Rebeca," was part of the Comisión Polítco Diplomática (CPD) between 1990 and 1992, and participated in the peace negotiations of the Peace Accords of 1992. She served as president of the National Assembly (Asamblea Legislativa de El Salvador) in 2015-2016. Known as a feminist, Peña was instrumental in the founding of the Movimiento de Mujeres Mélida Anaya Montes (Las Mélidas). In an 1994 interview by Marta Harneker, Peña discusses her perspectives on the women's movement and the importance of a struggle for the transformation of a society. She believes in creating the conditions beyond addressing the essential or basic needs so that women can strive to advance in a holistic and sustainable manner.[11]

Morena Herrera. "Political activist, mother, ex-guerrilla commander, and architecture student" – is how Lynn Stephen describes Morena Herrera in her interview, a chapter in her book entirely dedicated to Herrera's life. ("Morena Herrera: Women for Dignity and Life" in *Women and Social Movements in Latin America*, 1997.) Herrera and other women founded the feminist organization, known as *Las Dignas* in 1992, right after the war's demobilization and reintegration process began. Morena was a child when she would accompany her mother to political demonstrations such as the teachers' strike in 1968. As a high school student, she participated in Catholic youth group activities and then, joined Revolutionary Action of Secondary Students (ARDES). At this time, the Salvadoran military repression against civilians increased, and Morena witnessed first-hand the brutality. She remembers the shock in learning about the 1977 massacre that took place after a huge demonstration in downtown San Salvador.

The first time she was physically involved in a milieu, she and her school mates yelled at the National Guard who chased them with tear gas. She joined the Resistencia Nacional (RN) guerrilla organization and became a leader as a military and political strategist. Her life changed dramatically with *Las Dignas*. She embarked on a journey of self-discovery, and realized her passion in working with women, focused on feminist themes. Her participation in the women's conference in Argentina (1990) was particularly transformative. Upon her return,she enthusiastically shared everything she had learned with the women, who in turn, shared their newly found awakening with other women. Herrera is actively involved in the struggle for justice and equality and is currently one of the most high-profile feminists, not only in El Salvador but throughout Central America and México.

Mélida Anaya Montes (1929-1983), known as Comandante Ana María, was second in command, after Salvador Cayetano Carpio, of the Fuerzas Populares de Liberación (FPL). She was also a commanding officer in the FMLN. Montes was an educator and is best known as the founder of ANDES-21, the national teacher union that was a powerful force in the social movement during the war. After the 1972 national teacher strike, Anaya, who had witnessed the brutality of the repression against teachers, declared that she would be personally involved in the armed insurgency, since there was no other option. She joined FPL. Anaya was murdered in Managua, Nicaragua on April 6, 1983, and soon afterward, Carpio was accused of ordering her killing, and committed suicide. Her book is titled *Ana María, Combatiente de la Vida.*[12]

Norma Virginia Guirola de Herrera. In 1986, Norma Guirola founded *El instituto para la investigación, capacitación, y desarrollo de mujer* (the Institute for Research, Training, and Development of Women, or IMU). Guirola is a pioneer in the feminist movement in El Salvador. IMU provided support and training to women's organizations in the areas of communication, legal rights, and education. She was killed in 1989, but supporters and family continued her work with the opening of Centro de estudios de la mujer "Norma Guirola de Herrera' or CEMUJER. The organization is rooted in feminism and continues to support women's efforts in the areas of technical assistance, legal aid, and training for grassroots organizations.

Febe Elizabeth Velásquez, killed in a bomb attack in 1989, was secretary general for the trade union, Federación Nacional Sindical de Trabajadores Salvadoreños (FENASTRAS), was an outspoken leader and advocate for trade union activities, which the Salvadoran military fiercely opposed. The federation had become a very powerful, organized labor front since its inception in 1974. The headquarters were bombed twice in 1989, but the last one, on October 31, claimed the life of Velásquez and nine others. The October bombing occurred under President Cristiani's watch who at the time was in the middle of peace negotiations with the FMLN. As a consequence of the bombing at FENASTRAS and COMADRES headquarters, the FMLN suspended the peace talks under the protestation that the government was insincere and deceptive. The courage and bravery of Velásquez and her colleagues serve as a testament to the dedication of the federation to protect and advance the rights of the working class, especially the campesinos in the countryside.[13]

Alicia Panameno de García. On July 30, 1975, Alicia, who was working as a nurse at a maternity ward in a hospital, witnessed the brutal massacre of students peacefully protesting on the street in San Salvador by the National Guard. Afterward, her brother, who was amongst the student protestors, did not return home that day; the family learned that he had been "disappeared." In the course of searching for her brother, she encountered other families who had also lost their loved ones. She never located the remains of her brother, but she and others organized COMADRES, the *Committee of Mothers for People Who Have Disappeared*.[14]

Marianella García Villas, an attorney, served in the Salvadoran Legislative Assembly for two years (1974-1976). In 1979, she began to document the human rights abuses and disappearances that were reported by families of the victims. Her documentation included photographs and archival information, which she presented to the United Nations Commission on Human Rights. She was conducting field work with displaced refugees when she was assassinated by the Salvadoran Armed Forces. She was posthumously awarded the Bruno Kreisky Human Rights prize in 1984.[15]

Clara Elisabeth Ramírez (Eva) was born in 1949 into a middle-class family. According to Joaquín Chávez, Ramírez was a university student activist, who along with two other classmates, José Alejandro Solano and Andrés Torres, were co-editors of the notorious *Red Star* (*Estrella Roja*), a publication that advanced the ideology and strategy of the Fuerzas Populares de Liberación

(FPL) guerrilla organization.[16] The three students were part of the first generation of armed militants (early 1970s) in the FPL to engage in guerrilla warfare in urban sites. They were committed to the armed struggle because, according to Eva's sister, Victoria, "that was the path; there was no other path". On October 10, 1976, the three activist/militants were cornered by the military forces in San Salvador's neighborhood of Santa Tecla. A gun battle ensued, and clearly outnumbered, the three made a suicide pact rather than face the inevitable capture, detention, and torture.

***Lil Milagro Ramírez,* (1946 – 1979).** Ramírez was a student at the University of El Salvador when she became involved with a student group of poets and activists. She was one of the few female students involved, but she was committed to the revolution and was willing to risk her life. She was captured, detained, and tortured in a clandestine prison, where she died.[17]

Madeleine Lagadec was an international volunteer (from France) and had worked as a nurse for three years at a mobile FMLN hospital in the eastern El Salvador front. Celia Díaz was a radio operator and literacy instructor, María Cristina Hernández was a radio operator and nurse, and José Ignacio Isla Cásares was a doctor from Argentina. When the air strikes began, everyone evacuated except for the individuals including Lagadec who refused to leave the patients behind. All five were killed including one of their patients, Juan Antonio. The *Truth Commission* report details the attack and includes an autopsy summary report on Madeleine Lagadec, probably because it was demanded by her family.[18]

The *Truth Commission* report indicates that on April 15, 1989, two U.S. made A-37 aircrafts bombarded the hospital, which initiated the evacuation of the area. In addition to the A-37, the following military vehicles participated in the attack, all made available by the United States: three UH IM helicopter gunships, a Hughes-500 helicopter and a "Push-Pull" light airplane. The bombardment lasted for 15 minutes. Then, six helicopters carrying unknown number of paratroopers armed with M-16 rifles arrived on the ground. Lagadec was shot six times, twice in the head, two in the torso area and one bullet in each thigh. Her left hand was amputated, probably while she was alive. The report concludes that the state failed in its responsibility to investigate the case and punish those responsible for the heinous killings.

Dra. Begoña García Arandigoyen. At 24 years old, Dra. García had worked as a medical doctor for the FMLN for a year. According to the *Truth Commission* report, Begoña García Arandigoyen, a medical doctor from Spain, was captured along with other survivors of a unit of the ERP guerrilla. The circumstances surrounding how or why she was among the combatant guerrilla is unknown but she was unarmed and not in uniform. In fact, the report states that the Salvadoran military soldiers that captured her and others knew that she was a "foreigner" and a non-combatant. The autopsy performed by the Salvadoran forensic doctor omitted in its findings that Begoña had been shot close-range in the head. The military report had falsely concluded that she had been shot from a distance as if to suggest that she was caught in the cross-fire as the soldiers and the guerrilla engaged in a gun battle. The cover-up of Begoña's death was part of a pattern that the Salvadoran military devised to obfuscate their problems with human rights, which were frequently violated.[19]

Concluding Remarks

The Salvadoran people suffered grave consequences as a result of the 12-year war. Entire families were impacted by the immense loss of life, particularly among the youth. The collective memory of the despicable, horrendous crimes committed by the military units remains a powerful presence, sometimes in the foreground and sometimes buried in the unconscious minds of people. Despite the tragic and chaotic circumstances, women carved out a unique niche in their vision of a "new" beginning. Clearly, a change had transformed the entire populace, and women had experienced a significant shift in perspective. The idea of a 'point of no return' reinforced their collective stance that their lives would never be the same again. Among the pantheon of "feminist' heroines are *ghosts*, hovering over their constant work, consistently reminding them of the sacrifices made by women who wanted *to change the world.*

Discussion and Reflection Questions

1. Give examples of how women specifically experience multiple forms of discrimination that intersect with experiences of persons from racialized and marginalized minority groups. Discuss your personal beliefs concerning how gender, race and class play significant roles in gendered historiographies.

2. In your opinion, what are the "push/pull" factors central to the reasons why Central Americans seek asylum in the United States and elsewhere? What does the "American Dream" consist of for many of the migrants? What further research information is needed in the field of migration studies specifically related to gender?

3. What role does *context* play in analyzing historical events concerning gender issues? Give examples of events that illustrate how women's issues are treated differently based on contextual factors?

4. Give examples of how Salvadoran women experienced discrimination within a predatory culture, in subtle or blatant terms? Describe your views of *toxic hypermasculinity* environments.

5. What is the value of applying a genealogical approach to the study of discrimination and/or racism that women experience throughout their lifetime? Discuss how democratic institutions can best serve to address (and resolve) gender-based discrimination.

6. Describe the United States' foreign policy with El Salvador in the 1960's. Analyze its general effects on Salvadoran life and on the emergence of the military as a dominant fixture in the political arena in conjunction with the wealthy sector, also known as the oligarchy.

7. Share your thoughts about the brutal murders of the four American missionaries, and the assault on teachers during peaceful, legitimate protests

during the ANDES strike, as well as the kidnapping of the Catholic nuns, and on the near-death, machete assault of another nun. Discuss how factors related to misogynism and heteropatriarchy may have played a role in these atrocities.

8. Describe the participation and eventual integration of women into the armed conflict. Why did the women choose to participate when they understood the risks involved and the gravity of the situation and its lifelong consequences? Compare how the women in the urban and countryside mobilized their actions.

9. Describe roles that women in the guerrilla held as combatants and non-combatants. What sort of experiences did they have that prompted them to realize the deep-seated, gender inequities in the guerrilla? Although some of the women took some corrective actions, why do you think they were generally unable to take broad and effective measures?

10. Young girls in the guerrilla were particularly vulnerable because of their gender and age, and their precarious situation since many were separated from their families. What can the international community postulate so that in the future children are shielded from these traumatic experiences?

11. Analyze the evolution of the women's movement in El Salvador, beginning with the second wave phases (Table 1.5). Why were women initially hesitant to adopt a "feminist" philosophy and become engaged as advocacy for the advancement of Salvadoran women? The DIGNAS were challenged with the task of "unifying" and organizing women from varying experiences and backgrounds. What difficulties did they encounter and how did they work to resolve these? What else do you think they could have done to meet their goals?

12. The 2017 report submitted by the Committee on the Elimination of Discrimination against Women includes the following five recommendations in their proposed action plan:

1) The need to provide women who were victims of the armed conflict with reparation measures;

2) To improve the quality and speed by which to investigate and prosecute acts of harassment, discrimination, violence, and assassination of female human rights defenders, and offer remedies and reparation to the victims;

3) To allocate sufficient resources to the implementation of policies and action plans to ensure a violence-free life for women;

4) To improve an action plan to prevent and combat trafficking and sexual exploitation of women and girls, particularly in gang-related situations; and

5) To improve efforts to eradicate illiteracy, especially among women and girls in rural areas.

Discuss some issues that you think may prevent the successful implementation of any one of these recommendations in the action plan.

Chapter Three

The Winds of War and Change

*The telling of stories creates the real world. Is it possible
for stories to change us and the world we live in?*
Alberto Manguel

The history of the Women's Movement in Guatemala chronicles a trajectory that includes a broad spectrum of ideologies and agendas reflecting the diverse lived experiences of women, socially, culturally, and economically. While many women played important, integral roles in the 36-year Internal Armed Conflict, their experiences in the war appear to be less consequential than the struggles that women faced in the greater society of Guatemala.

Feminist writers, including Ana Silvia Monzón, have highlighted the October '44 Revolution (la revolución de octubre 44) as a significant event in the advancement of Guatemalan women.[1] It is important to note that the prevailing narrative frames often excluded Mayan women, as their perilous situation in surviving the armed conflict far exceeded a vision of themselves as part of the women's movement. The Guatemalan Women's Movement had its beginnings among women, mostly from the middle-class and those living in the capital city (*las capitalinas*), who were able to raise their voices and clamor for democracy. Over time, women from various sectors and with different motivations, joined in the organized struggle for freedom and justice, ushering in an unprecedented period of activism among Guatemalan women. By the 1990s, women had made significant progress, as described by Monzón, in achieving their demands for quality educational opportunities, particularly in higher education, the right to vote, and the ability to participate in the political arena. Furthermore, women in the workforce, such as teachers and unionists, made significant strides in the fight for dignified labor rights. Field laborers also gained advancements in accessing land for growing their own crops. While women's lack of reproductive rights remains relatively unchanged, there is a growing trend toward a favorable shift. The indigenous women's groups have remained steadfast in their demands for seeking collective autonomy.[2]

Undoubtedly, these advancements underscore the multitude of women's visions, and their formidable attempts to address the issues of discrimination and racism that have plagued Guatemalan society for centuries. The leaders of the popular women's movement continue to convey the message of *unity*, emphasizing that their work has consistently engaged in struggles for *just cause*, and against oppressive conditions experienced by all citizens.

What remains uncontested among the socially conscience voices is the importance of contextualizing history to aid in a comprehensive understanding on how the past persists in impacting the present, and how the challenges and efforts to address them shape the future.

***

The following section aims to provide an overview of the major historical events that have shaped present-day Guatemala and the role of women in advancing through struggle and resistance. The thematic strands are organized into four broad time periods: a brief summary of the Mayan civilization and the Spanish conquest in the 1500's; 1871-1944, the era of the modern dictatorships; the so-named October 44 Revolution and the 1954 coup; and the Internal Armed Conflict, beginning in the 1960's. These events serve to enhance our understanding and comprehension of Guatemala's history and its impact on women's rights.

***

The Grandeur of the Mayan Civilization

The Maya of Guatemala are descendants of the great Mayan civilization, which scholars believe has roots dating back to the Early Pre-classic period. The discovery of Mesoamerican settlements eventually led to a phenomenal field of study on a worldwide scale. The work of a cadre of international researchers and scholars since the latter part of the nineteenth century have resulted in discoveries that point to the grandeur of the Maya people.

The Maya civilization relied heavily on maize, which was domesticated from wild grasses between 5000-7000 BCE. This allowed for subsistence farming to replace a migratory lifestyle, which had a transformative impact on their society. With remarkable skill, they constructed magnificent cities with spacious and unique buildings. They established a functional social and economic system, organized around a hierarchical and sustainable mode of leadership. They also developed an advanced form of writing, which combined logos and syllables and eventually becoming standardized and widely used throughout Mayan society. The Mayans were among the first civilization to develop the concept of *zero*, which had a significant impact on the world's mathematical and scientific advancements.[3]

Mesoamerican history includes the stories of many civilizations, each one encompassing aspects of advanced scientific and mathematical accomplishments comparable and even, superseding to those of other continents around the world. Historical and cultural accounts of the Maya inscribed in archeological ruins contain numerous acknowledgements attributed toward the scholars, scribes, and artisans. The winds of change in the Mesoamerican world reveal societies devoted to knowledge and achievements, but they also confirmed the prevalence of warfare and how the outcome of such violence shaped the lives of people.

There is ample historical evidence that friction and conflict existed among and between various Mayan groups. It appears that certain groups held an upper hand and inflicted cruel and miserable suffering on their adversaries. However, no one could have predicted the kind of violence that would be instigated by the Spanish conquistadors. These invaders were solely interested in seizing valuable treasures for themselves and were intent on destroying everything else in their path. Some historians argue that the Mesoamerican civilization was a work in progress for at least 15,000 years before the arrival of the Spanish. However, the Spanish conquest aimed to destroy it in a very brief period of just a few years.

In 1519, the Spaniards arrived in Mesoamerica, landing on the shores of the Bay of Campeche in the Gulf of Mexico. They then traveled towards the valley of Mexico, where they encountered the great Mesoamerican civilization. While there are numerous tales, legend, and historical accounts of the conquest, one fact stands out as particularly interesting: the underlying motive behind the Spanish conquest was the pillaging of the "treasure" and destruction of a civilization, all in the name of spreading Christianity and paying homage to the Spanish Crown.

The Spanish Conquest Beginning in the 1530's

The Spanish conquest of Mesoamerica and Latin America, had a profound impact on the indigenous populations. The systematic seizure of land, forced labor, and debt servitude plunged these communities into poverty, making it difficult for them to survive on subsistence agriculture. The Mayas, who had relied on agriculture for thousands of years, were forced to adapt to a new way of life under foreign rule. They were forced to abandon their culture and identity, but they chose to survive by using their well-endowed mental and physical attributes to adapt to the invaders while maintaining their dignity and respect for their ancestral roots.

The Spanish Crown maintained a stronghold on power by establishing an elite social class of Spaniards and non-indigenous (ladino or mestizo) landowners who profited from the acquisition of Mayan ancestral lands and the use of forced labor among the indigenous people. This hacienda-based economy persisted for two hundred years until the 1724 abolishment of the system of encomienda (a forced-labor law), which required the Mayas to converted to Christianity in exchange for the end of forced labor. By this time, the indigenous population had been decimated by Old World diseases, and many families had fled to seek refuge in the mountains.

***

A Cycle of Oppression and Violence

During the Spanish rule, life in Guatemala was based on the conqueror's belief that the country was their personal possession, and they were entitled to live out their lives as if they were in Spain, and that the native population was to provide for them in every way possible.

The Spanish Crown invaders' ethnocentric approach guided their blueprint for a conquered Guatemala, which aimed to replicate the comforts of life they enjoyed in Spain. This involved replacing the Maya's spirituality with the Spanish version of Christianity, establishing a hierarchical political system where ruling Spaniards claimed uncontested governance over the Maya, and creating an economy of self-enrichment. This system turned the Maya people into subordinates within a caste-like system.[4]

Undoubtedly, the indigenous population suffered greatly under the oppressive rule of the Spanish conquerors, enduring long-term structural violence. The economic hardships and the psychological trauma of living in constant fear and control had significant consequences. However, another period of terror and torment was yet to come. Some historians argue that the internal armed conflict, known as the "civil war" of the 1970s, 80s, and 90s, had its roots in the period of the Spanish conquest, but specific events in the late nineteenth century pushed the country towards arms uprising. In particular, events in the late 1950s and 60s acted as fuel that accelerated the fury of bloody battles, putting the Maya Ixil directly in harm's way.

Historians agree that the Internal Armed Conflict in Guatemala lasted for a staggering 36 years, resulting in astronomical casualties. The majority of the 200,000 deaths were Mayan, and countless many human rights violations were committed, mostly by the military. At least a million people were displaced internally, adding to the already devastating impact of the conflict. Under the leadership of Gen. Romeo Lucas García, and later, Gen. Efraín Ríos Montt, the situation worsened. According to the Comisión de Esclaramiento Histórico (CEH1999) reported that 626 Mayan villages were completely destroyed between 1976 and 1983.

During a seven-year period, between 150,000-200,000 people were reportedly killed.[5] The Recuperación de la Memoria Histórica (REMHI) documented a total of 80 village massacres in one of the most affected regions, the Ixil region that includes Chajul, Nebaj, and Cotzal, within a three-year period from 1980-1983.[6] The case against General Ríos Montt in 2013 brought international attention to the genocide committed against the Mayas by the Guatemalan military. Ríos Montt was brought to trial and convicted for crimes against humanity and genocide. He was sentenced to 80 years in prison by the country's federal court, but died in 2018 during the appeal process. Many other ranking officers responsible for massive deaths and destruction have been convicted and are currently serving prison sentences, but many others have yet to be brought to justice.

***

The 1871 Liberal Revolution

The Liberal Revolution of 1871 mainly consisted of a change of "guard" led by the new ruling faction, García Granados and, later, Justo Rufino Barrios, who became president in 1873. The "new" guard was known as *liberal* because it replaced the 30-year conservative ruling faction that had resisted the kind of change needed to compete at a broader level, in lock step with the capitalism of the modernized societies around the world. Rufino Barrios was known as Guatemala's "Reformer," because of the "sweeping" changes he instigated at the social, educational, economic, and political levels. He presided over the development of a new constitution and brought under his government's control the powers of both the aristocracy and the Catholic Church. During Rufino Barrios' presidency, his administration played a pivotal role in promoting the privatization of Guatemala's resources, attracting foreign investments, and developing coffee as the country's main agro-export. However, some historians argue that these policies had a significant negative impact on the lives of the indigenous populations, jeopardizing their survival. He played a major role in the 1873 inauguration of the Polytechnic Institute, a national military academy that graduated many of the country's dictators. Under his leadership, the armed forces increased threefold to 15,000. The infrastructure he prioritized led to the construction of the railroad, and more telegraph lines. Rufino Barrios had a vision of creating a unified Central America, and even went to war with El Salvador which had refused to join. Unfortunately, he died in battle in 1885. Despite his passing, the *liberal* ascendency continued in Guatemala under the consecutive dictatorships of Barrillas, Reina Barrios, Manual Estrada Cabrera, and Jorge Ubico.[7]

Manual Estrada Cabrera, the dictator who served as president from 1898 to 1920, was known for using the military force as an instrument of terror. He embraced and supported the economic development of the United Fruit Company, owned by United States business and investment sectors. Estrada Cabrera was forceful in his dictatorship by persecuting his political opponents, shunning individual's human rights, and suppressing the news outlets. He was also accused of embezzling federal funds from the treasury. As a powerful dictator, Estrada Cabrera could not sustain his position without criticism and protests, and the eventual fallout from his supporters. He was removed from office, and within an eleven-year period, three other presidents were democratically elected, although not without controversy based on suspicions of fraud. A military coup d'état in 1931 marked the end of an era of presidencies wrought with conflict, and the beginning of General Jorge Ubico's term.

Ubico's thirteen-year tenure presidency (1931-1944) is well-known for its dramatic departure from the ideals of the Liberal Revolution that had set the course for the country in the 1870s. While he received praise for the country's advances in economic growth, his dictatorship led the country into a downward spiral that drastically undermined democratic ideals. He suppressed the freedom of speech and promoted the 1816 Decree that an indigenous member of the population would be assassinated for violating the laws. He used this law to resolve conflicts among community members, and appealed to the masses that he was their savior. He administered the Vagrancy Law that required the indigenous community field laborers to work for extended periods of time during the year and for low-paying wages. He maintained a positive, productive relationship with the United States, and used the economic aid toward increasing military power and for self-aggrandizement. Ubico's ability to manipulate the United States government to his advantage likely represented a standard modus operandi adopted by various dictators in their quest for diplomatic aid or support.

The "October 20, 1944" Revolution

During the summer of 1944, Ubico faced a nationwide strike led by a diverse group of individuals, including members of the middle-class, university students, teachers, and intellectuals. Ubico responded to the strike by deploying military forces, and during the confrontation, a young teacher, *María Chinchilla Recinos*, was shot and killed. The incident further inflamed the protestors, and the military was unable to maintain control. By the end of June, Ubico had resigned and one of his generals, Federico Ponce Viades became his proxy. On the first of October, the editor of an influential opposition newspaper, Alejandro Cordova, was assassinated. Twenty days later, on October 20, a military junta, led by army officers, including Jacobo Arbenz Guzmán, launched a successful, relatively bloodless coup d'état and forced Ponce Viades to resign. The events of October 20th became a rallying cry for future protests against military dictatorships for decades to come. Unfortunately, some of protests resulted in an unprecedented torrent of human rights violations.

The political party of the teachers, Renovación Nacional, had selected Juan José Arévalo as their candidate for president. Arévalo held a Ph.D. from a university in Argentinia and initially aspired to work in the Ministry of Education. However, he was unwilling to serve under the presidency of Ubico. Following his tenure as a professor in Argentina, Arévalo returned to Guatemala in the summer of 1944 and emerged as a prominent leader in the Renovación Nacional party. In the presidential elections held in December, 1944, and Arévalo secured a resounding victory and was declared the winner by a landslide.

Arévalo advocated for socialist policies, and despite claims by his opponents, he vehemently rejected communist ideals. His approach was characterized by a "spiritual socialism" that emphasized compassion and understanding in addressing the social and economic challenges faced by the indigenous population. Seventy percent of the population were illiterate, and malnutrition and health issues were rampant. The Liberal Revolution's policies concerning land holdings had been extremely biased against the indigenous communities, thus, the elite landowners owned three quarters of agricultural (fertile) land, leaving the peasant population in dire poverty. While Arévalo envisioned his country as capitalistic he focused on securing benefits for everyone. His ideas laid out the foundation for the reforms that his successor, Jacobo Arbenz Guzmán, would eventually integrate into his own vision.

Arévalo's government ratified a new constitution, known to be one the most progressive in Latin America. Included in the constitution were mandates for women's suffrage, and for organizing labor in order to promulgate laws that treat workers fairly and justly.

Jacobo Arbenz Guzmán, who had previously served as the Defense Minister during Arévalo's presidency, held democratic ideals that were in contrast to the dictatorship examples set my many of his predecessors, despite the fact that they had all graduated from the same national military academy, the Polytechnic Institute. In 1950, Arbenz Guzmán won the presidential election with sixty percent of the vote and his first priority was to modernize the agrarian reform bill. The bill was passed by the National Assembly in 1952 and promptly put into effect. Its primary objective was to transfer uncultivated land from wealthy landowners to the poverty-stricken indigenous families. This was a crucial step for the country, as the World Bank had refused to provide much needed funds until such reforms were implemented. Under the new law, landowners would be compensated with government bonds equivalent to the value of the expropriated land. The reform project was deemed successful on several fronts, however, in the final analysis, only a few families successfully completed the land transfers, leaving 80 to 90 percent of the contested landholdings with the previous owners. Some historians argue that while there were problems with the land reform laws, overall, they addressed the most urgent injustices experienced by the impoverish farmers. The way in which Arbenz Guzmán was ousted from the presidency highlights the complexity of achieving the terms of success, and raises many unanswered questions.

The Agrarian Reform Law had at its core the phenomenal potential of correcting the historical injustices perpetrated against the indigenous people. The period from 1944 to the passing and enforcement of the reform bill was hailed by many as nothing less than a revolution, and Arbenz' quote reaffirmed their belief: [the reform was not only] "the most precious fruit of the revolution and the fundamental base of the destiny of the nation as a new country, [but it also caused] an earthquake in the consciousness [of the Guatemalan people]."[8] Perhaps, it was the perception of Arbenz' remarkable success that alerted key opposition figures to assert their highest levels of power to cause his downfall. For example, the U.S. State Department's John Foster Dulles, and President Eisenhower, both of whom viewed Arbenz as a kind of threat to the United States, especially within the context of the Cold War. The Guatemalan military also perceived Arbenz as a president that would empower the indigenous population to rise and challenge their authority. Additionally, the various sectors such as the oligarchs, the politicians, and landowners would lose their positions of influence and power. It is often overlooked that the three factions eventually converged to create a theater of urban guerrilla warfare, which is a significant aspect of the historical armed conflict of Guatemala.

Guatemala's NEW Women's Movement

The killing of a teacher, María Chinchilla Recinos, during the June 25th protest in 1944, sparked a strong reaction from women, particularly those from the middle-class (known as *las capitalinas)*. Many of these women played an unprecedented role as activists during the social mobilization that followed.[9] Since post-colonialism, many women who participated in political and social protests were the first females in their families to do so, breaking away from the traditional, socially-ascribed gender roles. The election of Juan José Arévalo as president in 1945 buoyed many Guatemalan women beyond belief. In 1950, women exercised their right to vote in a national election for the first time, undoubtedly contributing to Jacobo Arbenz Guzmán's win that year.[10] They were instrumental in organizing presidential campaign activities in 1945 and 1950 under the banner, "por la revolución" (for the revolution). A surge of effervescence permeated the gleeful sentiments among all *capitalinos* (city dwellers), and proclaimed the 10-year historical period (1944-1954) in their country as "la primavera" (Spring).[11]

President's Arevalo's administration initiated new changes that would affect all Guatemalans, but particularly benefitted women. Many of these were deemed as essential in a democratic society, such as the creation of a Social Security system, labor laws to regulate the safety and protection of workers, childcare for working mothers, and educational support in building schools and teacher education programs. President Arbenz' (1951-54) contribution to institutional change had a distinctly positive effect at a grander scale. His political agenda called for the conversion of Guatemala as a dependent nation to one that is economically independent and modernized in capitalistic terms. His proposed policies envisioned a transformation on improving the quality of life for all Guatemalans. Women leaders/activists interpreted this vision of a "New Guatemala" (un *nuevo* Guatemala) as a movement to dismantle long-standing patriarchal laws that discriminate against women and impede their advancement in society. Furthermore, the Arbenz' policies addressed in theory the systematic racism and discriminatory laws that specifically target women and indigenous populations. Constitutional change at the structural level was necessary to effectively deal with problems such as impunity and repression.[12]

Although the ten-year "primavera" was relatively brief, women made remarkable advances, especially in education, employment, and in participating at the state level. Women were successful in organizing associations that addressed focal issues, such as the Alianza Cívica de Asociaciones Femininas (Civic Alliance of Women's Associations). In 1955, Rosa de Mora was the first (designated) woman to serve as a representative in Congress. When President Arbenz was forced to leave Office, women were among the social groups that believed they were expected to defend the revolution ("defender *la Revolución*"). In anticipation of a civil war, women were prepared to dutifully fight in order to save their country.[13] At the heart of their agenda, Guatemalan women were willing to serve in the interest of their country's democratic ideals, for the greater good of the public.[14] Although their accomplishments were short-lived, the Guatemalan women's movement created innovative pathways and new directions toward gender equality, demonstrating the emergence of feminism in society and the female voice in their country, and in Central American politics.

The United States and the Coup d'Etat

The blueprint for removing President Arbenz in the CIA's Operation PBSUCCESS has been the subject of numerous historical accounts, particularly by the authors/journalists, Stephen Schlesinger and Stephen Kinzer.[15] The descriptions of the events, timelines, and key players underscore the clandestine nature of Operation PBSUCCESS, but answers related to the reasons for launching the operation in the first place are less clear, unless of course, the intent was to create an ambiguous or conflated response to the question of motive. Undoubtedly, the Cold War's strategy used to control the expansion of communist played a huge role in the decisions made by President Eisenhower's administration, and State Department Secretary, John Foster Dulles. However, there was also the economic interest, namely, the United Fruit Company based in Guatemala, that was central to the decision-making process.

Since the 1954 coup, world leaders, especially from Latin America, have harshly criticized the United States involvement as political interventionism without a purposeful intent. Ultimately, official records revealed that Secretary Dulles and his brother, the CIA Director, Allen Dulles, benefitted financially from United Fruit Company, which was in violation of the Conflict of Interest laws. Secretary Dulles and his law firm, Sullivan & Cromwell, negotiated the land dealings between United Fruit and the Guatemalan government, and Allen Dulles was the director during Operation PBSUCCESS. Both men were on the United Fruit Company's payroll for 38 years. After being defeated in the 1944 coup d'état, the members of the

Guatemalan military junta, in conjunction with United Fruit, maneuvered their way back into power by using their connections with the Dulles brothers. In order to keep their financial dealings private, it was crucial to maintain a "political" message that justified the United States intervention as necessary to halt the "communist" government of President Arbenz. President Eisenhower, eager to fulfill his role as a powerful leader against the Soviet Union, wholeheartedly approved of the plan. The "economic" message was also incorporated in the military components, with specific language used to highlight the United Fruit Company as a significant investment that benefitted the United States.

The campaign to overthrow Arbenz' government was in full throttle when the State Department decided on John Peurifoy as the next ambassador to the Guatemala. Peurifoy, a life-long Democrat from South Carolina, was working in the State Department when he had a dispute with Senator Joseph McCarthy who alleged that communists were among his staffers embedded in the Department. Peurifoy vehemently argued to the contrary. Later, however, Peurifoy delivered to Congress the claim that a "homosexual underground" existed in the Department, which coincided with McCarthy's anti-gay rhetoric. He was appointed Ambassador to Greece in 1950, and three years later, he returned to the United States, leaving behind a reputation of being undiplomatic, and a meddler in their country's internal affairs.[16]

As Ambassador, one of Peurifoy's main goal was to convince President Arbenz that the United States had the sole interest of making assurances that his government was not communist. The public relations company hired by the United Fruit Company, John Clements Associates, had the exact opposite assignment of lobbying to powerful influencers, and convincing them that Arbenz' administration was intensely involved in communism. John Clements, a McCarthyite crusader against communism, developed a 300-plus page study, widely distributed to Congress, on why Guatemala's president should be removed. Clements also added another volume to his study, specifically addressing proposed strategic military maneuvers, and the selection of Col. Carlos Castillo Armas as the lead officer, later named by the CIA as "Liberator."

In November, 1950, Carlos Castillo Armas, a colonel in his forties and long-time enemy of Arbenz, led an army of 70 in an attempt to take over the Aurora Military Base in Guatemala. The operation proved to be a failure since 16 soldiers were killed and 10 were wounded, including Castillo Armas. He was sentenced to die by firing squad, but after six months in prison, he was granted asylum by the Colombian government.

Around Christmas in Tegucigalpa, Honduras, 1953, Castillo Armas began to broadcast and recruit for his "National Liberation Movement." He awaited official orders from the CIA in Nicaragua, with the assistance of the dictator, Samoza, who was involved in the collaboration. Allen Dulles, the CIA director, played a key role throughout the execution of Operation PBSUCCESS.

In their book, *Bitter Fruit,* authors Schlesinger and Kinzer offer a detailed and intriguing account of the coup. The initial steps of the Operation involved the smuggling of weapons, presumably purchased by Arbenz. While the Czech ship carrying the weapons was anchored at Puerto Barrios, Honduras, the CIA commenced their next strategy of alerting President Eisenhower and the National Security Council of the weapons. They presented them as proof of an imminent uprising and argued that a coup was urgently needed for the sake of saving Guatemala from the dangerous communists. Between June 18 and June 27, 1954, a series of bombings and gun battles ensued, causing the deaths of 17 soldiers and extensive property damage. The CIA used Honduran soil to launch ground troops and aerial attacks, employing improvisation tactics to create a scenario that the Russians were complicit in the attacks. They even disguised U.S. jet bombers as Soviet aircraft to further the deception.

The entire operation involved the CIA, the State Department and the Executive Branch, and together, on the behest of the United Fruit Company, conspired to launch an illegal coup d'état to oust a democratically elected president.

Under pressure, President Arbenz felt that he had no choice but to surrender. He left Guatemala for asylum in México on June 27, 1954. The United States' military force was overwhelming, and any diplomatic means by which to negotiate with such a powerful country were nonexistent. The most significant blow to Arbenz' leadership came from his leading military commanders, whom he had trusted and respected. They refused to support him, not because they sided with the United States, but because they were concerned about their survival as the dominant military force among the indigenous populations. Their military status had consistently allowed them to exercise privilege and power, and they feared that Arbenz' land reforms would threaten their position. Scholar/researcher, Jim Handy (1990), writes insightfully on the circumstances behind the military's position of dominance among the rural communities.[17] The general consensus was that the Agrarian Reform would essentially lead to the diminishing of authority, or the authoritative "grip" that the military had adapted for decades. Schlesinger and Kinzer described the ruling generals and their civilian backers as a "wealthy caste unto itself," in reference to the special capitalistic privileges that allowed them to achieve wealth and exclusive access to the upper echelons of society.

After the Coup

Col. Castillo Armas eventually took over the presidency as a dictator on September 1, 1954. Although he was CIA's third choice for the position, the "Liberator" became the ideal obedient loyalist, and tyrant, as was expected. Within a three-year period (1954-1957), he officially abolished the heart of the Reform Law, Decree 900, outlawed political parties, banned any and all organizations and unions, prohibited voting by the mostly poor and illiterate populace, and restored the Secret Police brigade. He also ordered the burning of literature he deemed "subversive," which were writings by leftists and revolutionaries, including Nobel Prize winner Miguel Angel Asturia's novel, *El señor presidente*, based on the life of Manuel Estrada Cabrera during his reign as a dictator. Castillo Armas encouraged foreign mining companies to purchase drilling rights, and indeed, welcomed capitalist investors; he yielded to the demands of the Catholic Church and allowed it to own property and include religious instruction in public schools, restoring ties with the conservative Catholic faction.[19]

Secretary of State Dulles seemed satisfied with Castillo Armas' overall performance, except for his obstinate refusal to arrest the 700 ardent followers of President Arbenz following the coup, that, as asylum seekers were protected in various foreign embassies. Dulles wanted to falsely brand these loyalists as criminals, or Russian agents. He wanted them expelled from Guatemala, and sent directly to Moscow. Perhaps, Castillo Armas recalled how the Colombian embassy saved him from the death sentence, and that asylum in a foreign embassy was the only legal mechanism by which the defeated ranks could find a respite from impending punishment.[20]

The Maya Pueblos After the Coup: Pragmatism and Solidarity

It was as though the 10-year "revolution" had never occurred, or perhaps, it was a dress rehearsal for the "real" one yet to come. Or, as Jim Handy explains, the Agrarian Reform movement put into motion the process of slowing down what was apparent since the 1950's: the gradual proletarianization of the campesinos. Certainly, the reform failed in achieving the most important objective, which was to allow the indigenous peoples' rights to their lands that had been illegally seized.[21]

But the Agrarian Reform served to expose the long-standing abuse of authority imposed upon rural communities largely populated by the indigenous peoples. Jim Handy's research reveals the systematic land grabbing by wealthy landowners, who were well-connected to the government's military, in an attempt to monopolize municipal land, and essentially pushing out the campesinos from their restricted planting areas. The campesinos were forced to pay in the form of "rent" for using the land, which only added to their economic constraints as subsistence farmers.[22]

The Agrarian Reform Law was not designed to expropriate all community lands. In fact, the large number of denunciations were made by those using the land, mainly, the campesinos, and not because of ancestral ownership.

Thus, allowable expropriations were based on usufruct, with the aim of benefitting the farmers that needed the land for survival.

The land expropriation during Arbenz' term came to a sudden halt after the 1954 coup. But, historians observed the accomplishments as well. David Stroll writes in his book, *Between Two Armies in the Ixil Town of Guatemala*, that the coup brought very few but important benefits to the communities.[23] Even though Castillo Armas reversed the right for farmers to unionize, the organizational structures were established and mandated during the Arbenz' presidency. The farmers essentially continued their organizational structures on their own, and proceeded to rally around their candidates in local elections. Stroll points to the way that the Maya Ixil leaders in the rural Quiché towns of Nebaj, Chajul, and Cotzal, were able to reassert themselves in town halls, which was considered a monumental achievement in a history dominated by colonial and post-colonial rulers and politicians. However, the politicization process wasn't completely favorable to the community as a whole since two distinct factions emerged in opposing directions: 1) the elderly men, or *principales* as they are called within the indigenous communal hierarchy, and at the other end of the pole, the elite oligarchy; and 2) the young, progressive, liberals, sometimes referred as "communists." These factions played a significant role in the years leading up to the 36-year Internal Armed Conflict and its aftermath.[24]

The Vagrancy Laws had been abolished as part of the reform, however, farmers continued to work at the plantations as before, but this time on their own volition because their families depended on their wages.

But the elite landowners continued waging their political battles against the Maya Ixil people. The nearby Finca La Perla in the Ixil region was one of the many haciendas that fell under the reform's expropriation mandate, and in their defense, the landowners accused everyone, including the entire Maya Ixil pueblo on the side of the reform, as "communists." This was the label for whom the *progressive* faction of the Maya Ixil could not deflect.[25]

No doubt, the Agrarian Reform Act rattled a hornet's nest, and hostile conflicts, once private and out-of-sight between the landowners and campesinos, became well-known in public spheres. The Maya Ixil had long struggled to maintain their livelihood as farmers, but their protests and denouncements consistently fell on deaf ears. Instead, the communities acquiesced in the spirit of solidarity, adapting to national norms but at the same time accepting them as their own. This was their way of life since the conquest, and survival was dependent on how well they succeeded.

The Women's Movement After the Coup

The Castillo Armas regime ordered the complete dismantlement of the previous administration's accomplishments. All social and economic improvement proposals were cancelled. Women transformed by their previous involvement felt a profound loss of purpose in their lives. Some of the leaders felt a need to self-exile to Argentina. The return of a harsh repressive state profoundly affected economically-strapped women since all of their support bases were abruptly removed. However, even more disheartening were the credible reports that indicated an increase in sexual and physical abuse cases among indigenous women.[26] By and large the indigenous women played a very small participatory role in the women's social movements, yet, they were visibly the subject of harsh, indiscriminate treatment and torture during the Internal Armed Conflict as discussed in the following chapter.

The Beginnings of the Internal Armed Conflict

The consensus among historians is that the Internal Armed Conflict began in 1960 and ended with the signing of the Peace Accords in 1996. However, the debates continue as historians posit various views and arguments. For example, some consider the October 20, 1944 coup d'état as the *actual* start of the Armed Conflict, not 1960. But certainly, key events during that period attributed to the turmoil that was later defined by historians as the underlying pillars that buttressed the Armed Conflict.[27]

The Cuban Revolution (1953-59) and its triumphant success for Fidel Castro's regime and its jubilant Cuban supporters against a well-defined enemy resonated deeply throughout Latin America, Central America, and México. It was the ultimate revolutionary, freedom-fighting bravery that was almost too perfect. Many young, idealistic intellectuals found their hero in Fidel Castro and Ernesto "Che" Guevara. Moreover, the revolutionary spirit swept up many young Guatemalans, who saw it as a sign that they too could fight and win a revolution in their home country. Fidel Castro's speeches declared that the Cubans now had the destiny in their own hands, that their freedom represents independence without foreign invasion or intervention. Castro immediately sought out a working relationship with the United States, but he was met with rejection and admonishment.

The U.S. Counter-Insurgency Expertise Comes to Guatemala

In 1960, five years after the start of the Vietnam War, the United States military and the CIA had committed to supporting the southern Vietnam region controlled by first, Bao Dai, then, Ngo Dinh Diem, against the Viet Minh forces, also known as Viet Cong, or the Vietnamese Communists. As in the case of the 1954 CIA-backed coup, the pressure wrought by the entanglement with the Soviet Union and the Cold War greatly enhanced the U.S. decision to intervene in the North-South Vietnam conflict. The United States overwhelming support for the South was imbued with the intent to crushing the North's pro-communist ideals and structure, which had been developed with the Soviet Union.

During the Vietnam War, the United States' military forces and the CIA developed specialized techniques and strategies to engage in a myriad of combat situations. The Green Berets were brought in as a specialized unit. Among these were forms of torture and covert operations to track down the enemy. Their counter-insurgency expertise was touted as among the best in the world, and they operated training camps in the U.S. (Fort Benning) and Central America (School of the Americas). This kind of training was welcomed by the Guatemalan military, but not for the reasons for which they were developed. Rather, the warfare techniques were used to harm, maim, and kill individuals, many of them civilians, targeted solely because of their opposing political views.[28]

The Uprisings That Marked the Beginning

After Castillo Armas assassination in 1957, General Ydigoras Fuentes stepped in as the next U.S.-approved dictator. Without using proper protocol, Ydigoras allowed the U.S. military and CIA to use Guatemala for their next operation, which was to train a selected group of soldiers, mostly Cuban exiles, and launch an attack against the Castro regime in an effort to regain control of Cuba.

Once the operation was in public view, the Guatemalan military's reaction was on high alert, and what happened next was clearly unexpected by the military. Three uprisings, starting in November, 1960 ensued. In the first instance, which took place at a military base in Guatemala City, the attack was instigated by an insurrectional group, made up of as many as half of the Guatemalan army, including 120 officers. A second one resulted in taking control of Puerto Barrios on the Atlantic, and a third one at the Zacapa military barracks, where 800 unarmed campesinos also participated. In each case, the attacks and raids were executed by dissident groups. A rebellion began taking root, one that vehemently opposed President Ydigoras' decision to allow the U.S. to use Guatemala to launch the operation, known as the Bay of Pigs, on the newly inaugurated government of Fidel Castro.[29] The United States, fearing that the uprisings would lead to a coup and ruin the Bay of Pigs operation, reacted with force. The military ordered several B-26 bombers, piloted by the Cuban exiles, to attack the rebels. On a patrolling detail off the Guatemalan coast were five Navy vessels, including an aircraft carrier. The revolt ended, but many of the soldiers chose to escape rather than face punishment. Among these were two young men that later worked together to form the leadership backbone of the rebellion at the start of the Armed Conflict. They were Lieutenant Marco Aurelio Yon Sosa and Lieutenant Luis Turcios Lima, both of whom had previously participated in the U.S.-sponsored military training. While their views or ideologies differed, they shared a criticism against the United States' position on Cuba.

They also shared the notion that the rural indigenous communities could rise to the level of combat necessary to overthrow the government. They believed in the "Che" Guevara model of combining social and military action, such as, educating the rural communities of their democratic rights, so that they would eventually assume appropriate action, including engaging in combat.[30] Yon Sosa and Turcios Lima moved to the eastern region of Guatemala, in the countryside, bordering Honduras. At that time, the grassroots, community action for social change was a popular approach for whom the Brazilian Paulo Freire is known in the literacy campaign for the masses. They had recruited the first wave of guerrilla fighters and called themselves the Alejandro de León November 13 Guerrilla Movement, (MR-13) in honor of their comrade killed in the November uprising of 1960. Several days before their second attack on February, 1962, they delivered a communiqué stating the urgency to overthrow the Ydigoras government and replace it with a democracy that represents human rights, and adopt a foreign policy based on self-respect. The group targeted the army camps near Puerto Barrios, but once inside the compound, they were swiftly chased out by the soldiers.

A month later, a second group of guerrilla fighters emerged. The former Minister of Defense in the Arbenz administration, Carlos Paz Tejada, led the group, the October 20 Front, so named as a tribute to the 1944 revolution. His message was similar to Yon Sosa and Turcio Lima's, which is, calling for the end of the despotic rule of Ydigoras, and particularly, the termination of foreign power intervention that he allowed, and to set up a government worthy of the people's trust.

As former military leaders, well-trained in the counter-insurgency field, Turcios Lima and Yon Sosa recognized the U.S. military as the most powerful and specialized force in the world, and their intentions in leading a rebellion was focused on a brief and well-strategized plan. Their plan was specifically modeled after Castro's successful revolution blueprint. However, once they left the leadership of the original group, the conflict evolved into a very different vision than they had imagined. Basically, it was hard-pressed to find anyone that predicted the intensity and scale of the counter-revolutionary violence, predicated and executed by the right-wing, and elite factions of Guatemalan society.

Ydigoras' Extreme Iron Rule

On March 16, 1962, hundreds of student demonstrators marched in protest and demanded Ydigoras' resignation. They represented the major opposition political parties, including the party founded by Castilla Armas. As predicted, Ydigoras' response was to call in the military and after the two-day raucous fighting and resistance, there were at least 20 students killed and 200 injured. The violent protests proceeded for at least two more months. Ydigoras doubled down by replacing his entire cabinet with appointed military officers.

The United States viewed the attempts to oust Ydigoras as a national security threat. The U.S. government offered to help, and Ydigoras eagerly accepted. The target was the eastern region of Guatemala, in Zacapa and Izabal, where the first guerrilla (MR-13) was founded. The aid was in the form of U.S. manufactured T-33 jets, that had been used for training purposes, and transport jets. Two American officers and five soldiers formerly trained in Vietnam as specialists in counter-insurgency, set up a base in Izabal for the purpose of furthering their techniques in specialized training of guerrilla warfare. Among the ranks of instructors were 15 Guatemalan military soldiers that had been especially trained in the Canal Zone camp.[31] By the end of 1962, Ydigoras, aided by the U.S. military and CIA, had managed to halt the student revolt and the guerrilla groups. The number of casualties began to escalate with hundreds killed or injured or arrested and detained. Among these were students, middle-class professionals, campesinos, community leaders, and former military soldiers. Ydigoras was removed from office and Colonel Peralta Azurdía replaced him. One of Peralta's first official action was on March, 1963, when he ordered a ban on all political parties, presumably to deter political unrest.[32]

***

The Organization and Disorganization of the Guerrilla

A crucial turning point in the early organization of the movement was Turcios Lima and Yon Sosa's joining the traditional, decades-old Partido Guatemalteco del Trabajo (PGT - the party of labor), after leaving the MR-13, which had a far-left ideological base. Then, between 1962 and 1965, the Fuerzas Armadas Rebeldes (FAR) was formed, and FAR became the guerilla front of PGT. But when César Montes became the newly elected leader of PGT, an ideological conflict flared up between the members, intensifying the conflicts between Turcios Limas and Yon Sosa. FAR had developed a strong following, and as the 1966 elections approximated, its members had their hopes on one of the progressive candidates. But, the PGT leader, César Montes, preferred his former law professor, a member of the Partido Revolucionario (PR), César Méndez Montenegro. A serious stand-off between the FAR and PGT members ensued, but ultimately, the FAR officially announced their support for Méndez Montenegro. After he was elected in 1966, the FAR began to partially demobilize. By then, Turcios Lima, angered over FAR's support for Méndez Montenegro had left the PGT. In 1966, he was killed in an automobile accident, and Yon Sosa, who had also left, was killed in 1970. So rancorous was the animosity between the FAR factions supporting or opposing Méndez Montenegro, that, once he became president, Julio César Méndez Montenegro allowed the U.S. military to intervene, causing violence, chaos, and death at an unprecedented scale. The PGT-FAR faction opposing Méndez Montenegro became the Fuerzas Armadas Revolucionarias (instead of "Rebeldes").[33]

The U.S. Military Aid, 1966-1970

Méndez Montenegro appointed a ruthless officer, Colonel Carlos Arana Osorio, as commander of the eastern region, in the state of Zacapa, where the guerrilla activity was most active. David Stoll labeled Arana Osorio, the "butcher of Zacapa," in reference to the colonel's notorious reputation of ordering the killings of so many people, some were guerrillas, but many, perhaps, most, were civilians.[34] It was known as the Zacapa-Izabal campaign, and the specially-trained military used anti-guerrilla tactics, including political kidnappings, disappearances, and assassinations. The targets were selected individuals that had been associated with the Arévalo-Arbenz presidencies, and who were prominent members of the PGT-FAR, such as students, intellectuals, activists, professionals. Anyone that was perceived as a leader, and as leaning toward "liberalism" was targeted. Paramilitary groups such as right-wing terrorists also participated by aiding the military in finding their victims while threatening others. As the violence increased with time, so did the terrorists' expertise in the precision by which they targeted "key" individuals. Within a seventeen-month period in 1966-1968, it was estimated that the Zacapa-Izabal campaign resulted in the deaths of between 3,000 to 8,000 people.[35]

Colonel Arana Osorio's ambition to eliminate the opposition led to a close affiliation with the United States. With the support of Méndez Montenegro, he allowed the U.S. Green Berets to conduct the specialized counter-insurgency training starting in October of 1966. The training included techniques similar to those practiced during the Vietnam War, such as interrogation and torture of prisoners, guerrilla warfare and jungle survival. The U.S. also granted the Guatemalan military a total of $17 million in funds and equipment. Vice-President Marroquín Rojas informed the media that a squadron of U.S. planes, flying out of Panama, had dropped napalm on certain guerrilla bases without landing their planes in Guatemala.[36]

The U.S. aid to Guatemala also included $2.6 million from 1966 to 1970 for equipment and training of police officers. The National Police increased their force from 3,000 to 11,000 members. By 1970, over 30,000 Guatemalan police officers had received the training. Guatemala had the second largest police force in Latin America; Brazil had the largest but its population was at least twenty times the size of Guatemala.

The Guerillas Attack the United States Military and Violence Escalates

The guerrilla forces were incensed by the assassinations, kidnappings/disappearances, and the overall blatant manner in which the President Méndez Montenegro and Col. Arana Osorio executed their campaign of terror and violence. After the ultra-right paramilitary tortured and killed a former beauty queen turned activist, Rogelia Cruz Martínez, the guerrilla killed two of their American targets: Colonel John Webber, director of the military aid mission, and military advisor, Lieutenant Commander Ernest Munro. In their guerrilla communiqué, an attempt was made to attribute the murders to the United States, accusing them of supporting the death squads that have inflicted an exceptionally high level of violence on the civilian population.[37]

The guerrilla also attempted to kidnap the U.S. Ambassador, John Gordon Mein, and use him as a trading chip for the release of one of their leaders, Comandante Camilo Sánchez. The plan failed and the ambassador was shot and killed as he fled from the guerrilla.[38]

By the time the next presidential elections were scheduled in 1970, Arana Osorio decided he had the best chance to win the presidency. His campaign message, riddled with distortions and misinformation, claimed that he had an impeccable record of upholding law and order, as he was widely recognized for, and that he had effectively eradicated the "communist" threat. Arana Osorio had also succeeded in coalescing the far-right into a well-defined constituency in an attempt to insure his win at the ballot box. The elites, oligarchs, wealthy landowners, and the influential military, along with their supporters, paved the way for his victory through election manipulation and substantial financial backing of his campaign. The first three years into his presidency, Arana Osorio maintained a steadfast and unwavering approach in his terror campaign, resulting in a significant increase in the number of murders, assassinations, and disappearances, often doubling or surpassing previous figures. Essentially, the Zacapa-Izabal campaign, which was launched in 1966, had evolved into an institution of its own. It had become the prevailing method of dealing with the opposition, setting a standard for handling dissenting voices in general.[39]

***

The Guerrilla Increases in Size and Power

During Arana Osorio's presidency, two formidable guerrilla groups emerged as splintered factions from the FAR revolucionarios: the Organización Revolucionaria del Pueblo en Armas (ORPA) founded by Rodrigo Asturias Amado in 1971, and Ejército Guerrillero de los Pobres (EGP), founded by Mario Payeras and Rolando Morán in 1972. It is worth noting that some members of the group had previously participated in the 1960 uprising in the eastern region.[40] ORPA's leaders justified their formation by highlighting their belief that FAR was racist and excluded the indigenous populations. On the other hand, the EGP adopted a strategy of combining the "social and military" actions, inspired by the Cuban revolution, to recruit members from the rural communities, which predominantly consisted of indigenous populations. The EGP strategically concentrated its efforts in the rural highlands of Huehuetenango and Quiché, where it played a significant role in the conflict that affected the Maya Ixiles from the mid-1970s to early 1980s. During this period, the guerrilla group began employing terrorist tactics, albeit on a smaller scale. Among their first targets, the EGP selected Jorge Bernal Hernández Castellón, a former advisor to Arana Osorio and previously known as "the strategist" who identified and ordered the disappearances and killings of people that were considered radicals. The guerrilla movement experienced a notable increase in its expansion, particularly following the kidnapping of the son from one of the prominent families. A ransom of five million dollars was paid upon his release.

Arana Osorio's Replacements

Arana Osorio's reign as the fearsome dictator continued with as much veracity as he could muster, but even the political right-wing faction viewed his actions as extreme. In 1974, a new military general, Gen. Kjell Laugerud García, was installed as a replacement for Arana Osorio. Despite his seemingly moderate administrative style, Laugerud García continued the campaign of terror established by his predecessor. In addition to the existing violence and chaos, Guatemala was struck by a devastating earthquake in 1976, resulting in the tragic loss of 25,000 lives. Despite the catastrophe,

Laugerud García refused to accept foreign aid and his government provided minimal assistance to the victims. The escalation of guerrilla warfare marked a perilous shift in the conflict, prompting the military to respond with even greater force to guerrilla aggression. This tit-for-tat pattern intensified as the armed conflict progressed, ultimately leading to a devastating and tragic catastrophe.[41]

In October 1978, Guatemala's capital witnessed a massive protest following the announcement of F. Romeo Lucas García, a wealthy landowner, as the fraudulent election winner as president. The initial cause of the protest was a dispute over the rise in bus fare. As expected, the military responded to the demonstration, resulting in several weeks of clashes between the protestors and security forces. Tragically, the casualties from this confrontation included 30 deaths, over 300 injured, and at least 600 arrests. Labor leaders responded to the situation by calling for a national strike, which further intensified and expanded the protest. Thousands of protestors joined the movement, demanding the end to institutionalized repression. On October 20th, the labor strike was officially declared, coinciding with the anniversary of the 1944 revolution. In a disturbing turn of events, the military specifically targeted a university student leader. While addressing a massive crowd gathered at the plaza opposite the National Palace, the young man was brutally shot down by the military, using machine gun fire. The assassination had the intended effect of not only killing a student leader but striking fear and terror in the hearts of the protestors, indeed, all Guatemalans. By the conclusion of Lucas García's presidency in 1982, a new wave of violence had surfaced, surpassing the brutality of previous attacks. This time, the killings were marked by their grotesque and monstrous nature, targeting innocent civilians, and impoverished families from indigenous populations residing in rural areas.[42]

Lucas García, along with his brother, General Benedicto Lucas García, whom he appointed as the military-in-charge, established a government with an unparalleled level of authority. Their actions, characterized by a sense of impunity and ruthlessness, reflected their belief that the power of the

Guatemalan state was unconstrained, even by the United States, the most influential nation.

The Response of the United States

In their book, Schlesinger and Kinzer provide insight into the communication presented to the United States Congress by Guatemalans, urging the legislators to re-assess the state of affairs in their country.[43] One notable figure, René de León Schlotter, a leader of the Christian Democrats political party, took the opportunity to address a congressional committee and provide an overview of the situation in Guatemala. In his speech, Schlotter aimed to bring clarity amidst the chaos and the "fog of war," emphasizing that the violence in Guatemala extends far beyond what is immediately apparent. He asserted that the root cause of the war can be traced back to the extreme right-wing political faction. Although Schlotter's affiliation with a center-left political party may have casted doubts among some cautious congressional members, his message, delivered to United States Congress in 1976, carries important credibility within a historical context. His speech highlighted the unwavering belief shared by the progressive factions throughout Latin America that the United States played a significant role in promoting and supporting three decades of dictatorship regimes which inflicted immense hardships on the Guatemalans and violated their human rights.[44]

President Reagan and Guatemalan President Ríos Montt

At the time when the political, social, and economic climate was already at its worst in modern history, another round of violence, terror, and death loomed on the horizon with the installment of another dictator, General Ríos Montt, in 1982. A year prior, in 1981, the United States, whose Congress hesitated to admit or take responsibility for its mistakes in facilitating the institutionalization of a repressive military regime in Guatemala, elected Ronald Reagan as President. President Reagan's campaign slogan, "Let's Make America Great Again," was built upon a platform of patriotism, asserting that the United States should take the lead in combating any semblance of communism, as exemplified in the Cold War. It particularly aimed to keep the enemy, such as the one behind the 20-year Vietnam War that ended five years prior to his election, at bay. President Reagan's administration dedicated a significant amount of energy, possibly an excessive amount to Central America. They provided substantial military aid and other resources in order to support the U.S.' efforts in "defeating" their opponents. After General Ríos Montt assumed the presidency of Guatemala in 1982, President Reagan visited him in December of the same year. During this visit, President Reagan praised Ríos Montt and reinstated economic aid that had been withheld by the previous president, Jimmy Carter, due to allegations of human rights violations. During the period of approximately one year, from 1982 - 1983, President Ríos Montt was responsible for the devastating destruction of numerous villages and the merciless killings of thousands of innocent people, primarily Mayan civilians including men, women, and children from the departments of El Quiché, Alta Verapaz, and Huehuetenango. Despite their starkly contrasting backgrounds, the two presidents managed to find common ground in their shared belief that military success was defined by such actions.[45]

'Saving Guatemala' Students' Uprisings

One of the key aspects of the Armed Conflict and its devastating impact on innocent people in the Ixil region revolves around the initial group of rebels known as the first "wave" of young insurgents. Who were these insurgents and what motivated them to embark on such a bold and perilous path? The young army lieutenants, Turcio Limas and Yon Sosa, along with their comrades took the initiative to organize and carry out the revolt against the the Ydigoras dictatorship in 1960. At that time, a new wave of ideological fervor had swept through their generation, igniting a new way of thinking. The Cuban revolution had brought attention to the growing desire for freedom and self-expression, as well as alternative perspectives on the global social and cultural order. These ideas resonated deeply with the educational aspirations of public university students across Latin America, including in Guatemala.

The leaders of the insurgency emerged from the University of San Carlos (USAC), attracting the most passionate and determined students who joined the revolutionary movement. They were young, around mid-twenties, and had possessed a vision for change that surpassed their limited understanding of the realities they faced due to their youthful idealism. Among the recruits were former military soldiers, as well as young women and students aspiring to pursue a pastoral vocation. Over time, the guerrilla units underwent significant transformations. By the time they reached Ixil country in 1972, they had evolved into a formidable military force, undeterred by the fact that the Guatemalan military held far superior power that they could never hope to match. In terms of proportion, the US-supported military posed as a colossal opponent. They were fully trained and equipped with weapons, such as the Israeli's M-16s in 1989, helicopters, jets, artillery and mortar power.

The Guerrilla of the Poor, the EGP

David Stoll's comprehensive volume on the Ixil towns of Guatemala, details the military tactics utilized between insurgents and counterinsurgents that occurred from the 1970s to 1990s. He incorporates information from the work of an ex-guerrilla member, Mario Payeras, in order to accentuate the authenticity of his facts and provide contextualization.[46] Stoll adheres to his established thesis, that the guerrilla was principally responsible for the armed conflict, mainly in the beginning stages where, in his view, they stirred up and manipulated the Maya Ixil to join their revolution. However, Stoll's insistence on laying blame on the guerrilla is eclipsed by the overwhelming, well-documented information that he interjects throughout his book, establishing the fact that the Guatemalan military committed most of the worst atrocities against the indigenous peoples, especially the Maya Ixil (in the Department of Quiché).

The Ejército Guerillero de los Pobres (EGP) chose to establish their base in the Ixcan region of northern Quiché in 1972, close to the Mexican border, amongst the Cuchumatanes mountain range and its dense forest, close enough and within striking distance to the Ixil towns of Nebaj, Chajul, and Cotzal. The guerrilla, primarily composed of indigenous soldiers rather than mestizos, had started to undergo a transformation, becoming the "second" wave of recruits. While they adhered to the *foquismo* model, which believed that a small group of "outsiders" could ignite the flames of revolution, their understanding of achieving success had expanded to encompass a prolonged struggle, in contrast to the two-year timeline of the Cuban revolution. What they stood for was crafted in the names they adopted for the two column fronts: "Che" (after Che Guevara) and Ho Chi Minh, so named in honor of the popular North Vietnamese revolutionary hero.[47]

The Assassination of Luis Arenas

Three years after the EGP's arrival in the Ixcan, the assassination of Luis Arenas took place. He was an hacienda boss at La Perla, known for his respected character in the region. This incident marked the guerilla's first politically motivated killing. The assassination that occurred in 1975, along with its motives and consequences, has been the subject of intense debate among credible sources. Some argue that it was the EGP's most significant and costly mistake. However, the assassination garnered attention from two distinct groups: those who believed it was a justifiable act and those who strongly disapproved of it. The latter group primarily consisted of hacienda workers who relied on Arenas for their livelihood and wages. In the subsequent year of 1976, the army apprehended a man whom the EGP had relied upon as a trusted intermediary for bilingual communication in Ixil and Spanish. He was known as "Fonseca," a fair-skinned Cotzaleño (resident of Cotzal). Following four days of intense interrogation and torture, the army managed to extract from Fonseca the identities of his contacts. Subsequently, the army rounded up hundreds of innocent families and transported them to an army base in Santa Cruz del Quiché. Unfortunately, their fate was never revealed. The town folk blamed another man, Gaspar Pérez Pérez (a political boss), for presumably "welcoming" the army to their town. The utilization of torture as a means to coerce captives into implicating others was just one of the numerous brutal tactics systematically employed by the army against innocent individuals. Within the Cotzaleños were the initial EGP recruits, and credible sources indicate that the Maya Ixil, including the Cotzaleños, endured some of the most severe repression throughout the Armed Conflict.[48]

The Promises They Could Not Keep

One possible explanation for the resistance of the Maya Ixil to the guerrilla's recruitment efforts could be attributed to their recent progress in local politics. The 1944 revolution had left the campesinos without the fertile lands they depended on, but they made some headway in figuring out their power base and using it to their advantage. The guerrilla's campaign of promises convinced only a small constituency of the community, mostly progressive young males. However, the older members, conservative, *costumbristas*, were against any kind of substantial change to their lives. The message of the guerrillas was both clear and inspiring, offering the villagers the hope of reclaiming their lands, obtaining constitutional rights to combat discrimination, and thriving in a society characterized by freedom and democracy. By the early 1990's, the hardship and tragedy of a brutal war had taken their toll on the last-standing insurgency, extinguishing any remaining hope of fulfilling their promised objectives. In hindsight, it becomes evident that the guerillas assurances of a revolutionary future were primarily built upon deceit and propaganda.[49]

However, when the conflict escalated into a full-scale armed conflict, the Maya Ixil found themselves in a precarious position where their survival hinged on which side to align with – the guerrilla or the state. Unfortunately, the Maya Ixil were at a distinct disadvantage as the guerrilla's strategy of embedding themselves with the population proved highly successful. Unbeknownst to the Mayas Ixil, their mere association with the guerrilla, or vice versa, sealed their fate and led to their tragic demise.

The 1981-83 Genocide

The guerrilla group, EGP Ejército Guerillero de los Pobres, relied heavily on ambush tactics as their preferred mode of attack. With the inclusion of local bilingual recruits, they possessed a significant advantage in their knowledge of strategic areas within the expansive terrain. In response, the army would swiftly retaliate by carrying out massacres in villages, falsely alleging the involvement of all civilians in some capacity. Similar to the urban warfare tactics employed during the 1960s and 1970s, the state military responded with severe retaliation against the insurgency's attacks, consistently delivering a significantly more powerful and deadly response. In one particular incident in February, 1981, the insurgency targeted a state army vehicle, prompting the army to retaliate by setting fire to houses within the community. Tragically, this resulted in the death of 45 individuals who were burned alive. Subsequently, the state army began carrying out massacres in villages without any provocation from the insurgency. They adopted a military strategy that involved falsely labeling all Maya Ixiles as guerrilla soldiers, designating their communities, villages, and towns as being in the "red" zone. This term, in military jargon, denoted the regional presence of the perceived internal enemy.[50]

Massacres Without Provocation: The Death Toll Rises

The presidency of General Lucas García (1978-1982) marked the conclusion of a period characterized by brutal oppression. However, the despotic regime that was systematically established since the 1954 coup d'état was far from being eradicated. Under the command of his brother, Benedicto Lucas García, the regime persistently employed assassination death squads as a means to eliminate their perceived "opposition." Additionally, they utilized civil patrols or PACs, which were portrayed as "voluntary" military units, and constructed what were essentially prison camps referred as "model cities." The Lucas García regime's astronomical scale of violence and oppression was atrocious, and, yet, without rebuke from the United States, the elite military guard would not change its course.[51]

Gen. Efraín Ríos Montt, Chosen by God

A military triumvirate replaced the Lucas García regime, and after a brief period of political wrangling, one individual emerged as leader. General Ríos Montt, was initially chosen as superintendent at the military academy, however, according to the general, he was chosen by God. The general, who had undergone a religious transformation and was temporarily exiled by his military colleagues, returned to his country as a member of the Church of the Word. As a leader of the nation, his religious beliefs greatly influenced his style of leadership. He adopted a populist persona, advocating for the dismantling of elite police forces that were instilling fear among the middle and upper classes in urban areas. Furthermore, he proposed a general amnesty for the insurgency, albeit with carefully scripted limitations. The guerrilla rejected the amnesty offer, and the urban warfare of forced disappearances, death squads continued. Ríos Montt's appearance and demeanor were reminiscent of previous dictators, but what set him apart was his manipulation of religious fervor to deceive the masses and justify the horrific killings of thousands of civilians. He would then ask for their forgiveness, claiming he was deserving of God's mercy.[52]

1982: The URNG Combined Forces and the Year of Death and Destruction

The Ejército Guerrillero de los Pobres (EGP), having suffered significant losses in their ranks, joined with other guerrillas to create a better equipped and formidable force: the Unidad Revolucionaria Nacional Guatemalteca (URNG). Combining their forces with the Fuerzas Armadas Rebeldes (FAR), the Organización Revolucionaria del Pueblo en Armas (ORPA), and the Partido Guatemalteco de Trabajo/Fuerzas Armadas Revolucionarias (PGT/FAR), the URNG strategized a renewed plan to seek political amends for the oppressed masses, mostly the indigenous populations. Recognizing its shortcomings as a military force, the guerrilla umbrella sought a win-win solution in its negotiations with the State, but it was too little, too late since the Guatemalan army had become an unstoppable power giant.[53]

The scorched-earth (*tierra arrasada*) military tactic or policy, initiated by the Lucas Garcia regime and continued by Rios Montt, resulted in the devastating destruction of hundreds of villages, causing catastrophic damage of homes and communities, and leading to the loss of thousands of lives. Despite the armed conflict that began in 1960 appearing to reach its peak, much to the dismay and anguish of those most affected, the intense destruction and killings persisted for at least another five years.[54]

Official Reports on the Acts of Genocide, 1981-83

The United Nations Report of the Commission for Historical Clarification (CEH) released in 1999, titled *Guatemala Memory of Silence Tz'inil Na'Tab'al*, declares with substantial accuracy and diligence, the claim that as a State, Guatemala committed acts of genocide between 1981 and 1983.[55] The legal framework that formed the basis for the charge of genocide is stated in the *Convention on the Prevention and Punishment of the Crime of Genocide*.[56] Other documents such as *Guatemala Nunca Más*, by the Office of the Human Rights of the Archbishop of Guatemala (REMHI), provide documentation with precise details of the various human rights violations committed during the armed conflict.[57]

Campaña Victoria '82: The Campaign to Destroy Life

During the Ríos Montt regime, a plan was devised that allowed the president to authorize the military to carry out actions involving the indiscriminate and unlawful killing of non-combatant civilians in their efforts to eradicate guerrilla forces. Ríos Montt unlawfully seized the constitutional powers of the three branches of government, enabling him to abuse his authority, inflict severe harm, injury and death upon innocent individuals, all the while evading accountability and enjoying the protection of impunity. The National Security and Development Plan in the *Campaign Victoria 82* encompassed objectives in military, administrative, legal, social, political, and economic domains. It specifically targeted three specific geographic departments as targets: Quiché, Huehuetenango, and Chimaltenango. The document's guide, the *Manual of Counter-insurgency Warfare*, classified the enemy as communist, criminal, and subversive. General Gramajo Morale, one of the three strategists that designed the plan, claimed that the military strategy was meticulously designed and developed, down to the last detail. In the initial phase, certain population areas were designated as "red zones" to signify the perceived threat level posed by the "enemy." This classification effectively marked these areas for destruction, with the intention of annihilating entire villages and eliminating every inhabitant, leaving no evidence of life behind. The Ixil region found itself at the very heart of the military's focus and attention. The level of clarity exhibited in the documents regarding their plan of action indicated that every military member, regardless of their rank, was well-informed about the concept and specifics of "scorched-earth" destruction. This suggests that the overall and detailed message of this destructive approach was effectively communicated throughout the military hierarchy. Researchers have discovered archival data containing declarations from military officials, in which they congratulate each other for the brutal and aggressive tactics in targeting and killing non-combatants. The language used in these declarations is filled with racism and hatred towards the indigenous people.[58]

The plan for *Campaign Victoria '82* was deemed a national priority, with all available resources directed towards its execution. As part of this effort, the army added 10, 000 new recruits, bringing the total to 36,000 personnel. Notably, at least 20 percent of these recruits were young men from the rural indigenous communities who were obligated to fulfill a two-year military service conscription.[59]

Operation Sofía: Evil and Deadly

If there were any doubt regarding the precise intentions behind the military operations in the Ixil region, they were unequivocally dispelled during the infamous Operation Sofía. Led by President Ríos Montt and his operation commanders, the mission's objective was to annihilate, exterminate, and erase the indigenous population, specifically targeting the Maya Ixil. *Operation Ixil*, a 1981 military document, is widely recognized as a meticulously researched psychological analysis and assessment report that reveals a distinct bias against the Maya Ixil.

Information based on archival documents of *Operation Sofía* reveals that between July and August of 1982, 500 specialized "Kaibiles" soldiers parachuted into the Ixil town of Nebaj. These soldiers were trained to carry out the extreme forms of warfare and were given explicit orders were to "exterminate" the indigenous population. The entire Ixil community was labeled as "the internal enemy," regardless of whether or not the guerrilla were present amongst them. The "scorched-earth" operations intensified as the army perfected its strategy.[60]

The Massacres of 1982: Mass Killings of Innocent Civilians

During the period between April and November of 1982, was the deadliest. The United Nations Report of the Commission for Historical Clarification (CEH) concluded that 81 percent of human rights violations were committed between 1981 and 1983. The data show that 83.3 percent of the victims throughout the duration of the armed conflict were Maya, 16.51 percent were ladino or mestizo, and .16 percent were of another origin.[61]

The CEH reports 18 cases of massacres which are specifically attributable to President Ríos Montt that took place in Chel and Ilom, in the Ixil region.[62] These are recorded in the context of the most brutal and deadly, with 1,400 victims. The Archdiocese REMHI report, includes a total of 451 massacres in 1982. Particularly illustrated from this list as horrendously cruel and extreme in human rights violations were 180 massacres. These reports chronicle the testimonies of survivors, carefully detailing the most egregious crimes committed against a civilian population. Reports of killing innocent women, children, and the elderly, are incomprehensible; but the cruel, malicious torture of these individuals without purpose except to inflict suffering, is emotionally devastating. In almost every report that involves massacres, there are cases of sexual abuse and assault, on girls and women of all ages.[63]

Thousands are Forced to Flee for Their Lives

The army was ordered to completely annihilate the villages, assuring that the inhabitants would abandon their homes and become moving targets for execution. The people, in panic and terror, fled toward the mountain tops and sought refuge in dense vegetation. However, the army was relentless in their pursuit. The CEH concludes that about a third of the people that fled from the violence and sought refuge in the mountains died from starvation, decease, injuries, and/or grief.[64]

The number of civilians that took refuge in the mountains between 1980 and 1983 is estimated at 50,000. The three guerrilla-friendly areas where the refugees settled were known as "refugee zones:" Amajchel, Xeputul, and Sumal. Of the three, the Sumal area was at the highest elevation of the Cuchumatanes Sierra, and where the army maneuvered their next operation, the *Campaign Plan Firmeza 83*, beginning in August of 1982, until January, 1983.[65] A specialized unit called, the *Gumarcaj Task Force,* was ordered to attack the encampments of refugees, numbering between 18,000 and 25,000. The military ground troops surrounded the Sumal region as aerial bombardments triggered a chaotic response from the large groups of refugees. Some of them immediately fled the area but were executed by the army soldiers waiting in camouflage. Many of the captured refugees were taken to Nebaj and ordered to serve in the civil patrols and/or to construct the army-controlled settlements. The Sumal and Amajchel were the last EGP-friendly settlements. Other settlements that sheltered the displaced refugees were organized as Communities in Population as Resistance (CPRs). These settlements eventually received some international aid, particularly from the Catholic Church. Among the diverse indigenous groups, the majority consisted of the Maya Ixil. Even a decade after the establishment of the refugee settlements, there were still approximately 25,000 people residing in the CPRs. Nebajeños (residents of Nebaj) were among the last refugees to eventually return from the mountains. It is important to note that while the army coerced the refugees to return, using the pretext of amnesty, the campaign of terror persisted in the rural communities.[66]

The United States' Aid and Support for the Army

Post-conflict research and reports have raised significant questions regarding the catastrophic death toll and damages inflicted upon the Mayan groups. These inquiries have pointed to the Guatemalan military as the primary perpetrators the atrocities, and the United States playing a supportive role.

Archival data strongly supports the accuracy of the reports drawn by the CEH, that the Guatemalan Army was responsible for 93 percent of the human rights violations and acts of violence.

From the Maya Ixil perspective, there are far too many important factors that contributed to the tragedy, rather than solely blaming one group. The compulsory participation of the male population in the army's civil patrols and the guerrilla's Local Irregular Forces (FIL) raises questions about the individual and collective responsibility of those who participated in the violence. Those that joined the guerrilla and survived, had similar views since their soldiering requirements included acts of violence. However, it is notably important to mention that the carefully constructed strategy of "spreading the blame," tactic was used by the Guatemalan army to deflect from the extreme cruelty in carrying out the mission to "exterminate" the targeted non-combatant population.[67]

The CEH report contains archival data, including declassified communiqués between the U.S. and the Guatemalan military. President Reagan's Secretary of State, George Schultz, had a more significant involvement in the politics of Nicaragua and El Salvador compared to Guatemala. Schultz' focus throughout his administration from 1982 to 1989 remained aligned with President Reagan's commitment to end the Cold War. The Reagan administration maintained its support for the Guatemalan military's involvement in the armed conflict until at least 1989. It is important to note that the aircraft and artillery equipment used in field and aerial bombing raids, which resulted in village and refugee massacres, were supplied from the United States. The declassified communiqués between the CIA and Guatemalan State officials provide evidence that the U.S. officials were aware of and supported the "scorched-earth" policies. These policies involved intentionally targeting non-combatants and civilians as a means to defeat the guerrillas. The CIA communiqués concerning the burning down of multiple villages downplay the significance of non-combatant casualties. Instead, they focus on the number of guerrilla insurgents, supporters, or collaborators who were killed. Notably, none of the declassified communiqués express any concern or alarm regarding the large-scale killing of civilians in indigenous communities.[68]

Charges of Genocide and Crimes Against Humanity

The deliberate and systematic planning and execution of thousands of civilians by influential military generals, with the support of wealthy elites, sparked international outrage during the post-conflict period of the late 1990s and 2000s. The question of how to hold those responsible accountable for their actions was of utmost importance. However, the survivors of the armed conflict were hesitant to revisit the agony and suffering they endured during that shameful and painful period of their lives. On the other hand, there were strong demands for the punishment of those responsible, seen as a necessary step towards the healing process. To this date, only a few high-profile cases have been tried in Guatemala's tribunal courts, while many military officials accused of related crimes are still at large and remain on the list of wanted fugitives.[69]

The trial of Ríos Montt, who was charged with genocide and crimes of humanity, was the most significant trial. It was a remarkable achievement to bring a high-ranking official to justice, made possible by the determination and perseverance of numerous Guatemalan human rights defenders who were eager to handle the case in their own judicial courts known as "tribunales de alto riesgo." The Ríos Montt trial commenced on March 19, 2013 and by May 10, 2013 he was found guilty and sentenced to 80 years of prison for both counts of genocide and crimes against humanity.[70] However, the Constitutional Court of Guatemala overturned the verdict, citing certain technical issues, and ordered a retrial. Ríos Montt died during the retrial proceedings, on April 1, 2018. One of the most notable outcomes of the case was the courageous testimonies given by the men and women survivors, which showcased their strength and fortitude. This was powerfully depicted in the documentary, *500 Years: Life in Resistance*.[71]

Another prominent case that ended with a guilty verdict was the murder of Catholic Archbishop and human rights defender, Juan José Gerardi

Conedera.[72] Gerardi was a vocal advocate against the human rights violations perpetrated by the army during the armed conflict. As a bishop in the department of Quiché, he openly criticized the administration of President Lucas García for authorizing the 1980 military's attack on the Spanish Embassy, which resulted in the tragic deaths of 39 individuals. As an activist and staunch defender of human rights activists, Gerardi became a target of right-wing political groups. On April 24, 1998, Gerardi released the highly anticipated book, *Guatemala Nunca Más* (a project of the Interdiocesano de Recuperación de la Memoria Histórica and the United Nations). This extensively researched book documented the human rights violations committed against the Mayan people by the state army during the armed conflict. Tragically, just two days after the book's release, Gerardi was murdered in his home. Eventually, three former military officials were convicted and sentenced to prison on June 8, 2001. Among them, Col. Byron Disrael Lima Estrada played a key leadership role as the commander of the Gumarkaj Task Force during Ríos Montt's period of "scorched-earth" atrocities. All three have since passed away including José Villanueva, and the colonel's son, Byron, Jr. Author Francisco Goldman's book, *The Art of Political Murder: Who Killed the Bishop,* writes an insightful narrative behind the crime and mentions the possible involvement of but never convicted, Otto Pérez Molina, another retired military officer, and former President (2012-2015), who is currently serving a prison term for corruption charges.[73]

The CIA's Involvement Revealed

The case of Efraín "Everardo" Bámaca Velásquez, a former ORPA guerrilla leader and spouse of the American lawyer and author, *Jennifer Harbury* is one of the most significant cases that addresses the question of the extent to which the United States' CIA played a role in the armed conflict. Bámaca was kidnapped by the army in 1992, a year after he and Harbury got married. The search for her husband, dead or alive, became an arduous, dangerous, and heartbreaking journey for Harbury, which she describes in her book, *Searching for Everardo*. Her involvement in fighting civil rights cases against the CIA, the State Department, and the National Security Council led to the release of documents which proved that the United States had previous knowledge of Bámaca's kidnapping. The astonishing and disturbing fact was that the military personnel responsible for the crimes committed against Bámaca were actually paid CIA assets. Once this information became public, a campaign was launched, leading to the disclosure and declassification of thousands of records These records revealed that the U.S. and Guatemalan authorities were collaborating to a greater extent than previously known in the human rights violations committed during the armed conflict. Harbury eventually learned about her husband's fate but the whereabouts of his remains are unknown.[74]

The Long and Winding Road Toward Peace

The journey towards peace in post-conflict Guatemala is a complex and extensive process, involving multiple narratives from various perspectives. The central question at hand is how a nation can begin to heal itself after experiencing the devastating consequences of an armed conflict. The conflict that resulted in the loss of 200,000 lives, predominantly indigenous peoples, countless physical injuries, the displacement of over a million families, 40,000 disappearances, and the enduring, psychological and emotional trauma suffered by survivors. The objective of the *Peace Accords*, also known as the Firm and Lasting Peace, (*Acuerdo de Paz Firme y Duradero),* was to establish a peace treaty that all parties could agree upon. The aim was to address past injustices, enhance institutional structures, and foster the promotion of democratic rights and responsibilities.[75]

The United Nations team responsible for the UN Verification Mission in Guatemala or MINUGUA were tasked with this assignment from September, 1994 to November 15, 2004. The Peace Accords, which consisted of several agreements, particularly the agreement on socio-economic and agrarian rights, as well as the agreement on the rights of indigenous peoples, were not significantly distinct from the international human rights declarations previously promulgated by the United Nations.[76] For example, the UN specialized entity, the *International Labour Organization Convention 169,* promotes the protection of rights of indigenous and tribal peoples as exemplified in their 1989 revision of the 1957 convention.[77] The significance of the Peace Accords lies in the State of Guatemala's willingness to accept the mandate for a democratization of the Guatemalan government, insuring the rights of all its citizens, and the strengthening of the institutions that protect these rights.

***

Twenty-seven years after the signing of the 1996 Peace Accords, Guatemala faces an economic crisis that poses a significant threat to the future of the younger generation. According to the World Bank, approximately 59.3 percent of the population lives below the national poverty line, with 23.4 percent living in extreme poverty. Furthermore, Guatemala has one of the highest levels of income inequality in Latin America, with a Gini coefficient of 0.55 in 2019. Socially, Guatemala faces various issues, including violence, crime, and social exclusion. Indigenous communities, which make up 41 percent of the total population, often face discrimination and marginalization, leading to social disparities. Additionally, access to basic services such as healthcare, clean water, and sanitation remains limited, especially in rural communities.

Improving access to quality education is vital for Guatemala's development. The literacy rate stands at around 81.5%, with notable disparities between urban and rural areas. Access to education is particularly limited for indigenous and rural communities, leading to high dropout rates and limited educational opportunities. The quality of education is also a concern, with low levels of student achievement and inadequate infrastructure and resources in many schools.

Guatemala's judicial system has long been plagued by issues of corruption and impunity, which have undermined the rule of law and hindered the country's development. High levels of impunity have contributed to a culture of lawlessness and have eroded public trust in the justice system. This has allowed criminal networks, including drug traffickers and organized crime groups, to operate with relative impunity.

Guatemala has been a significant source of migration to the United States, with a large number of Guatemalans seeking better economic opportunities and escaping social and political challenges. Additionally, social and political challenges contribute to migration from Guatemala. The country has experienced long-standing issues such as violence, crime, and gang-related activities, which pose threats to personal safety and security. In 2019, Guatemala reportedly had one of the highest homicide rates in the region, with a rate of 22.4 per 100,000 people. It is important to note that migration from Guatemala to the United States is not without risks and challenges. Migrants often face dangerous journeys, including crossing borders irregularly and relying on smugglers. They may also encounter discrimination, exploitation, and legal barriers upon arrival in the United States. According to the U.S. Census Bureau, as of 2019, there were approximately 1.5 million Guatemalan immigrants residing in the United States.

Women in Guatemala face significant disparities. The World Bank reports that the labor force participation rate for women was 50.6 percent in 2019, lower than that of men. The gender wage gap remains a concern, with women earning approximately 70 percent of what men earn for similar work. Gender-based violence and limited access to healthcare is particularly alarming. According to the United Nations, Guatemala has one of the highest rates of femicide in the world, with an estimated 10 women being killed each week. Access to reproductive health services and family planning is also limited, contributing to high rates of teenage pregnancies. Efforts to address gender inequality, promote women's empowerment, and ensure their access to education, economic opportunities, and social services are crucial for achieving a more equitable and inclusive society in Guatemala.

Transforming the Women's Movement: Finding Common Ground

The women's movement during the October 44 Revolution paved the way for the establishment of safe spaces where women could assert their own unique expressions of feminism. The most significant challenge for women in post-conflict Guatemala is the reconstruction process, particularly for marginalized groups such as the Mayans who suffered the worst consequences of war. The investigations conducted by the CEH reveal compelling data, demonstrating that war crimes such as rape, torture, and murder were widespread, with Mayan women comprising the majority. This violence is deeply ingrained in the social memories of the communities, especially where women were sexually tortured in mass.[78]

Collective feminism aims to challenge and dismantle systems of oppression by centering the experiences and perspectives of indigenous women. It recognizes that the struggles faced by indigenous women are interconnected and cannot be separated from the their cultural, historical, and social contexts. By embracing feminism, indigenous women seek to reclaim their agency and challenge the dominant narratives that have marginalized and silenced them. They recognize that their liberation is intertwined with the liberation of their communities and the broader society, This collective feminism also acknowledges the importance of intersectionality, understanding that indigenous women face multiple forms of oppression and discrimination based on their gender, race, class, and sexuality.

Through their activism and organizing, indigenous women aim to create spaces for dialog, empowerment, and solidarity. They seek to challenge the patriarchal structures that perpetuate inequality and violence against women, while also reclaiming and celebrating their indigenous identities and cultures.

The purpose for organizing collective or community feminism (*el adelante comunitario*), adopted by groups such as the Asociación Mujeres Indígenas de Santa María Xalapá, is to open the possibilities for "seeing" through the eyes of indigenous women (*ver con ojos de mujer indígena*). A *collective feminist's* vision of freedom stems from the perspective of inferiority as a result of racism, capitalism, and homophobia, as well as ancestral oppression and subjugation.[79]

Socially-active indigenous women in organizations prefer alliances with groups that are not associated with western notions of feminism, such as the

European and U.S. Their interests are grounded in social and economic issues that concern indigenous women in areas of racism, ethnicity, and social class. Collective feminism embodies the mission of *reindicación*, the right to engage in *multiple resistances* in the struggle for autonomy and self-determination. Thus, women create their own pathways within the cosmovision to construct social transformations leading to a renewed society. [80]

The concerns over divisions based on race and identity within the women's movement in Guatemala reflect the broader challenges faced by feminist movements globally. While feminism aims to challenge and dismantle systems of oppression, it is not immune to internal divisions and power dynamics. However, as in the case of Guatemala where indigenous women have historically faced multiple forms of discrimination and marginalization, it is crucial to address these divisions and work towards a more inclusive and intersectional feminism. This means recognizing and valuing the diverse experiences and perspectives of women from different racial and ethnic backgrounds.

Originally created in 2007, the *Asamblea Feminista*, the first high-ranking political conference of its kind began the process of constructing a *Guatemalan feminist agenda* in 2010.[81] The Confluencia Nuevo Baqtun (The Confluence of the New Baqtun) was created (2012-2014) as a mechanism for providing a space for generating dialog and gathering information from social movement feminists and organizations of women self-identified as primarily indigenous and campesinas.[82] The two-year process engaged women who represented feminist social movement organizations and the Mayan (*pueblos*) perspective. The following is a representative statement from one of the participating women:

> *Nos encontramos en múltiples espacios de lucha, y actuamos juntas y juntos, no solamente en el espacio de la Confluencia, sino en actividades de reflexión y acción política alrededor de nuestras propuestas fundamentales: la defensa de los cuerpos, el territorio, la dignidad, la memoria, las cosmovisiones, el cuidado de la vida*

(personas, seres, naturaleza), como propuesta que nos identifica y une.[83]

English Translation:

We find ourselves in multiple spaces of struggle, and we act upon these not only within the Confluencia, but also in activities of reflection and political action congruent with our fundamental proposals: in defense of our bodies, our territories, our dignity, collective memory, the cosmovision, the protection of life (persons, beings, nature), all of which are like proposals that identify and unite us.

The statement reflects an acceptance of the proposed expressions of differences and similarities in women's perspectives, as well as an inclusion of the multiple layers of identity that are uniquely tied to a nationalistic entity. Incorporating the diversity within the feminisms that represent the voices of women from the vast regional and pluralistic cultural corners of Guatemala is a phenomenal task that may be best described as work in progress and a labor of love. Understanding the complex nature of transforming their world, the Guatemalan women have demonstrated that engaging in *change* can be a unifying process. Ultimately, the goal should be to build a feminist movement that is not only united in its fight against patriarchy and oppression but also recognizes and addresses the specific needs and experiences of different groups of women. This requires ongoing reflection, dialog, and a commitment to intersectionality and inclusivity.

Concluding Remarks

In many ways, the substantial advances made by Guatemalan feminists serve as metaphors for the country's vision beyond a post-conflict era. As they develop a blueprint for the future, they reflect upon the past and present: the past that was like a dagger that tore into their hearts and souls, and how today and every day, women are determined to rise like a phoenix from the ashes, reclaiming their lives with renewed energy and a spiritual awakening.

From a social science perspective, Guatemala's story is often characterized as a study of how power dynamics overwhelmed a society and contributed to its extensive, ultra-destruction. This destruction raises concerns about the integrity of our civilization as a whole. Thus, the crux of this chapter underscores the analysis that in order to understand the dynamics of power situated at the core of domination and subjugation, considerable attention to historical detail is essential and integral to the development of a thoroughly imbued perspective. Certainly, our memory is not comprised of detailed historiographies; however, although r*ecall* is important in the storing of what is memorable, it is the *remembering* at a personal level that achieves the intended objective. When Guatemala's story becomes *our story*, we can better approximate an adequate response to Alberto Manguel's question included in the chapter's epigraph: Is it possible for stories to change us and the world we live in?[84]

***

Discussion and Reflection Questions

1. <u>Colonialism in Guatemala</u>: What do you think were the most striking consequences as a result of the conquest of Guatemala by Europeans, mostly Spaniards, from 1523 to the country's independence in 1838?

2. <u>Post-colonialism period and beyond</u>. Describe and analyze the alliances and/or business ventures between Guatemala and the United States in the following periods: (include in your assessment some of the most important outcomes for each)

- 1871-1885, President Rufino Barrios
- 1898 – 1920, President Estrada Cabrera
- 1931-1944, President Jorge Ubico

3. <u>Transitional period of 1944-1954</u>. What were some of the significant advances during this period by women and the indigenous communities under the presidencies of Arévalo and Arbenz Guzman? Analyze the role of the United States during this period: what were the objectives in the U.S. involvement and the outcomes?

4. <u>The beginnings of the Internal Armed Conflict in the 1960s</u>. Describe in your own words the events that led to the armed conflict. What were the motivations that compelled the two lieutenants, Yon Sosa and Turcios Lima, to take the decisive actions? Do you think their actions were justified?

5. Describe and analyze the role of the United States and its involvement in the military actions taken by the Guatemalan dictators during the Internal Armed Conflict.

6. During the most violent periods of the Internal Armed Conflict, women were particularly targeted and as a consequence, it is believed that as a whole, indigenous women suffered the gravest injuries. Analyze the historical facts surrounding these attestations, and describe how you think the surviving women were impacted.

7. Discuss your views about the feminist movement and their advances made on behalf of women in Guatemala during the presidencies of Arévalo and Arbenz Guzmán. Most recently, the indigenous feminists have added their voices to the movement, however, their perspective is distinctly different from the "traditional" feminists. Share your thoughts about the diversity, specifically the inclusion of indigenous women, in the expansion of feminist thought and action in Guatemala.

Chapter Four

The Change from Within: Maya Women's 'Journey of Hope'

> *Estoy aquí, sobreviví, estoy viva.*
> *(I am here, I survived, I am alive.)*
> *Doña Julia*

oña Teresa, a Maya K'iché woman, relaxed and pensive on a mountain slope in Zacualpa, reflects upon her life-changes and transformations from the last three decades.[1] She shares with me the story about how she and her family survived the Internal Armed Conflict. She was a teenager when the state military forces' violent confrontations of terror and chaos shocked her community and thousands of others, causing death and destruction at a unprecedented scale. Historians compare the 36-year catastrophic Armed Conflict in Guatemala with the near-total devastation during and after the conquest of 1524 by the Spanish conquistadors.[2] Doña Teresa and her family grew up subsisting in the mountainous part of Zacualpa, an area deemed as excessively impacted by the military forces, so reported by the United Nations report, *Comisión para el Esclarecimiento Histórico (CEH)*.[3] Zacualpa and two other, K'iche'-speaking pueblos, Joyabaj, and Chiché, constituted one of the four geographical areas in Guatemala that were identified by the state military as the *"internal enemies,"* a term used to define civilians as insurrectionists. It was a false tactical assessment that served to justify their use of indiscriminate military power, killing and injuring thousands of innocent people.[4]

Doña Teresa's healing practices are rooted in the Mayan ancestral spirituality and cosmovision, which form the guided principles that she embraces in every aspect of her life. She learned the Mayan way of life through the cultural transmission process within her extended family and community.

But when the Internal Armed Conflict erupted violently, the cultural and social foundations of life became fragmented and weakened.[5] As a result of the tragic destruction of so many lives, as well as the loss of physical property and personal possessions, Doña Teresa turned her attention toward basic survival, for herself and her family.

Several decades later, her long, strenuous journey of self-healing has closed a circle, and Doña Teresa's vibrant and positive outlook on life is a testament of her determination to regain her spiritual strength, and to help others realize their journey of self-healing as foretold by their ancestors. The effects are far beyond the rewards of basic health and well-being. At the core of the principles that she espouses is the belief that a cultural reconstruction of the Mayan culture as gifted by her ancestors is the best antidote for the affliction that many people continue to suffer, especially the survivors of the war. As a member of a woman's organization devoted to using native plants for alternative medicine, Doña Teresa is a *change agent* in the cultural reconstruction process. Her story is part of a broader scope of Guatemala's history during which women suffered in one of the most egregious and widely encompassing scope that the world has ever known. Their stories live amongst us as a reminder of the strength of the human spirit.

Women as Victims and Protagonists

As discussed in the previous chapter, women were violently targeted, specifically during the genocidal events between 1981 and 1983. The *CEH,* the United Nations report on the Guatemalan 36-year Armed Conflict, concluded that at least 25 percent of the human rights violations and acts of violence were *directedly attributed* to women. However, children were also impacted as a result of the violence that women experienced. The *CEH* reported that a "large number" of children were also victimized, citing atrocious acts of torture, rape, and forced disappearances. Another document detailing the Armed Conflict, the *REMHI* investigative report, supported by the Archdiocese Office of Human Rights in Guatemala, includes first-hand accounts of several massacres in which the state military forces, in direct knowledge of villages whose male members had left for work in distant labor jobs, descended upon pueblos of innocent families, mostly women and children, and proceeded to torture, rape the women and young girls, murder them, and destroy their entire farms, their homes, crops and farm animals.[6] Several hundreds were killed instantly, or died from prolonged illnesses, while many more fled to the mountains for refuge. Disturbing images of graphic violence perpetrated against women and children are included in the internet version of the *REMHI* document.[7] However, these massacres were not isolated instances of violence, nor were the brutal massive sexual assaults on the women. The conclusions in the *CEH* report refer to the systemic genocidal operations as deliberate actions deeply embedded in a policy that could only have been executed with the *specific mandate(s)* of the highest governmental bodies. Indeed, the *CEH* includes statements regarding their investigation's conclusions that the State of Guatemala is undeniably responsible for "human rights violations and infringements of international humanitarian law."[8]

The violations perpetrated against women are underscored in the *CEH* report, and argues the case of *genocidal killings* committed by the State and that the official military plan, "Victory 82", was part of the overall state's *National Security Doctrine*. The report emphasized that the mission was to "annihilate the guerrillas and parallel organizations," of which the "internal enemy" had been identified as *the inhabitants or civilians of the specified locations*.[9] The State acted to intentionally destroy as many of the Mayan communities as it could, and to inflict serious injury to women as a whole and specifically targeting their reproductive capabilities. The data reveal that 89 percent of sexual assaults were committed against the Mayan women, and mostly in the massive sexual violence during the massacres or invasions.[10]

Documenting Women's Experiences

The documentation of the horrendous acts of crimes against women in violation of their human rights impels investigators to use extensive research methods and analytical lenses by which to study these actions.

Two recent reports, one published by Luz Méndez Gutiérrez and Amanda Carrera Guerra, *Mujeres indígenas: clamor por la justicia*;[11] and another, *Tejidos que lleva el alma* by Amandine Fulchirone,[12] highlight the women's traumatic events as well as their healing and recovery from their personal perspectives.

Luz Méndez Gutiérrez and Amanda Carrera Guerra's study includes two groups of women: the survivors of the Sepur Zarco invasion during the Armed Conflict which occurred between 1982 and 1988; and the survivors of the massive sexual assaults that occurred in Lote Ocho in 2007 during an invasion by the Policía Nacional Civil and Military (government) forces and security units employed by the HudBay transnational mining company, a subsidiary of Compañía Guatemalteca del Niquel (CGN). Both groups of women reside in Q'eqchi' communities of el Valle del Polochic (El Estor, Izabal, bordering Alta Verapaz) in the towns of Sepur Zarco and el Lote Ocho, respectively. The authors interviewed almost 60 women all together, individually and/or in focus groups. Their pre-established premise forms the basis of their study, that in Guatemala's institutions the indigenous population is systematically discriminated against, and that racism against the Indigenous people is at the root cause of inequality. In their stories, many of the women subjects gradually gained a consciousness of understanding the gender-based injustices they experienced. Thus, the patriarchal system that dominated their lives was integral to their understanding of how they were (and continue to be) systematically and socially excluded, and discriminated against. The investigation sought to document the human rights violations perpetrated against the women, and how the women pursued justice for the crimes committed against them.

The Lote Ocho Case: Justice in the Court of Law as a Form of 'Healing'

The Peace Accords document was signed in 1996, purportedly ending the devastating 36-year Armed Conflict. Yet, eleven years later, in January of 2007, the war had *not* ended, at least not according to the inhabitants in the remote community of Lote Ocho. Their story speaks of the tragedy that forever changed their lives.

An incendiary land dispute between the Q'eqchi' community members and owners of the HudBay Minerals and HMI/Skye mining company in charge of the Fenix mining project, came to a halt when the corporation ordered the eviction of the residents they claimed were blocking the construction of their mining project. The Fenix project security guards (the Campañía Guatemalteca del Níquel or CGN), the police, and army took charge of the violence and destruction on January 7th and 8th, according to the lawsuit summary filed by the legal counsel representing the affected Q'eqchi' women.[13] A week later, the same kind of callous force was repeated by the three enforcement units. However, the soldiers' uses of violence became increasingly brutal and extreme. In the January 17th eviction, the uniformed soldiers attacked viciously, and the terror and destruction tactics they employed were strikingly similar to those used by the state military units during the Internal Armed Conflict. According to the survivors' description of the events on that day, the armed guards and soldiers surrounded the homes, and everyone took cover, paralyzed with fear. After the soldiers broke down the front doors, they asked the women, many with their children, the whereabouts of their husbands. The women bravely stood steadfast against the armed soldiers that had surrounded the entire community. They believed that since their husbands were all gone to work in the distant fields, the soldiers would not harm them. But, unbeknownst to them, the commanding officers knew in advance that the men would be absent, and strategically targeted the community in their absence. As they ordered the inhabitants to leave their homes, they were doused with tear gas; soldiers with automatic guns sprayed bullets everywhere, barely sparing the lives of family members as they frantically escaped their homes. Before their homes were completely torched, the soldiers destroyed their essential belongings such as the grinding stones, dried corn in storage bins, their beds, clothing, tables and chairs. Then, they destroyed their crops and killed their domestic animals. They stole food and any materials they found of value.

Just as they had terrorized the families and destroyed their possessions and valuables, the uniformed soldiers proceeded to torture the women and girls. The sexual assaults were massive. The women suffered long-term consequences, such miscarriages among pregnant women, infertility caused by internal injuries, and permanent scars from psychosocial, emotional trauma.[14]

A documentary film, *Defensora*, includes an explanation behind the three lawsuits brought against the proprietors of the Canadian mining company. In the first case is plaintiff Angelica Choc, whose husband, Adolfo Ich Chaman, was murdered in 2009 by a security guard with the mining company. Second, the case of Rosa Elbira Coc Ich, representing herself and the women that were sexually assaulted during the unlawful eviction of 2007, and lastly, the case of German Chub Choc, who was shot and paralyzed by a security guard in 2009.[15] The fact that the cases are litigated in the Canadian court of law sets a precedence, and the long-held belief that foreign investors cannot be held accountable for their crimes is in jeopardy. Even if the cases don't reach an absolute resolve, for the families and community of Lote Ocho, their long journey toward justice has finally reached the pinnacle.

The Sepur Zarco Case, 1982-1988

The women in this study, known as the Sepur Zarco *abuelas* (grandmothers) from the *aldea* (the town) of the same name, endured a six-year, torturous imprisonment during the Internal Armed Conflict.[16] The state military and paramilitary forces had established several army bases near their community on the fincas (large plantations) owned by finqueros who welcomed the military. The women's husbands were "disappeared," a term commonly used to indicate that they were murdered and buried in a clandestine grave. The military officials informed the women that, as widows, they were legally obligated to work as servants for the soldiers. They were threatened with death or injury to their children or themselves if they refused. The women endured indescribable emotional and physical pain while being subjected to physical abused and sexually assaults. The women were compelled to work as domestic laborers, performing tasks such as cooking and cleaning for the men, while their own children were left unattended. In addition to the loss of their husbands due to military assassinations, their teenage sons had been kidnapped, and their homes had been deliberately burned down, resulting in the destruction of all their belongings. Consequently, the women had to construct basic, makeshift shelters in close proximity to the military base for themselves and their children. They were subject to twelve-hour shifts of unpaid labor, enduring the horrifying ordeal of being sexually assaulted at gunpoint. The reign of terror and imprisonment, which lasted for six years, finally came to an end when the military bases were ultimately closed in 1988.

Many of the women believed that they were targeted due to their husbands' (the campesino leaders who were "disappeared") lodging formal complaints against government officials. The husbands had questioned the officials' claims of legitimacy over their land claims and titles. The large landowners, known as "finqueros," were willing to collaborate with the government in order to suppress the campesinos' pursuit of their ancestral lands. The finqueros felt threatened as their land titles were fraudulent or illegal, just like the "widow's" law imposed by the military to force the women into compliance with their criminal activities. The military base in Sepur Zarco, where the women were enslaved, prominently displayed the United States trademark on various items, such as weapons, ammunition, vehicles, and communication devices. Additionally, the well-equipped army personnel had received training originating from the United States. Despite being prepared for combat on a large scale, the military base primarily served as a transitional station for their soldiers and faced a minimal, if any, threat, from counterinsurgency attacks. The military justified their use of extreme military tactics by claiming it was necessary to prevent guerrilla infiltration and the contamination of the indigenous population. This explanation aligned with the interests of the United States, which aimed "to keep the communist from taking over, and keeping Guatemala safe and secure."

***

El Consorcio de Victimas y Actoras de Cambio: From Victims to Change Agents

Although the 1996 Peace Accords authorized the initiative to open up a space for advancing women's rights, the government lacked the resources or the will (or both) to create mechanisms by which to appropriate justice for human rights violations committed against the women.[17]

However, autonomous feminist organizations began to propose actions that addressed the critical need of women whose human rights had been violated during the Internal Armed Conflict. In 2003, feminists Yolanda Aguilar and Amandine Fulchirone sought the collaboration of four organizations to develop a project of support, development, and investigation related to the human rights violations committed against the indigenous women.[18] These associations were *Mamá Maquín*; *Mujeres Petén Ixqik*; *Unión Nacional de Mujeres Guatemaltecas (UNAMG)*; and *Equipo de Estudios Comunitarios y Atención Psicosocial (ECAP)*.[19] The key goals and objectives of el Consorcio revolved around *breaking the silence* ("romper el silencio") and *recovering the history* (of human rights violations), and guiding and supporting women in transcending the complex psychological and social obstacles in order to develop self-validation, self-affirmation, and self-esteem. These were extraordinary goals, considering that the participating women initially felt unable to share their most intimate and tragic experiences. Additionally, they refused to subject themselves to social backlashes like the types they had experienced in the wake of the violations when they felt stigmatized, of no fault of their own, for having been sexually assaulted. The women had lost their place of dignity and respect in the social realm of their communities and as widows, they were left without the prospects of land ownership. But as members of a *collective (el Consorcio)*, the women courageously seized moments of challenge and opportunity, and reached out to other women that sought their help, sharing their journeys of self-healing.

***

The Formation Stage of el Consorcio, 2004-2008

The *Consorcio de Víctimas a Actoras de Cambio* program involved sixty-two women from four different Mayan *pueblos*: Chuj, Mam, Kaqchikel and Q'eqchi'. The group leaders consisted of Guatemalan feminists who served as facilitators, supporters, and confidantes. Their foremost task was to build *trust* between and among each other. From the outset of the formation period, the women shared their stories, and gradually, they began to feel confident enough to share their most frightening and private experiences, which included the sexual assaults. Clearly, the women's successful participation was largely due to the group's dynamics that eventually engaged everyone to support each other and learn from one another, creating a consensus-building spirit with intentions of overcoming the individual tragedies, and developing *solidarity and sisterhood.*

As a part of their investigation, the Consorcio (or *Colectivo*) guided the women in developing biographical profiles and personal narratives, and then, published them on their website.[20]

The women's recognition of their responsibility to assist others who have experienced similar suffering during the Armed Conflict has greatly influenced their approach to addressing these issues. Their voices carry a powerful resonance, not only because they speak from the heart, but also because of the profound message they convey – one of renewal and self-affirmation. Their efforts are specifically directed towards women whom they feel a strong obligation to support and console, letting them know that *they are not alone.*

The Women's Voices

The three women highlighted in this section not only endured the horrors of the Internal Armed Conflict, but also achieved remarkable accomplishments that surpassed even their own expectations. Their extraordinary lives are held in high regard by those close to them, as well as other women who learn about their past and witness how they have triumphed over seemingly insurmountable challenges.

Doña Julia

Doña Julia resisted the move to a refugee camp in México, but it was her only option in order to stay clear from the violence triggered by the Internal Armed Conflict of the 1970s and 1980s. Once she and her family fled from her home, the Maya Chuj aldea of Subajasum, near Nentón Huehuetenango, they were unable to return until after the violent skirmishes subsided. Tragically, by then, their home had been completely destroyed.

Doña Julia's childhood and adolescence were "normal and typical" of females in her pueblo. At birth, she was disdained by her father who preferred a male child, and the extreme poverty that they experienced caused the usual predicaments of hunger, malnutrition, and lack of education. In her community, it was customary for fathers to have the option of "selling" their daughters to men who would eventually take them away. However, when faced with this prospect, a young Julia made a courageous decision. She refused to accept this arrangement and instead chose to leave her home and live with relatives.

Doña Julia came to realize that escaping from her difficult situation was the most effective solution. Throughout her journey, she endured severe physical, emotional, and psychological abuses. However, the most devastating experience she faced was a sexual assault by a guerrilla soldier. Although she survived the attack, the profound psychological and emotional wounds it inflicted upon her were enduring and profound.

At the Mexican refugee camp, Doña Julia found solace and empowerment through her involvement with the women's organization, Mamá Maquín. This transformative experience had a profound impact on her life. Through her participation, she gained valuable literacy skills in Spanish, deepened her understanding of human rights, and discovered her legal entitlements, including land ownership and the workings of the justice system. Previously, she had believed that her gender stripped her of any rights. Her active engagement with the organization spanned six years, during which she achieved numerous milestones. Today, she takes immense pride in her accomplishments and possesses unwavering confidence in her ability to overcome any obstacles that may arise on her path to achieving her goals She explains her awakening in this quote (English translation follows:

> "Yo era una persona dormida, inconsciente, pero gracias a Mamá Maquín aprendí cosas buenas y a dejar atrás todos esos obstáculos que no nos permiten hacer muchas cosas." *(I used to be an uneducated person, but thanks to Mamá Maquín I learned so many good things and I left behind the obstacles that impede our efforts to accomplish so many good deeds).*[21]

Initially, Doña Julia harbored fear and reluctance when it came to discussing her own experience of sexual assault. However, as she became more involved with the women's group, she discovered that many of her fellow members had also endured similar traumatic experiences. Realizing the shared pain and sorrow they carried, Doña Julia empathized deeply with their struggles.

Over time, Doña Julia embarked on a mission to empower these women, helping them recognize their rights to speak out against the crimes committed against them and pursue justice. She highlighted the unfortunate reality that the perpetrators of these heinous acts often evaded punishment, while the women who suffered at their hands were left to bear the brunt of social consequences and enduring psychological wounds.

In expanding her role from student to teacher in the Mamá Maquín organization, Doña Julia acquired a kind of re-birth that she had not expected: a genuine sense of self-validation, confidence, and self-esteem. Her empathy toward women who have been sexually assaulted or physically abused was sincere; in every case she felt as though *she* was the victim. But, she's not running away from the problem anymore because she has learned how to cope and resolve.

Her spirituality is at the base of her strength. She describes her prayer in this quote:

> Me pongo a rezar con candelas, veladoras y pom, pido por el corazón del agua, de la tierra, del aire y de la naturaleza, enciendo mis velas por todo lo que existe en la naturaleza, yo misma voy a buscar el copal y lo enciendo, cuando hago eso, me alegra mucho el corazón.
> *(I pray with candles and incense; I ask for strength from the heart of water, the earth, the air, and nature; I burn my candles for everything that exists…. When I do this, my heart feels so happy).*[22]

Doña Julia's words, though simple, resonate deeply with the women, encapsulating their shared sentiments and experiences:

"Estoy aquí, sobreviví, estoy viva." (I am here, I survived, I am alive).[23]

Doña Dorotea's Inner Strength

The traumatic experience of being forcibly taken and sexually assaulted by soldiers during the six-year period in the early 1980s left Doña Dorotea devastated, not only in terms of material loss but also in terms of her spiritual well-being. The soldiers' actions not only stripped her of her home, possessions, and beloved family members but also shattered the spiritual practices that had been an integral part of her life since childhood.[24]

The Maya Q'eqchi' attribute their very existence to a unique and profound relationship with the land and the mountains that surround them. According to their beliefs, each mountain is regarded as a living entity, housing a sacred spirit that possesses person-like qualities. These spirits, known as Tzuultaq'a, are seen as integral members of the Q'eqchi' community. For the Q'eqchi' people, caves hold significant spiritual importance and serve as sacred spaces where they engage in various rituals. These rituals involve acts of sacrifice, expressions of gratitude, and offerings of food to reciprocate the blessings bestowed upon them by the spirits. Maintaining a strong bond between the

Tzuultaq'a and the people is crucial for ensuring good health and prosperity within the community.

The act of utilizing the land for planting and harvesting is deeply intertwined with the Q'eqchi' religious practices. It is considered a religious event in which they perform their rituals, seeking permission from the Tzuultaq'a through prayer and expressing their unwavering gratitude for the abundance they receive. This connection to the land is not merely a practical endeavor but a spiritual one, reinforcing their belief in the reciprocal relationship between humans and the sacred spirits that inhabit the mountains.

Anthropologist Richard Wilson explains that "as long as the Mayans are alive in the mountains, each community's claim to be the rightful owner of the land remains alive too"[25]. Doña Dorotea survived the Armed Conflict, but after her community was demolished, she joined thousands of people as refugees in search of a new life.[26] Without her community, the respected elders, and the collective traditions and customs of spiritual manifestations, Doña Dorotea relied on her own strength and beliefs as part of the healing process. She alone summoned the Tzuultaq'a in her dreams and interpreted their words for guidance. She found her inner strength in the ancient traditions of her culture to resolve the painful lingering problems that impeded her ability to live her life to the fullest. As an integral member of the Colectiva, Doña Dorotea is known for her spiritual devotion, believing that everything in our natural world has life and the need to show our appreciation by offering our positive energies. Her inner strength and self-respect are well-noted in her leadership abilities, and she is a dutiful, passionate advocate against domestic violence.

Doña Carolina

Doña Carolina's story began with her journey of grief, as she tirelessly searched clandestine graves for the remains of the eight members of her family who were violently killed during the Armed Conflict. Her story serves as an exemplary testament to the transformative power of women, as they emerge as beacons of light in a journey filled with hope.[29]

Doña Carolina, a Maya Kaqchikel "war widow" from Chimaltenango, endured years of anguish following the 1996 Peace Accords as she tirelessly sought answers about the whereabouts of her loved ones' final resting places. Despite the government's refusal to assist the war widows' pleas, Doña Carolina took it upon herself to shoulder the burden of this responsibility. The devastating loss she experienced included the torture and murder of her husband, the killing of her father and two-year-old son before her eyes, as well as the deaths of her sister, brother-in-law, mother-in-law, sister-in-law, and husband's brother. Miraculously, she and her mother survived. Throughout the arduous search process, Doña Carolina was consumed by grief, sadness, and a shattered heart. She played a pivotal role in organizing the exhumation of 35 bodies, an endeavor that nearly claimed her life on multiple occasions.

Doña Carolina's unwavering determination to locate the graves of her missing family members became the driving force behind her life's mission. Collaborating with Rosalina Tuyuc, the founder of CONAVIGUA (The National Association of Guatemalan Widows), she embarked on a journey to share her poignant tale of grief and service, inspiring others along the way. Together, they worked tirelessly to recover collective memory, uncover the truth, and advocate for justice. Additionally, Doña Carolina played a crucial role in organizing the war widows of San José Poaquil, supporting them as they bravely spoke out against the sexual assaults perpetrated by the army. She also spearheaded efforts to demand the removal of the military base from their municipality, seeking to create a safer environment for her community.

The processes of self-validation and self-affirmation are evident in Doña Carolina's remarkable journey of overcoming immense pain and finding the strength to become a passionate advocate for justice and reparations. Despite the challenges she faced, she emerged as an intrepid and courageous leader, unwavering in her commitment to her cause. In her own words, she boldly declares, "Even if I go to jail, I will continue moving forward." *(Soy fuerte, no tengo miedo. Aunque me vaya en la cárcel puedo salir adelante).*[30]

In their *journey of hope*, the women relied on their collective strength to attain unity as well as self-reflection. They engaged in a process of *accompaniment* ("el proceso de acompañamiento"), as an integral part of the collaboration between the women and the feminists, blending their support and guidance throughout the stages of the women's development.

Seeking Justice Through the Healing Process

The road toward recovery for the eleven Maya Q'eqchi'women survivors of the Sepur Zarco sexual assault case was excruciatingly painful, explains Luz Méndez Gutiérrez in a documentary film about the Sepur Zarco case.[31] The women felt shame and guilt; they kept this "dark" secret to themselves which further exacerbated their emotional, psychological, and physical injuries. Twenty-five years later, between 2004-2011, the women began to share their heart-rendering stories publicly, eventually marking the end of a difficult metamorphosis transformation, enabling them to acknowledge their life as victims in the past, and their newfound freedom as change agents ("actoras de cambio") in the present.

The women's decision to demand justice for the crimes committed against them was a remarkable accomplishment. Once they had taken this important first step, the national and international human rights and feminists organizations provided assistance and support. A support network was organized in 2010, called the *Alliance to End Silence and Impunity*, specifically to address the human rights and gender inequality (UN Women) and Mujeres Transformando el Mundo (MTM); to lend psychological and social support to the women by el Equipo de Estudios Comunitarios y Atención Psicosocial (ECAP); and to establish political precedence at the national and international levels, i.e., la Unión Nacional de Mujeres Guatemaltecas (UNAMG). The fifteen women asked the court to charge those responsible for the crimes, to reveal the truth of the events and the consequences, and to apply the necessary jurisprudence so that the crimes would not be repeated. The women insisted that no other woman or girl should be subjected to such violence as they experienced.[32]

The *Court of Conscience* was formed to serve as a symbolic form of justice. It is known as "el tribunal de consciencia contra la violencia sexual hacia las mujeres durante el conflict armado de Guatemala," *(the tribunal court of conscience against the sexual violence of women during Guatemala's armed conflict).*[33] The Court of Law that normally processes these types of crimes was yet to be formed by the Guatemalan legal system, nevertheless, the Tribunal Court served the purpose of allowing the case to go forward.

A three-year investigation yielded substantial evidence to charge two former military officers: Lt. Col. Esteelmer Reyes Girón and military commissioner Heriberto Valdéz Asij. Both men also faced additional charges of *murder*.

On February 26, 2016, presiding judge, Yasmin Barrios Aguilar, the president of the High-Risk Court of Guatemala, handed over the verdict of *guilty* for both men, including a prison sentence of 120 years for Reyes Girón and 240 years for Valdez Asij. Reparations that addressed the health and education needs of the community were also included.[34] The Sepur Zarco case brought to justice those responsible for the crimes of sexual slavery committed against the women during the course of an armed conflict. It was the first of its kind in Guatemala and the world.[35]

The Sepur Zarco case is a significant step forward in the pursuit of justice for many women who experienced sexual assault during the Armed Conflict. Despite the State of Guatemala formerly agreeing upon declarations that serve as laws to protect women and prevent crimes of violence against them, many human rights advocates are disappointed with the inadequate enforcement that renders these protection measures meaningless. Resolution 1325, adopted by the United Nations Security Council on October 31, 2000, declares that the government has the responsibility to end impunity and prosecute those responsible for "genocide, crimes against humanity, and war crimes including those relating to sexual and other violence against women and girls." In a communiqué by Immunity Watch, a statement of support is mentioned concerning the Sepur Zarco case, however, it also reiterates the need to specify reparation measures for the victims, to "overcome the structural conditions that allowed the public security forces to perpetrate sexual violence against women."[36]

On February 21, 2018, two years after the decisive verdict, the Ministerio Público de Guatemala and the United Nations Women (UNO) awarded the 14 surviving *abuelas* a special recognition, including a Medal "Naxjolomi," signifying their courageous leadership, "aquella que lidera," in Q'eqchi'.[37] The (remaining) survivors are: Matilde Sub, María Ba Caal, Felisa Cuc, Margarita Chub, Cecilia Xo, Catarina Caal, Manuela Bá, Candelaria Maaz, Rosario Xo, Carmen Xol, Antonia Choc, and Demesia Yat. María Ba Caal's main concern is that because of her advanced age, she may not see the reparations that were included in the verdict.[38]

'In Defense of the Indigenous Women's Rights'

The work of women who served as human rights defenders played a key role in facilitating the indigenous communities in their struggle to bring justice against their perpetrators, many of whom believed that their crimes would never be exposed. Among these were Luz Méndez Gutiérrez, Mamá Maquín, and Rosalina Tuyuc Velásquez.

***

Luz Méndez Gutiérrez

Luz Méndez Gutiérrez' prior experiences in the counterinsurgency movement during the Internal Armed Conflict and in the post-conflict period, Peace Accords process were instrumental in the development of key aspects of the investigative report, *Mujeres indígenas: clamor por la justicia: violencia sexual, conflict armado y despojo violento de tierras*. In the 1970s, Méndez was an activist with the Guatemalan Labor Party (el Partido Guatemalteco del Trabajo or PGT), which became part of the Guatemalan National Revolutionary Unity (Unidad Revolucionaria Nacional Guatemalteca or URNG) in the 1980s. In 1991, she was appointed *Political Diplomat* by the URNG as a representative in the Peace Accords process. As the only female in the committee, she began to understand her vital role in representing women, and in particular, the indigenous women, for whom she had deep regards for the suffering they had endured during the Internal Armed Conflict. However, understanding that her depth of knowledge about their experiences was insufficient, she became a dedicated researcher, collecting data from multiple sources, including first-hand information from the affected women, and the organizations that supported the women. As part of the peace negotiators, Luz Méndez played a crucial role in the inclusion of an *"Office for the Defense of Indigenous' Women's Rights"* in the Peace Accords' official document.[39] Included in her research were feminist organizations, such as the National Union of Guatemalan Women (Unión Nacional Asociación de Mujeres Guatemaltecas or UNAMG) and human rights authorities such as the United Nations Women (UN Women). Her leadership, along with others, played a crucial role in ensuring that the Peace Accords included significant advancements in the rights of indigenous women, particularly their right to demand justice against all forms of violence.[40] In the report that Luz Méndez co-authors with Amanda Carrera Guerra, Méndez highlights a quote from one of the women that she interviewed. The women's message, which is clear and concise, appears to resonate with Mendez' compassionate yet profound perspective in her capacity as a researcher, writer and activist: "Que todos sepan lo que sufrimos las mujeres. sufrimos destrucción de nuestras cosas, violación, nos dejaron sin tierra," (*Everyone should know what we went through... we suffered the destruction of our personal belongings, sexual assault, and we were left without land.*)[41]

Mamá Maquín: A Community Leader that Inspired Thousands of Women

At the time that Mamá Maquín joined the march of Maya Q'eqchi' protesters in the heart of Panzós, Alta Verapaz on May 29, 1978, she was known as a respected leader and spokesperson for the campesinos who were fighting for their rights to obtain land titles that had been passed down from their ancestors over a century ago. Unknown to her and the rest of the large group of unarmed, peaceful protestors - men, women and children - was that the army was waiting for them at the end of the street. In a surprise attack, the soldiers opened fire on the crowd. Although, everyone scurried to safety, hundreds were killed or injured. Some, including women and children, jumped into the Río Polochic in desperation and drowned. This event later became known as the *"Panzós Massacre."*

María Maquín, granddaughter of Mamá Maquín, recounts her experience on the day of the march. She was twelve-years old at the time, and was with her grandmother when they were fired upon. Her grandmother was shot and killed, but María managed to dodge the bullets and pretended to be dead until she was able to escape with the others to the mountain.

The soldiers who were ordered to quash the rebellion were trained as assassins at the Zacapa military base, which was headed by former military president, Carlos Arana Osorio (1970-74), known as the "butcher of Zacapa."[42] Approximately, 140 to 150 unarmed, peaceful protesters were killed and later, buried in clandestine graves by the soldiers.[43]

Mamá Maquín, whose real name was Adelina Caal, earned the title *Mamá*, as a sign of respect and admiration due to her leadership in the fight for the campesinos' rights to land titles that had been revoked or stolen by the government. The May 29 March was part of a series of protests carried out by campesinos, including farmers, activists, and community leaders from various Mayan pueblos, who all share similar grievances such as lack of land, discrimination, forced conscription, and low wages. The land that the campesinos relied on for their livelihood had been illegally transferred to wealthy landowners who claimed to have purchased the titles. These titles were issued under the auspices of the government agency, the Guatemalan Agrarian Transformation Institute, which administered by Hans Laugerud, the brother of the Guatemalan president, Kjell E. Laugerud García (1974-78). Fraudulent titles were regularly given to wealthy landholders, many of whom held high-ranking positions in the military and/or the government. The "zone of the generals," an area of personal interests to them, had extensive oil and nickel deposits and was suitable to raising cattle.[44] Only a small number of wealthy landholders (two percent) claimed ownership of 57 percent of arable land, which the Mayan pueblos considered extremely unfair and unjust. Under these circumstances, they were unable to sustain a living without resorting to migratory work as field hands.[45]

In 1974, campesino leaders and activists began to build a support base after the fraudulent presidential election of the military-supported Kjell Laugerud García. However, it was the spectacular success of the 150,000-strong, nine-day Ixtahuacán Miners March in November 1977 that compelled the Committee for Campesino Unity (CUC) to take the affirmative steps in becoming an organized, liberally-oriented organization dedicated to the struggles of the rural Maya pueblo campesinos.[46] Against this background of peaceful protests, the Panzós May 29th March was organized by the community leaders, including Mamá Maquín.

In a historical panorama, the "Panzós Massacre" was a crucial event that provoked and accelerated forward the Armed Conflict. Two years later, in January of 1980, a group of K'iche' and Ixil men peacefully occupied the Spanish embassy in the hope of garnering international attention to the killings of civilians, particularly in the north Quiché pueblo communities.[47] The government, presided over by President Fernando Lucas García (1978-82), acted brutally and burned down the embassy, killing everyone inside, including the protesters. Just a few weeks later, the Committee for Campesino Unity (CUC) organized a leadership conference that introduced a document known as the "declaración de Iximché," which, as author Arturo Arias asserts, was actually a declaration of war against the state forces.[48]

Mamá Maquín originated in México as an organization that provided refuge for hundreds of Mayan families fleeing the violence in Guatemala. Among these groups were the inhabitants of Santa María Tzejá, a K'iche' community that had been devastated by the conflict. In her book, Beatriz Manz describes their journey through the horrendous years of the Internal Armed Conflict. Despite the hardships and tragedies that dominated their lives, Manz makes a concerted effort to focus on the strengths and accomplishments of a people that lost everything but fortuitously embraced the opportunity to apply fresh ideas to a new start in life.[49] The promoters of the Mamá Maquín organization offered post-conflict workshops to help women learn a broad and deep perspective of the chaotic and complex Armed Conflict, and to understand, protect, and defend their rights.

Rosalía Hernández was a founding member of Mamá Maquín in México and took great lengths to help women in all aspects of self-help, including the use of birth control. Of course, some of the women were in opposition to what Hernández proposed, but many others benefitted from the organization, such as Doña Julia.[50]

Rosalina Tuyuc Velásquez, CONAVIGUA

Doña Rosalina Tuyuc Velásquez is a prominent human rights activist and defender who founded CONAVIGUA (The National Association of Guatemalan Widows) in 1988. The organization is dedicated to seeking truth and justice for women whose husbands and loved ones were assassinated or disappeared during the Internal Armed Conflict.[51] Rosalina Tuyuc's father and husband were killed during the early 1980's of the Armed Conflict, and she began the painful ordeal of searching for their remains. Since then she has devoted her time to helping women, known as the "war widows," not only find the graves of their loved ones but also seek justice.[52] Tuyuc is a compassionate community leader who understands the healing process that Guatemalans must endure, and mostly leads by example.

Concluding Remarks

The "success stories" of women who participated in the *Colectiva* and whose narratives are presented in this chapter, are imbued with a unique significance when analyzed from the historical and social perspective of survival. Guatemala's 500-year-old history of conquest, colonialism, and armed conflict is replete with countless stories of struggle for justice, which often seemed untenable for the majority of Guatemalans against a backdrop of institutionalized racism and discrimination. The women's stories in the *Colectiva* are representative of their *journeys of hope*, not only because of their singular accomplishments, but for the powerful messages they emit to the world. As a whole, they share a story of profound sadness, tragedy, pain, anguish, and frustration. But they also demonstrated to the world how each one overcame their multiple, near-death experiences, and resisted what could have been a life sentence of extreme psychological and emotional debilitation. Instead, they radiate with a keen sense of love for life and the natural world around them. There is no greater hope than that, especially for women.

***

Discussion and Reflection Questions

1. <u>Colonialism in Guatemala</u>: What do you think were the most striking consequences as a result of the conquest of Guatemala by Europeans, mostly Spaniards, from 1523 to the country's independence in 1838?

2. <u>Post-colonialism period and beyond</u>. Describe and analyze the alliances and/or business ventures between Guatemala and the United States in the following periods: (include in your assessment some of the most important outcomes for each)

- 1871-1885, President Rufino Barrios
- 1898 – 1920, President Estrada Cabrera
- 1931-1944, President Jorge Ubico

3. <u>Transitional period of 1944-1954</u>. What were some of the significant advances during this period by women and the indigenous communities under the presidencies of Arévalo and Arbenz Guzman? Analyze the role of the United States during this period: what were the objectives in the U.S. involvement and the outcomes?

4. <u>The beginnings of the Internal Armed Conflict in the 1960s</u>. Describe in your own words the events that led to the armed conflict. What were the motivations that compelled the two lieutenants, Yon Sosa and Turcios Lima, to take the decisive actions? Do you think their actions were justified?

5. Describe and analyze the role of the United States and its involvement in the military actions taken by the Guatemalan dictators during the Internal Armed Conflict.

6. During the most violent periods of the Internal Armed Conflict, women were particularly targeted and as a consequence, it is believed that as a whole, indigenous women suffered the gravest injuries. Analyze the historical facts surrounding these attestations, and describe how you think the surviving women were impacted.

7. Discuss your views about the feminist movement and their advances made on behalf of women in Guatemala during the presidencies of Arévalo and Arbenz Guzmán. Most recently, the indigenous feminists have added their voices to the movement, however, their perspective is distinctly different from the "traditional" feminists. Share your thoughts about the diversity, specifically the inclusion of indigenous women, in the expansion of feminist thought and action in Guatemala.

Chapter Five

Nicaragua, Our 'Beautiful' Country: From a Liberating Revolution to a Repressive State

The Revolution started in the stars, millions
Of light-years away. The egg of life
Is one. From
The first bubble of gas, to the iguana's egg, to the New Man.
Sandino was proud he had been born "from the womb of the
Oppressed"
(from the womb of a Niquinohomo Indian woman)
From the womb of the oppressed the Revolution will be born.
(Ernesto Cardenal, translated by M. Zimmermann)

It was a moment of rebirth. The victory of the Sandinistas over the Somoza regime in the summer of 1979 was met with awe and jubilation not only in Central America and the Caribbean region, but around the world. Historians hailed it as a *revolution*, a testament to the immense popularity among Nicaraguans who believed that their dire conditions of poverty and repression would finally be alleviated. Nicaraguans endured a brutal a dictatorship for forty years (1937-1979), followed by an exhaustive and bloody revolution and almost immediately after, another violent and deadly armed confrontation known as the Contra War. Both conflicts lasted from 1979 to 1990 and claimed at least 88,000 lives, a significant number in a country of about 6.5 million inhabitants.[1] Another notable fact is the revolution's compelling social mobilization efforts of the masses, as well as the stories of sacrifice and heroism of many people, especially young adults, who risked their lives for the promise of a democratic society.[2] Ten years after the 1979 victory, Nicaragua's governance was in serious disarray. In 1990, the Sandinistas lost their grip on power after the national elections. Seventeen years later, the Sandinistas are back in power, and Daniel Ortega continues to rule with a very different vision than what was imagined by the original Sandinista revolutionaries. An integral part of the Nicaraguan revolution was the essential role of women before, during and after the revolution. Historical data indicate that female combatants and non-combatants in the Sandinista guerrilla comprised a third of the total number of soldiers. Some of these women are known as revolutionary heroes. Their fight then, as it is today, is an uncompromising struggle to defend the right to live in a democratic society and to construct a future commensurate with their vision of a *new Nicaragua.*

The current state of affairs, fourteen years into the Ortega regime, demonstrates the reality that ascertains the worst fears of so many Nicaraguans, i.e., that the Ortega-Murillo regime is a dictatorship whose predominant vision for Nicaragua is a government ruled by the powerful Ortega-Murillo family for years to come. By controlling the electoral laws and procedures, and taking measures to keep viable candidates off the ballots, the regime conveys the false impression of a democratically-elected government.

The Building Blocks of a Dictatorship

A historical perspective of Nicaragua brings into focus multiple and varied series of events and developments that combine war and conquest with phenomenal cultural, social, and economic changes--all within a physical and geographical environment known around the globe for its extraordinary bio-diversified regions and of course, its natural beauty. The intervention and subsequent conquest of the Nicaraguans by the Spanish conquistadors in 1523 led to the rise of colonialism that lasted far beyond the time the country gained its independence in 1838. Once an indigenous nation where numerous distinct tribal groups claimed their longstanding ancestral roots, some as far back as 900 AD, today, Nicaragua is a country with 6.5 million inhabitants, and 95 percent speak Spanish.[3] Only about five indigenous languages remain (most belong to the Macro-chibcha family), and these are spoken in the far eastern part of the country and along the littoral region of the Caribbean Sea.[4] Despite their efforts to lift their country out of poverty, Nicaragua is the poorest country in the Central America and second poorest in the Western Hemisphere.[5]

In highlighting the current state of affairs in Nicaragua, a historical survey of key events of the past several years provides the context for processing a discourse of analysis and critique. Several questions that focus on the *how* and *why* are rooted in the overall understanding on how Nicaragua became the country it is today. Related topics focus on the roles of women and their struggles and acts of heroism and resistance, as well as a critique on Rosario Murillo, the vice-president who yields as much power as Daniel Ortega, and could have lifted women's causes for the development of the country but instead chose the regime's path of thwarting women's advancements. And, lastly, the discussion on the prominent role of the United States in Nicaragua's history is of important significance that cannot be overlooked.

Nicaragua as a Sovereign Country

In its early stages as an independent nation, Nicaraguan politics seemed to adopt a democratic option but change in governmental control usually involved the conservative faction taking over the liberal faction, and vice versa. It wasn't long before the political parties seeking power turned their attention to the United States as a potential ally. The election of the liberal president, José Santos Zelaya (1893-1906), and his government's attempt to "modernize" the country caught the undivided attention of the U.S. president, Theodore Roosevelt (1901-1909).[6] President Roosevelt, known as the champion of the Spanish-American War (1898), created and administered the *Roosevelt Corollary* to the *Monroe Doctrine* (1907) that invariably engaged the United States in interventionist maneuvers to ensure that American capitalist investors would reap the rewards. Nicaragua was amongst several countries throughout Latin America affected by the ambitious and invasive U.S. foreign policy. The multi-faceted policy also included President Taft's administration (1909-1913) in what was known as the "dollar diplomacy," allowing the U.S. to exercise full control over Nicaragua's banks and transportation agencies, including railroads and canals. The conservative faction seeking to overthrow the popular Pres. Zelaya, rallied around the prospects of a shared power grab with the well-equipped American military forces. Upon the request of the conservative leadership, the U.S. deployed a marine unit in 1909, entering the country through the Caribbean coastal town of Bluefields. Once a British protectorate in the 18th century, Bluefields had been declared the capital of the Department of Zelaya in 1903, shortly after it was incorporated into the country in accordance with the new 1894 constitution. Negotiations between the conservative party leaders and the U.S. resulted in the ouster of Zelaya's replacement, José Madríz Rodríguez, and in exchange, the Nicaraguan leaders agreed to a multi-million-dollar business transaction deal. Although the conservative leadership had selected Juan José Estrada, Adolfo Díaz challenged the decision and then, was eventually elected. In 1912, President Díaz transferred the control of the country's National Bank to the United States' Commercial Bank owned by the Brown brothers. Benjamín Zeledón, a military general pertaining to the liberal faction, adamantly opposed Díaz' controversial dealings with the U.S. and in response, organized a rebellion. Díaz requested military intervention, and the U.S. responded--again. After Zeledón was defeated (and subsequently assassinated), the United States assumed a dominant role in Nicaragua's government with a strong military presence for twelve years, until 1924, and again from 1927 to 1933.[7]

Zeledón's Stance Against Imperialism

The story of Benjamín Zeledón, whose letter to his wife reveals his impassioned plea for a revolution, and from which the title of this chapter is excerpted, has a plausible storyline. It is a story that unveils the strength and courage of a people who believed in change by any means possible. The letter includes the following excerpt:

> *"But if that sentence is carried out I will die serenely, because each drop of my blood spilled in defense of the nation and its freedom will give life to a hundred Nicaraguans who, like me, will take up arms against the betrayal of our beautiful but unfortunate Nicaragua." (Benjamín Zeledón, 1912)*[8]

Zeledón was a former school teacher, a lawyer/judge and a military general. He was a patriot and like many others, and he shared the indignation toward the unencumbered American military intervention. His life and heroic patriotism inspired others, especially Augusto César Sandino, who upon learning of his heroic death, followed in his footsteps and eventually, became a legendary, revolutionary hero in his own right.

Sandino's Rebellion Against the U.S. Marine Corps

As a young man barely twenty years old, Augusto César Sandino left his country to seek his fortunes in Honduras and México. He worked in various American-owned companies such as United Fruit. His involvement in the labor unions steered him toward activism, advocating for workers' rights and agrarian reform. He learned from his fellow workers and union activists about how his country had agreed to the extraordinary demands by the Americans to take over the financial institutions and become deeply indebted to American businesses. Indeed, the United States' intrusion was evident all over Mexico and Latin America, but Nicaragua, according to Sandino's circle of union laborers, exemplified the worst-case scenario. Sandino was thirty-one when he returned to Nicaragua (1926) and headed directly to the mining industry where he knew he could successfully talk to the downtrodden miners about joining an insurrection. His message was clear, engaging, and convincing, that the United States Marines must be dislodged from the country, and as proud Nicaraguans, take back their freedom and independence; and that the Americans had robbed them of their possessions and turned their people into slaves.

Sandino insisted that he was anti-imperialist and a nationalist, but not a Marxist. After all, Agustín Farabundo Martí, the Salvadoran legendary hero who had joined Sandino in Nicaragua for a brief period, returned to his country and told his fellow comrades that he was unable to convince Sandino to adopt Marxist tenets.

Several hundred men, many of them boys, joined Sandino's army and began attacking the U.S. military outposts, but as expected, the U.S. Marines fired back with a vengeance. In their first major attack in Ocotal in the Segovia highlands, Sandino's guerrilla unit managed to push the marines toward the outer perimeters of the town. No one expected aerial bombardments, but soon, two American planes dropped bombs all over the town killing at least 300 people, many of them women and children. This tragedy has the distinction of being the "first" aerial bombardment of its kind in all of Latin America.

The conservative party had elected Adolfo Díaz as their president for a second time (1926-1929); the same President Díaz that had made the business deals and a military pact with the United States in 1912. Under his presidency, more U.S. Marines were deployed, strategically located, and instead of Zeledón, his new enemy was Sandino.

Battle skirmishes with Sandino at the helm continued for several years. Then, in 1933, Sandino traveled to Managua to sign a Peace Treaty with President Sacasa. Included in the agreement was that certain state lands along the Coco River would become accessible to the farmers. Later that year, as the United States grappled with the Great Depression, the American Marines withdrew from Nicaragua. Sandino was overwhelmed with celebratory cheers from his many supporters. As a poorly equipped insurgency, they had managed to evict the U.S. Marine Corps from their beloved country and sign a peace treaty. This image and its implications lay deeply ingrained in the collective memories of Nicaraguans.[9]

Somoza Eliminates His Rival and Unwittingly Solidifies the Struggle Against Imperialism

Anastasio Somoza García, just a year older than Sandino, was the son of a wealthy family of coffee plantation owners. At the time the U.S. Marines were withdrawn (1933), Somoza had achieved a superior rank as a military officer. Thus, when the conditions for removal of American military personnel required a Nicaraguan officer to replace the American general, Somoza was chosen for the position. However, Somoza was also a politician with presidential aspirations, and he perceived the popular Sandino as his rival. On February 21, 1934, Somoza ordered his National Guard to capture and assassinate Sandino while he was attending a dinner with President

Sacasa in Managua. Sandino and his entourage had just left the presidential event when the National Guard carried out Somoza's orders. The Guard transported their corpses and buried them in an unknown location. However, Somoza's plan to eliminate his rival also included the murder of hundreds of men, women and children in the eastern semiautonomous region, all of whom were Sandino's supporters. Somoza used fraudulent electoral tactics to gain presidential positions, from 1937 to 1947, and again from 1950 until 1956, when he was assassinated in Panama. He was replaced by his son, Luis Somoza Debayle from 1956 until his death in 1963. (His death was due to illness.) Somoza's other son, Anastasio Somoza Debayle became president from 1967 to 1972 and again from 1974 to 1979. During the interim periods when the Somoza father and sons were not presidents, the presidency was held by politicians for whom many believed acted as their "puppets."[10] The United States response to the assassination of Sandino was not publicly disclosed, although anyone that had a substantial or even peripheral understanding of the current events in Somoza's political orbit understood the repercussions quite clearly, especially in Latin America. According to historian, David Francois, the United States' animosity toward Sandino, along with his subsequent assassination, caused a furor across the revolutionary landscape of Latin America. The Alianza Popular Revolucionaria Americana (APRA), one of many organizations whose prime focus was to fight North American aggressive imperialism, declared Sandino as the symbol of the Latin American struggle.[11]

Somoza's Blind Ambition

Somoza's calculations for staying in power and accumulating wealth amounted to what historian, Thomas Walker, describes as a simple formula: "maintain the support of the National Guard, cultivate the Americans, and co-opt important domestic power contenders."[12] The well-trained National Guard of the United States was the prize that kept on giving for Somoza since he had intimate knowledge on how he could maintain the soldiers' loyalties while coercing them to commit heinous crimes against innocent people, mostly the elderly, women and children. Corruption was an integral part of Somoza's authoritarian rule and to hold on to power, the well-mannered,

English-speaking ruler created a special image of himself for the Americans as the benevolent, astute, rule-abiding, and promoter of human rights for everyone, including women. His two sons, Luis and Anastasio, Jr., both highly decorated in military rank and file, were equally adapt to playing the roles as powerful, pro-American dictators, although Anastasio, Jr. or "Tachito" received the worst criticism. After the devastating earthquake in 1972 that killed at least 10,000 inhabitants and leveled 600 square blocks in the heart of Managua, Anastasio Jr. created a colossal fiasco at a scale that only a corrupted dictator could achieve. While the international community responded with compassion and generosity, Anastasio Jr. used the donations to line his pockets and those of his loyal guard members and supporters. At first, the public was unaware of the plunderage but Somoza's deception and lies were particularly noticed by those in the business and private, elite sectors. The anti-Somoza sentiment began to escalate as more middle-class and wealthy people participated in the FSLN revolutionary organization. The red-and-black flag, once the symbol of the revolutionary Sandino, appeared increasingly dominant as it became the adopted emblem of the Sandinista Front of National Liberation (FSLN).

A Victorious Euphoria and the End of the Somoza Dynasty

Somoza Jr. stepped down from the presidency for two years (1972-1974), presumably to create a deceptive appearance as a proper presidential candidate complying with electoral law. But, as predicted, he became president for a second time from 1974 to 1979. The revolution spiraled into an excruciating rage in its final years, from 1977 to 1979. The Sandinistas' persistence, determination, and perseverance resulted in an extraordinary victory against Somoza's giant war machine. Chávez sums up the contrast between the two rivals:

> *"This is another distinctive element in Nicaraguan history – that the fragile but heroic resistance of a small guerilla army commanded by a visionary--could become such a symbolically important factor to denounce and counter the designs of the emerging imperial power of the United States for decades to come."* [13]

By July 20, 1979, the Somoza family departed Nicaragua and sought refuge in their property in the United States, taking their wealth and valuables. Meanwhile the Nicaraguans celebrated their hard-won victory. The Somoza's family financial worth was estimated at one billion dollars by the time they left. They owned more than ten thousand square miles of fertile and grazing lands throughout the country and in Guatemala, Honduras, and Costa Rica. They also had investments in numerous capital ventures, such as railroad lines, steamship travel, fisheries, mining industries, lumber, and brewery companies. However, most of these financial sources were considered as illegitimate.[14] The possessions of the country's oligarch families, known as the "piñata" at the stage of disbursements by the state, were now in the hands of the triumphant Sandinistas.[15]

Feminism in Transition

Although the term "feminism" is commonly used to describe an organized movement that advocates for gender equality in political, civil, and social spheres, it is worth considering whether it's readily applicable in all contexts that recognize women's efforts to feminize their work. The life and work of Josefa Toledo de Aguerri (1866-1962) serves as an example of the feminist role in the historical First Wave of Latin American feminism.[16] Toledo de Aguerri, a teacher and writer by profession, belonged to the upper-middle class, much like many of her contemporaries. As a highly influential feminist, she encouraged women to participate in the suffragist movement of the early twentieth century, although she lacked a deep understanding of the true meaning of feminism. Therefore, women typically aligned themselves with the political movement that best served their interests as members of the elite social and economic classes. Zelaya's liberal presidency from 1863 to 1909 was especially enlightening for feminists that had the resources to connect with like-minded individuals outside of Nicaragua. In the years preceding the passage of the suffrage bill in 1955, various groups of feminists engaged in public debates regarding the bill's provisions. The liberal feminists, who were aligned with Somoza's regime, actively supported the suffrage bill in a partisan manner. Meanwhile the conservative feminists, who were appalled with the "morality" issue, sought to remove the Somoza family from power as a means of reforming Nicaraguan politics. Ultimately, the bill was passed and Somoza was able to present himself as politically correct and in line with the suffragist movement, which was a boon for his image and his closest ally, the United States. As a result, his administration successfully enacted the voting rights law for women. A year later, a significant number of Nicaraguan women registered to vote, among them were the members of the *Ala Femenina*, a right-wing female faction of the Somoza regime. The group campaigned for his re-election, but Somoza was assassinated. In 1957, his son, Luis Somoza Debayle became President. Despite maintaining a female membership, the *Ala Femenina's* focus was political and pro-Somoza. They targeted women from all social and economic classes for recruitment.[17] Conservative feminists, among others, objected to the lack of moral standards regarding the treatment of women by Somoza's political party, the National Liberal Party, and by extension, the *Ala Femenina*. In her research, Gonzalez-Rivera describes a toxic social environment where women in the professional leadership of *Ala Femenina* were scandalized for being "mistresses to the Somozas," and some of the women, such as Josefa Toledo de Aguerri, "were accused of presenting virgin teenage students as 'gifts' to Presidents Zelayo and Somoza García."[18] Men were not admonished for engaging openly and publicly in extramarital affairs, while women, under similar circumstances, were accused of prostitution. Gonzalez-Rivera also points out that after the state institutionalized prostitution, the Somoza regime established a brothel business in conjunction with the National Guard.[19] However, the most disturbing disclosures are those that reveal how rape was systematically used as a weapon to torture women who opposed the Somoza dictatorship.[20]

The Somoza dictatorship touted its record of employment opportunities for women. While this was a welcomed economic relief for many women, the fact that the jobs paid very low wages amounted to exploitation rather than an equal opportunity. Women were encouraged to work outside the home, however, the women should not give up their traditional roles as mothers and wives. The government's underlying message was that working outside the home should not interfere or disrupt the existing patriarchal foundation. But women were criticized nevertheless, and more so if they wore lipstick.

Wearing make-up, which started in the Somoza era, was associated with the U.S. military occupation during the 1920s and 1930s, who were blamed for bringing unwelcome change and disorder to the sexual lives of Nicaraguan women.[21]

It should be pointed out that discrimination against women based on misogynism and sexism was not uncommon in all of Central America. However, the Somoza dictatorship was notorious for its corrupt practices in dealing with civilians; their tactics were cruel and torturous, resulting in unnecessary deaths and the sexual assault of women. One way to understand how women were particularly affected is through their stories that address critical questions about their experiences, challenges, and problems.

The Women and Their Stories

By the time the Sandinista Front of National Liberation, (the FSLN, also known as the "Front" or "Frente") was in the conceptual phase--constructed, developed and led by Carlos Fonseca, Silvio Mayorga, and Tomás Borges in 1961, the Somoza dictatorship or "dynasty" had ruled for twenty-four years. The Somoza governing hand print was starkly obvious in the economic, social, and cultural divisions of the country, where the well-off consisted of a small fraction of the entire population and the majority of Nicaraguans were poor, illiterate, underemployed, and in some cases living in extreme poverty where families were barely surviving.

Nora Astorga

In 1969, Nora Astorga was a law student at the Catholic University when she came into direct contact with members of the FSLN. Thus, began a clandestine relationship with the organization. Almost a decade later, Astorga and her comrades hashed out a plan to kidnap one of the most notoriously brutal, high-ranking National Guard members, General Pérez Vega.[22] Astorga's story reveals how she used her sexuality against a man who considered her as a sexual object; a very powerful military officer that has consistently (and successfully) used his rank and privilege to exploit and abuse women without consequence. To Pérez Vega, Nora Astorga, was just another beautiful, young, intelligent woman that he would have to "conquer."

The plot was to take place on March 8, 1978. The plan was to lure Pérez Vega to her house where three comrades awaited in hiding for the right moment to seize the general and proceed with the kidnapping plot. Then, the general would be traded for imprisoned comrades. Astorga had no difficulty leading the general into her bedroom, and while he was undressing, the three comrades attempted to subdue him. But, he was exceedingly strong, and after a violent struggle, the comrades felt they had no other option but to kill him. By then, Astorga had managed to send the general's chauffer, waiting for him in the car, to the liquor store for the general's favorite drink. Astorga's final step was to "disappear," leaving her two young children, her home, her family and her job. After the revolution, Astorga continued to work with the FSLN in overseeing the jurisdiction over the thousands of cases of former National Guard members, and as a representative to the United Nations.[23]

Nora Astorga grew up in an upper middle-class household.[24] Her father was a rancher and as a close associate of Anastasio Somoza, he held a ranking position in the National Guard. He wasn't pleased with his daughter's dedication to teaching young children in the poor neighborhoods. The prevailing thought concerning the working "masses" amongst the bourgeoisie was that education was a product of communism. The oldest of four children, Astorga recalls in her autobiographical story that she experienced a profound transformation while studying at a private Catholic school. She credits the nuns for introducing her to an entirely different world from her own, giving her an opportunity to apply her Christian values in praxis, as a volunteer in poor, marginal communities. At that time, the Catholic Church in Nicaragua was beginning to transform itself as result of the influence of Liberation Theology, the historic declaration of change by the Catholic Church in its pastoral duty toward the poor and disenfranchised. The direct contact with the community members compelled Astorga to reflect upon her social work and her future, and while she had more questions than answers, she determined that her role in life was very different from what she had imagined as a child. The attraction toward the Front (FSLN) was based on her conviction that life is meaningful when you belong to a community of shared values and ideals, and together work toward change that is anchored in one's political consciousness.

Doris Tijerino's Courage

Doris Tijerino was one of the first females to fight in the frontlines as a ranking officer with the Frente. She was captured three times between 1967 to 1978. In an article that draws together a review of Tijerino's book, *Somos millones* with a biographical profile, the author Kristine Byron describes the impossible and agonizing position of the incarcerated females.[25] Tijerino is a daughter of a wealthy family, the granddaughter of an English colonist, whose mother is caring and loving and whose father dominated her life in the tradition of a patriarchic society. Her mother gave her a special collection of classical books, which inspired and guided Tijerino to develop into an independent intellectual. Tijerino's praise for "motherhood" is based on her beloved mother's image, the selfless mother such as in Maxim Gorky's novel, *Mother*, that above all and despite everything, loves her child profoundly, a raison d'etre behind the unconditional love for the son or daughter.

Yet, in prison she was treated like an animal. She was tortured like the rest of the male prisoners, however, as a woman in the guerrilla, she had to endure the cruel and savage methods that targeted her *sexuality*.[26] She was repeatedly raped, her breasts and vaginal area were electrocuted; the guardsmen sexually abused her while naked; they humiliated her and made her feel as though she was a despicable female, a "communist whore." The author explains that when she was captured for the third time in 1978, many people, including author Margaret Randall, feared that she would be killed. Randall had the unpublished, Spanish language manuscript, *Somos millones*, detailing the life of Tijerino as a female FSLN combatant. She believed that by publishing it, Tijerino's imprisonment would bring international attention to her case. An English-translated version of the book was published within months of her capture in 1978. A photojournalist's documentation with photos and audio recordings revealing Tijerino's harrowing experiences also contributed to her eventual release and safety.

Dora María Tellez, the 'Revolutionary Hero'

Dora María Tellez was sixteen years-old when she entered the university in León to study medicine. She knew that the university was known for the radical student organizations, and before long she became a member of the FSLN. Her initiation activities were fairly risk-free – procuring food, supplies, medicine, clothes, weapons, and identifying safehouses. Then, around Christmas Eve, the earthquake hit taking 10,000 lives and destroying 600 blocks in a downtown area of Managua. Even so the Sandinistas continued their work and two years later in 1974, the FSLN pulled off a hostage takeover at the Castillo Christmas Party effectively causing intense negotiations between Somoza and the commanders. The Sandinistas asked for the release of prisoners, a hefty ransom, a broadcasting of a prepared communiqué over the public radio waves, and safe passage to Cuba. Somoza complied. One of the prisoners released was Daniel Ortega, convicted for bank robbery and had spent seven years in prison. The FSLN commander was Eduardo Contreras and next in command was Hugo Torres. Edén Pastora, Hugo Torres, and Dora María Tellez commanded the next hostage operation, *Operation Pigpen*, in August, 1978 with Tellez as the principal negotiator. Later, in 2021, both Tellez and Torres were incarcerated by the Ortega Murillo regime on false charges that amount to a politically motivated vendetta.

Tellez was one of the lead commanders of the Western Front. Her comrades were killed while planning their next operation in a "safehouse" in León, thus, she was tasked with unifying the units and taking command in the liberation of León, which had become one of the National Guard's stronghold. In the summer of 1979, she led her unit in a highly intense battle for several weeks, pushing and dispersing of Guards at the street level while escaping aerial and mortar bombardments. It was a phenomenal feat considering that the National Guard had major weapons and many more soldiers; the FSLN guerrilla were far short in both numbers and weaponry.

However, by this stage of the revolution, thousands of civilians had joined the FSLN as supporters, setting up barricades, and using anything they could to fight off the Guard. There's no doubt that their involvement was a contributing factor to the FSLN victory.[27] At twenty-two years old, Dora María Tellez who went to León to study medicine, and instead, led a squadron to liberate it, was a heroic figure.[28] In the following quotes, Tellez shares some of her most intimate thoughts as a result of her experiences in the guerilla.

"What makes a woman believe that she is capable of anything? No one taught us. That is one of the great mysteries about the Revolution. They don't teach it to you at school. You don't learn to believe in humanity on the streets. Religion doesn't teach it. It teaches us to believe in God, not in men and women. So, it's difficult to awaken that belief in yourself and in others. But in spite of all that, many women and men did develop that commitment."[29]

"All we knew was that we were going to make the Revolution, however long it took. Ten, 20, 30, even 40 years. Most of us thought we'd never live to see the day. It's still hard to believe that we've done it."[30]

"It's through experiences like these that our values have changed. We've had to live through things most people can't even imagine. All of this has called into question values and beliefs that used to be taken for granted. How could values not change in families where sons and daughters were killed, where a mother lost what she loved the most? I mean, what couldn't change in a home where a woman was already capable of seeing her children fight for the Revolution, accepting their death, burying them, and then often having to pretend they were still alive so the repression wouldn't fall on them all the harder? Anything, even the role of women—so deeply rooted—can change."[31]

***

Amada Pineda

In her story, Amada Pineda relates how she and her husband worked long and arduous hours picking coffee beans for a pittance, subsisting on a meager diet for themselves and their nine children. Amada's narrative, full of struggle and tragedy, as told to Margaret Randall, coincides with those of thousands of others during the sixties and seventies when Somoza's attempts to quash the increasingly vocal *campesino* uprisings developed into a brutal repression.[32] Amada's husband joined the Nicaragua Socialist Party and then, began to participate in labor union meetings. After the union leader, Bernardino Díaz Ochoa, was violently killed by the Somoza's National Guard, Amada began to get involved. She learned from the fledgling FSLN members about Somoza's repressive regime. She joined the Women's Organization associated with the Socialist Party. As the Guard hunted down the families suspected of supporting the guerrilla, people would disperse throughout the countryside. Amada's husband left the country for the Soviet Union, and Amada took her young children to a safehouse (her infant son died in a rainstorm while they attempted to flee). But the Guard tracked her down, and at dawn one day, Amada awoke to find her dilapidated house where she was sheltering surrounded by guardsmen with weapons pointed at her. The Guard was looking for her, and not necessarily for her husband. In her reluctance to surrender, she refused to give up her child that she was carrying in her arms. She was forced to let go of her child, and as soon as she did, several guardsmen began beating her with gang style force and violence until she could hardly stand up. They threw her in a prison cell with six other men, her comrades, and then, the Guard began to interrogate her, mostly about the whereabouts of her husband and other "subversives." Amada claimed she knew nothing about the union, the leaders, and their activities.

Several guardsmen proceeded to violently sexually assault Amada. She recalled that within a few days the men had raped her seventeen times. She managed to stop the assaults by pleading with them to consider the fact that she is a mother and wife and not a prostitute, and she had had enough of their brutality. To her astonishment, the men stopped, leaving her with painful injuries, and alone in a locked room.

Amada's story, one of several in Randall's *Sandino's Daughters*, concludes with a hopeful but tragic message. The revolution had finally reached closure and Amada's determination to impact the gross inequalities amongst the working poor affected her perception of the roles that women assume in the insurrection. She now believes that women are as capable as men in making important decisions in labor unions, and in fighting alongside their male counterparts in the Frente's frontlines. Amada's father prevented her from attending school, which she strongly regrets, but now believes that women should have the same or similar educational opportunities as men. The loss of her children during the war was the most emotionally, heart-rendering for Amada. The Frente had just declared victory when she learned that her seventeen-year old son had been violently killed while collecting firewood for cooking. The teenager was wounded, tortured and then shot to death. His corpse was found in a shallow grave alongside those of a woman and her baby. Her sentiments reflect a profound sense of a mother's sadness: "What's there to say? War is like that. You lose and you win, and sometimes you lose what you loved the most. But what really upsets me is the way he died. If he'd been killed in battle, with a gun in his hand, maybe I wouldn't feel like I do."[33]

Rosario Murillo: Ambition, Power and a Revolution

Rosario Murillo's self-proclaimed powers equal to her husband's, Daniel Ortega, has been scrutinized by many historians and journalists.[34] Murillo began her political career alongside Ortega immediately after the 1979 Sandinista Revolution. As the official spokesperson for Ortega, she has remained in the public's eye for over forty years, long enough for the world to adjust a broad lens upon which to examine and analyze her actions and decisions as both First Lady and now as the powerful Vice President to her husband, President Daniel Ortega.

Murillo is the VP, "groomed" by President Ortega to replace him if the need occurs; so, what should the public expect if she would inherit the presidency? Is she the benevolent, stately "queen" that deeply and genuinely cares about all Nicaraguans, especially the poor, struggling and suffering "la gente del pueblo." Or, is she the heartless "dictator" whose ambition is paramount and will use (and abuse) whatever political maneuverings in the toolbox to gain that power? What kind of ambition—besides president? Does Murillo harbor the desire for the accumulation of wealth? And, perhaps, significantly, does Murillo promote the empowerment of woman especially since she possesses a position of power? The responses to these inquiries are in Murillo's past, her background, her personal and professional relationships, and in her actions and decisions as a powerful member of the Sandinista political party.

Murillo's family was a member of the petit bourgeoisie. She attended a private high school in Great Britain, the Greenway Convent Collegiate School. At the *Institut Anglo-Suisse Le Manoir* in Switzerland, she was an art student; while at the University of Neuchatel also in Switzerland, she earned a French language certificate. At the University of Cambridge, she acquired an English language certificate. Upon her return to Managua, she attended the National Autonomous University and afterwards, became a language professor at the Instituto de Ciencias Comerciales and the Colegio Teresiano. About that time, at the age of sixteen, Murillo gave birth to her daughter, Zoilamérica, whom she named after her maternal grandmother.[35] Like so many other Nicaraguan families with privileged positions, both educationally and economically, Murillo's ambition was based on a European tradition with an international connection. A teaching career wasn't in Murillo's horizon and after two years she began instead, to support the FSLN, setting up her house as a clandestine shelter and also, becoming politically involved. She was caught by the National Guard in 1976 because of her political activities and detained for a short time. Upon her release she fled to South America, Panama, and then, to Costa Rica where she met and fell in love with the future president of Nicaragua, Daniel Ortega.

Daniel Ortega's working-class parents were fierce opponents of Somoza. He and his two brothers were young revolutionaries socialized by their parent's rhetoric and political activities.[36] Ortega joined the Frente at age fifteen and three years later in 1967, he was convicted of armed bank robbery and imprisoned for seven years. Murillo knew about Ortega's imprisonment and reportedly, sent him some of her poems. His release from prison was due to the Frente's armed operation at a Christmas party hosted and attended by Somoza's government dignitaries. Among the commanders of the 1974 guerrilla unit were Eduardo Contreras and Hugo Torres. Their operation was successful in collecting a hefty ransom and in forcing the Somoza government to release the FSLN prisoners, which included Daniel Ortega.

Perhaps, one of the most enduring qualities of mutual attraction between Ortega and Murillo was their shared ambition—the notion that they could become the country's most powerful couple seemed to be a formidable reality. After the war ended on July, 1979, Murillo and Ortega, now a couple with children, moved to Managua where their political trajectory had its beginnings.

***

In 1932, the newspaper *La Prensa*, owned and operated by editor-in-chief Pedro Joaquín Chamorro Zelaya, became the established news outlet and the critical voice of the conservative, wealthy sector against the government of President Sacasa and then, Anastasio Somoza García. Pedro Joaquín Chamorro Cardenal (the son) took over the business after the death of his father in 1952 and followed a similar course of opposition and critique against the Somoza dictatorship.

During the 1940's and early 50's, in other Central American countries like Guatemala and El Salvador, the voices of the discontent were rising, especially amongst women leaders, and the middle and upper-middle classes began to stand against their despotic leaders.

Chamorro and a co-editor, Pablo Antonio Cuadro, both of whom were members of the conservative, wealthy elite, began to use *La Prensa* as a platform to publish stories with varied literary genres specifically intended to unify the anti-Somoza opposition and create a viable coalition against the dictatorship.[37]

Many young and aspiring writers were direct beneficiaries of the opportunities that La Prensa afforded them. *La Prensa Literaria* was the major source of Nicaragua's published poetry during the 1960's. Eventually, a group of writers whose diverse works focused on anti-somozacismo within the forceful, pro-revolution rhetoric, emerged as frontrunners in the category of poet-combatants. Some of the most popular works were writings by Carlos Fonseca, Ricardo Morales Avilés, Leonel Rugama, Ernesto Cardenal, Sergio Ramírez, and Doris Tijerino, to name a few.[38]

In the early 1970's Murillo began working as a reporter with *La Prensa* and at the same time was a member of *"Gradas,"* a group of politically oriented artists, consisting of poets, singer/songwriters such as Carlos Mejía Godoy, painters, and others. As a reporter, Murillo took on the assignment of writing up Amada Pineda's story, which Chamorro then published with full knowledge that the Somoza regime would retaliate for this act.[39]

Amada Pineda had tried in vain to seek justice against the perpetrators that committed the brutal torture against her and others. She made a personal plea to Chamorro as the last resort, and her published story reached a wide, economically diverse readership. As expected, Amada Pineda's story, in full display in the country's major newspaper, was received with outrage by Somoza and his supporters. But its publication was also perceived as a bold and powerful statement against the dictatorship's brutality and repression. Chamorro was assassinated by the National Guard in 1978. His murder sparked a tsunami of violence: the National Guard increased its terror of fear and death against the revolting populace, and the FSLN responded with a massive and forceful mobilization.[40]

***

Murillo played an important role as a featured poet during the late 60's and early 70s. She was a member of a group of middle and upper-class women known as "The Six," and their writings were called the *new women's poetry*.[41] "The Six" included Murillo, Michele Najlis, Yolanda Blanco, Vidaluz Meneses, Gioconda Belli, and Daisy Zamora. The women shared

183

similar backgrounds and experiences: a Catholic school education throughout their youth, including at the (modernized) private universities, and some studied abroad as did Murillo; all were influenced by early vanguard poets, including Ernesto Cardenal; their poems were published in *La Prensa Literaria*; and they benefitted from the support of the international community by which they gained greater access to the world-class literary field as women at the universities and in career training. Their poetry was not "feminist" per say, but the overtones were obviously encased within a unique female voice. In as much as their poetic expressions contained images of the female emancipatory identity and the revolution, in general, their feminist themes were consistent with the Nicaraguan society that upholds women's social traditions as primarily mothers, daughters, and wives. Their poetic inclinations of advancing women's liberating process from the Somoza patriarchal grip was exhilarating but far removed and out of the grasp of the majority of women in Nicaragua that lived in poverty and repression.[42]

Murillo published seven poetry books from 1975 to 1992: *Gualtayán* (1975); *Sube a nacer conmigo* (1977); *Un deber de cantar* (1981); *Amar es combatir (antología)* (1982); *En espléndidas ciudades* (1985); *Las esperanzas misteriosas* (1990); *Angel in the deluge* (1992) translated from the Spanish by Alejandro Murguía.[43]

Murillo's Maneuvering for Sustainable Power

After the revolution in the early 80s, Murillo positioned herself alongside the leadership of her compañero, Daniel Ortega, the coordinator of the Junta of National Reconstruction.[44] She was director of a union of cultural workers, the Asociación Sandinista de Trabajadores de la Cultura (ASTC), and the editor of the literary supplement of the Sandinista newspaper, *Barricada*. She believed that the artist should always be prepared to defend the revolution through their art—music, painting, writing—but, also in combat fighting with the guerrilla.[45]

The Ministry of Culture at the State level was directed by the vanguard poet, Ernesto Cardenal. He and his brother, Fernando Cardenal, the director of the Ministry of Education, worked together to administer two of the most important projects of the era. Ernesto Cardenal organized the poetry workshops (talleres de poesía) based on his previous work known as the Solentiname writing project.[46] Fernando Cardenal's work involved the organization and deployment of thousands of volunteer literacy educators to areas of Nicaragua that had experienced extreme social, cultural, and educational neglect throughout Somoza's reign.[47] Both projects introduced poetry writing and literacy development at the grassroots level, using techniques advanced by Paulo Freire.[48] Particularly important was the inclusion of the narrative, testimonial poetry techniques developed in the Solentiname Project.[49]

Murillo and other established poets of the Vanguard era, were highly critical of Ernesto Cardenal's writing project. Murillo used her authority and arranged for the airing of a televised program, which she hosted, to publicly discredit Cardenal's work and the writings of the workshop participants. Essentially, she asserted in her opinion that the substandard quality of the poetry was "too simplistic". However, Cardenal was also a Catholic priest and as a liberation theologian his work at the Solentiname lay monastery (which he founded), had as its core foundation the pastoral duty to bring the teachings of Christ into the daily lives of the poor and oppressed, which was a spiritual/religious process in the revolutionary act of liberation.[50] Cardenal's response was that the goal of the project was to introduce and teach the expressive arts to the disadvantaged and disenfranchised populace. But Murillo's preference for a system of cultural brigades, i.e., taking the arts-in-performance to the people, over Cardenal's writing workshops, i.e., nurturing creative writing at the grassroots level, eventually, pushed Cardenal out of the Ministry. Whether the conflict between Murillo and Cardenal was personal rather than substantive remains unanswered, although Murillo's overreaching ambition could not be ignored.

***

On July 20, 2018, in a ceremony, commemorating the 39th anniversary of the Sandinista victory over the Somoza regime forces, Amada Pineda stood on a stage platform with Daniel Ortega and Rosario Murillo. In front of a huge crowd of Sandinista supporters at the Plaza la Fe, Ortega pins the Augusto César Sandino medal on Pineda's blouse. The special honor is bestowed upon Pineda as an award for her heroism as a fighter for the Sandinista Revolution. Pineda took the microphone to thank the Commander for the honor and then, proceeded to tell the story of how the Somocista Guard assassinated her son in 1979, and now her other son, Francisco Arauz Pineda was recently assassinated by those that want to end the Revolution. "I want to say to the young people," she stated, "to continue forward, don't hold back, work hard for the Revolution, since it has given us so much." Comandante Daniel is here to stay," she added. In referring to the assassins, she remarked that she wanted to yell at the *golpistas* (the persons that attempted the "coup") that they were murderers but "they will not finish off the Revolution."

Murillo, standing by her side, listening intently, waits until she puts down the microphone and then embraces her. The two women pose for photographs; Murillo's expression shows compassion and warmth, as if to offer Pineda her most profound condolences.[51]

The Chaos Behind the Killing of Francisco Arauz Pineda

In one of the deadliest events during the June, 2018 uprising, Francisco Arauz Pineda, the 55-year old son of Amada Pineda, was struck with gunshot and then, partially incinerated at the site of one of the multiple barracks in Managua that had been erected by the civilian protestors. He and his three companions, all workers with the Sandinista government, were part of the "clean-up" crew tasked with dismantling the barracks. The protest had started peacefully on April 18th, and by most accounts, there was no intention of violence on the part of the protesters. However, violence erupted, and the back and forth skirmishes between the unarmed protestors and the armed Sandinista police and paramilitary (called voluntary police by the government) lingered intermittently for several months.

Although Arauz Pineda's perpetrators were captured the following month, very few details about the crime were available to the public. The following paragraph contains the information published in the Sandinista news outlets.

Four adolescent men were charged with participating in the assassination of Arauz Pineda, as well as injuring one of his fellow workers. According to the digital article in *El 19*, the court hearing took place on November 14, 2018, while Amada Pineda sat somberly in the audience. Two of the young men stand accused of killing Arauz and wounding his co-worker with an AK rifle. The other three were each charged with carrying an illegal fire arm and incinerating the lifeless corpse of Arauz Pineda. The young men, wearing a passion purple-color uniform, sat confused while conferring with their legal counsel.

Just seven months later, on June 11, 2019, *Confidencial.com.ni* published an article with photographs of jubilant men celebrating their release from prison.[52] The opening paragraph informs the reader that dozens of political prisoners were recently released due to an amnesty proclamation. In this particular group (alluding to the fact that another group of fifty prisoners were previously released) were campesinos, ex-military members, journalists, and student leaders of the April 18th (2018) "rebellion." The student leaders had been imprisoned by the Ortega Murillo dictatorship on false charges of terrorism, organized crime, and even murder. Reportedly, some had served a prison sentence of 380 days.

Among the 56 names of prisoners released were the four men that had been recently charged with the murder of Arauz Pineda. Questions about the men's judicial process remain unanswered without additional information on the circumstances by which these men were charged, tried, and sentenced. However, if they gained their release based on the premise of "amnesty," then, it appears that Amada Pineda lost the justice she sought for the assassination of her son. She believed that the murderers were part of a scheme to overthrow the Sandinista government; and that imperial forces financed the agitators and paid assassins to murder Sandinistas. This was the official message communicated by Ortega and Murillo, and hardly anyone had any reason to question its integrity. News outlets throughout the country are obligated to disseminate official Sandinista communication since most, if not all, are owned or controlled by the Ortega Murillo government. One of Murillo's responsibility is the management of communication networks and systems, ensuring that *her specific message* is widely broadcasted on a daily basis.

The Questioning of the Amnesty Law

The Amnesty Law grants "broad amnesty to all people who took part in the events that have taken place throughout Nicaragua from April 18, 2018, until this law enters into force." The Inter-American Commission on Human Rights (IACHR) raises its objections to this law, not only because of its ambiguity, but because it purports to grant amnesty to those that committed serious human rights violations.[53] Over 300 people lost their lives as a direct result of the April 18th Rebellion, and thousands were injured, some seriously, and many of the hundreds of people that were detained and imprisoned were subjected to torture. In an article, a journalist writes that there were credible reports that women were picked up by the police, taken to jails, brutally beaten with clubs – in the legs, stomach, chest, face – and interrogated endlessly.[54] They were denied medical assistance that they desperately needed, and two pregnant women suffered miscarriages. According to international human rights law, the government is obligated to "investigate, identify, and sanction" the individuals responsible for the human rights violations.[55] If the court determines that grave human rights have been violated, the perpetrators must be held accountable.

Murillo's Repression Against the Mothers of April Association (AMA)

Amada Pineda lost her son during the violence in the 2018 protestations, and although her case for justice is yet unresolved, she has the support and admiration of Rosario Murillo. But it's another completely different story for the mothers of victims who were also killed as a result of the 2018 April

Rebellion. Dozens of mothers and their family members of the victims who were shot and killed by the police and/or paramilitary-style forces have desperately sought the truth. They followed every protocol and procedure in filing formal complaints with the state authorities, but were repeatedly turned away. They finally realized that the Ortega Murillo regime would never concede to their demands, and to make matters worse, some group members began to suspect that they were being targeted and persecuted. When they understood the uphill battle against the ironclad and repressive regime, they realized the need to create their own power of defense. They launched *La Asociación de Madres de Abril* (April Mothers Association) or AMA, which not only formed a base of support for the members, but it also constituted a means by which to seek truth and justice, using every available resource, including those offered by the international community.[56]

In a historical context, the binding circumstances of the mothers and their families in *La Asociación de Madres de Abril* are reminiscent of the mothers whose children were killed in the Sandinista Revolution, and who became the most vocal critics against the Somoza regime. Their indefatigable campaigning was forceful and their presence was perceived as honorable and courageous by the Sandinistas. It became their fight, and their struggle to abolish the brutal torture, and to free the prisoners of war. The mothers' sorrowful voices were refrains in the revolutionary marches where young men and women proudly and bravely fought and died for their freedom—in Nicaragua, but also in Chile, Argentina, and El Salvador.

***

AMA's first major task was to provide support for the grieving mothers and their families. Many of the victims were teenagers whose sole purpose was to participate in a peaceful protest as part of their civic duty. The April 18th March (2018) was started by people (mostly older adults) protesting the government's decision to cut back their pension checks. But then, the students joined in and the police responded; the violence escalated, especially when the police began to use deadly force. The families learned that their loved ones were unarmed and didn't pose any threat of violence.

The police refused to render aid to the wounded, causing some of the victims to bleed out. They were appalled at the brutal assault on defenseless young people that didn't deserve to be killed or even wounded.

The families chose to create a museum, which they named, *Ama y No Olvida: Museo de la Memoria Contra La Impunidad*, to dignify the lives of their loved ones and to remember them.[57] They also wanted to publicly denounce the circumstances by which the victims lost their lives. They insisted that they were not criminals, nor were they conspiring to overthrow the government, as the Ortega Murillo government claimed. With the assistance of the commissioned, Interdisciplinary Group of Independent Experts (GIEL), an entity of the Inter-American Commission on Human Rights (IACHR), the AMA members are able to declare, with their own documentation, that the offenses committed by the Ortega Murillo government constitute *crimes against humanity*.

***

The museum opened on September 30, 2019 and closed a year later, December, 2020, due to the constant harassment by police and their agents. The virtual museum features the 70 victims killed during a five-month period in ten departments.[58] Each department features a custom-made map of the municipality where the victims were shot, and illustrates the location of the police that committed the assassinations. Many of these killings occurred at the site of the barricades where protestors were positioned. These *barricades*, once hailed as heroic symbols of resistance during the Sandinista Revolution, were re-named by the Ortega Murillo regime as "tranqueros de muerte" (blockades of death).

Murillo's words and deeds were closely aligned with Ortega's accusations that the protesters were paid by foreign agents and the killings were justified to end the attempted coup. Murillo's similar message to the mothers of the victims was intended to discredit their complaints against the police, and despite their unfortunate loss, the Sandinista government would only acknowledge the loss suffered by Sandinista women like Amada Pineda.

In a news release (dated April 21, 2021) by the Mesoamerican Initiative of Women Human Rights Defenders, several incidents of aggression and assault were reported toward members and supporters of the AMA as they commemorated the third anniversary of the April 2018 Rebellion.[59] Between the 14th and 17th of April, about 75 women (human rights defenders) associated with AMA (and their families) were subjected to harassment by police, preventing them from leaving their homes. On April 19th, a similar group of women in Masaya and Carazo were also harassed by the police. Their commemorative books were confiscated, their purses and bags were searched, and they were threatened with incarceration.

On April 20th, the police physically assaulted and then, detained a female human rights defender and the president of AMA, her mother and three other women. While in police custody, the women were physically and verbally assaulted.[60] They were eventually released but were never told the reason for their detention.

A video (*YouTube*) released by the BBC News service features women outside of the El Chipote Prison where their children and other family members were detained.[61] According to "Betsy," speaking anonymously, the women were demanding the answers to their basic questions: where are their loved ones, why are they detained, and when can they see them. Their detention is illegal and the accusations against them are false. On that day, the women were ordered to voluntarily leave the premises or face the physical aggression by police. Betsy reiterates the group's response, that contrary to the government's false claim, their family members in detention are not "*golpistas*," and neither are their families.

Murillo's Propaganda and Distortion of the Truth

The Ortega-Murillo dictatorship is dependent on key governmental authorities, and the expanded core of Sandinista supporters to apply the regime's manifesto accordingly. In the case of the paramilitary or parapolice, which Ortega calls the "voluntary police," their actions reflect an autonomous interpretation of responsibilities and expectations. Thus, their repressive actions against civilians, regardless of the extent of aggression or brutality that they exercise, are in acquiescence to the order established by the National Police, which functions exclusively under the Ortega Murillo directive. From all indications, the government allows the paramilitary forces (or voluntary police) to act with impunity.

As *VP*, Murillo had strict control over the content that's broadcasted throughout the country. The precise language she used to describe the 2018 April Rebellion is echoed in various formats by different governmental functionaries. For instance, they refer to the protestors as *golpistas*, who aim to overthrow the government, and/or allege that they are paid by foreign interventionists, or the imperialists like the United States. Additionally, they claim that their families of the protestors are also terrorists. Essentially, individuals that are pro-government and embrace the Sandinista rhetoric and propaganda have the support of the Ortega Murillo administration, but the anti-government populace, or everyone else, is abhorrently rebuked.

The human rights violations committed against those associated with the April Rebellion have been documented in various reports including the following: two Human Rights Reports: *Human Rights Violations and Abuses in the Context of Protests in Nicaragua, April 18 to August 18, 2018* and *Situation of Human Rights in Nicaragua: Report of the United Nations High Commissioner for Human Rights.*[62] An additional document was produced by the *Comisión de la verdad, justicia y paz,* as ordered by the government's National Assembly.

Denying the truth became a tactic to create chaos and confusion. In the wake of the reports the Nicaraguan government authorities refused to acknowledge the violations of human rights as the first step toward reconciliation and reparations. The reports mentioned above highlight some of the most severe violations, including: 1) the disproportionate use of force by the police, and in some cases resulted in extrajudicial killings; 2) enforced disappearances; 3) obstruction to access medical care (particularly of victims of gunshot); 4) widespread, arbitrary, illegal detentions; 5) prevalent ill-treatment and instances of torture and sexual violence in detention centers; and 6) criminalization of social leaders, human rights defenders, journalists, and protesters considered in opposition of the government.

The OHCHR reports consistently conclude that over 300 people were killed as a result of the April Rebellion, with about 2,000 injuries. The July, 2018 *Comisión de la verdad, justicia y paz* report, the official document commissioned by the National Assembly, includes the total deaths of 222 as a result of the April Rebellion and 2,225 wounded. The autopsy reports issued by the Instituto de Medicina Legal (IML) include information that of the 81 corpses examined, 71 of these were killed violently by gunshot. The report also concludes that the deceased received gunshot wounds to the head and chest, suggesting that they were killed by "tiradores expertos" (francotiradores or sharp shooters). This evidence puts forward the idea that the gunmen were either members of or were contracted by the state's National Police. They had the training and the weaponry to carry out these kinds of killings. Barricades or "tranques" were reportedly assembled by the protesters, which obstructed vital routes throughout the cities. The National Police ordered the paramilitary groups called "fuerzas de choque" or shock forces, to attack the barricades with military-style weapons. These confrontations caused the deaths of 108 victims, which presumably were mostly protesters since they only had hand-made, crude weaponry to defend themselves. Numerous complaints by victims and their families were filed; besides extrajudicial killings, these included extreme beatings resulting in fractured bones, sexual violence, and some were burned to death.

The Case of Cristiana Chamorro Barrios: Two Perspectives – Vilma Nuñez and Rosario Murillo

When *La Prensa* editor, Pedro Joaquín Chamorro, was arrested in mid-1970s for publishing Amada Pineda's story, which was written by Rosario Murillo, Vilma Nuñez de Escorcia was a human rights defender and lawyer. She recalls in an article "Ni Somoza: la destrucción judicial del gobierno Ortega Murillo" (*Not even Somoza: The Destruction of the Judicial System in the Ortega Murillo Government),* that Pedro Joaquín Chamorro was allowed due process, and his court proceedings were open to the public, allowing journalists, family members, human rights defenders and activists in the courtroom. Daniel Ortega was also allowed similar judicial proceedings after his arrest for bank robbery in 1967. In contrast, Nuñez argues that Cristiana Chamorro Barrios, illegally arrested on June, 2021, was detained for three months before any proceedings were allowed. Subsequent to her arrest were at least thirty others that were similarly detained. Clearly, their rights were violated, and Nuñez contends that Chamorro's arrest was political as were the others, and that the judicial process is so corrupt that a fair trial is unlikely to materialize.[63]

Cristiana Chamorro Barrios, the daughter of Violeta and Pedro Joaquín Chamorro, founded the Violeta Barrios de Chamorro Foundation in 1987 with the expressed mission of promoting free speech and freedom of the press. On September 11, 2020, Chamorro Barrios bestowed the Foundation's prestigious award to the Association of Mothers of April (AMA) for their diligent work in the creation of *Museum of Memory Against Impunity in Nicaragua*. The museum became the target of cruel harassment and threats by the Ortega Murillo regime's supporters, and on December, 2020, the museum closed its doors but retained its website as a virtual exhibition. In the same month, the Sandinista National Assembly approved controversial laws that were consider in violation of international human rights norms and standards. One particular law, *Ley 1055, The Defense of the Rights of People to Independence, Sovereignty, Self-determination for peace*, developed on the behest of the Ortega Murillo regime, was obvious to many government critics as a means by which to attempt to silence the opposition that threatened their electoral victory in the November 2021 elections. On February 5, 2021, Barrios Chamorro publicly announces that her foundation had to shutter because Ley 1055 specifically targets her NGO, which receives international funding. The Ley 1055 is so ambiguous and broad that a partial judge can readily amplify the "treasonous" interpretation of Barrios Chamorro's support of associations like AMA.

It seems that Barrios Chamorro's fate was sealed, probably even before she was actually arrested. After a few days of her arrest, according to the news article, *"Murillo clamors for justice, against corruption and la huaca golpista,"* Murillo broadcasted her opinion of Chamorro in her daily radio show, saying in effect that Cristiana Barrios Chamorro is a "huaca golpista," (a coup leader) and "receives blood money to kill, to quash, subordinate, to create chaos, instability, insecurity… [it is] money to destroy, and she will pay." Murillo adds that Barrios Chamorro "receives money from those that believe they are powerful (presumably from the United States); it's a crime and the "pueblo" (the Nicaraguan people) demands justice and reparations." However, Murillo refuses to reveal the nature of Barrios Chamorro's crimes, although "money laundering" is on the potential list, which human rights defenders and Sandinista opposers claim are all false and thus, deliberately intends to obfuscate the judicial process. Barrios Chamorro was considered by many political analysts to be the viable front-runner as a presidential candidate, which posed a serious threat to the Ortega Murillo aspirations for a November electoral win.[64]

Vilma Nuñez, her two siblings and their mother, grew up in a single parent household in Acoyapa, Chontales.[65] Their father and his wife (not their mother) were wealthy; their father was a stern critic of Somoza's dictatorship. Vilma and her siblings had to be home schooled by their mother because they were born out of wedlock.[66]

They were refused enrollment at a public school and, then a private Catholic school, as well as at a neighborhood social club. After the death of her father, their mother was excluded from receiving the inheritance, but had to collect the monthly check from a designated guardianship on behalf of her children. Eventually, the siblings lost all of their inheritance when a judge gave approval to the guardian in charge of selling their property. From these discriminatory experiences, Vilma learned about injustices, and at a very early age began to ask questions, which only deepened her quest to find the answers from a personal level. In Managua, she was able to study law and eventually, obtained her law degree. In 1990, after the election of Violeta Barrios de Chamorro in a stunning defeat of Daniel Ortega, she founded the Centro Nicaragüense de Derechos Humanos (CENIDH), and continued to practice law in the area of human rights.

In contrast to Nuñez, Murillo's wealthy, elite upbringing included the best private schools in Nicaragua and abroad. Even when Murillo became part of the Sandinista movement, her family's wealth offered her economic security. After Ortega assumed the leadership in the Sandinista government, Murillo benefitted from the properties and possessions that the Somoza family left behind.[67] Today, Murillo, Ortega, and their children are reportedly millionaires. Their businesses are set up as anonymous companies to hide their identity and their wealth.[68]

The Extraordinary Power Behind Ortega

Murillo used her position as VP and the numerous, privately-owned communication outlets at her disposal to disparage her adversaries, including mothers, activists, professionals in their own right, scholars, and in the case of Dora María Tellez, as a revolutionary hero. She used propagandistic schemes to denounce the women's efforts in raising their voices in opposition to the Sandinista dictatorship. Her main targets are female leaders/activists, particularly those actively preparing for the November, 2021 elections. Murillo's plan was to silence the key female members of the political opposition in a deliberate, synchronized tactical strategy. First, she had to convince her supporters that the women were "enemies of la patria," or traitors that should be charged and convicted for their treasonous acts. Cristiano Barrios Chamorro was the first victim of her nefarious campaign strategy. Currently, there are approximately 11 female political prisoners. They include the following:[69]

Dora María Tellez (arrested on June 13th): Born in Matagalpa in 1955, Tellez joined the FSLN in León when she was twenty years old. Her initial move to León was to enroll in the School of Medicine. She was twenty-three years old and commander number three when on August 22, 1978, she participated in the *Operation Pigpen*, the takeover of the Somoza regime's National Palace that resulted in the release of FSLN prisoners and a ransom. She was chosen as chief negotiator amongst her comrades, illustrating their confidence in her remarkable abilities. Then, under her command, the FSLN unit in León "liberated" the department, defeating the powerful, well-trained and equipped Somoza National Guard. Her success as a female commander was perceived as one of the most heroic acts in the Sandinista Revolution. The international feminist communities took special interest in her achievements. She was awarded an honorary doctorate by the University of Helsinki, and she was invited as a Visiting Professor by the Harvard University's Robert F. Kennedy School of Theology, although she was unable to attend due to problems with a U.S. visa. After the Revolution, Tellez served as Vice President of Parliament and in the Ministry of Health. In 1995, disillusioned and disappointed over the direction of the FSLN political party, Tellez and many other stalwarts of the FSLN, left the party and created their own movement based on democratic ideals. The Movimiento Renovador Sandinista (MRS) was established and later "cancelled" by Ortega in 2008. A new version of MRS emerged as the Unión Democrático Renovadora (UNAMOS). Her writings have been well-received by international audiences; her publications are catalogued in the centers of investigation such as Instituto de Investigación y Desarrollo Nitlapan (UCA), the Institute of History in Nicaragua an Central America (IHNCA), and the *Envió Digital Journal*. She was in charge of coordinating the project Memoria Centroamericana, an academic platform in the field of Social Science. Dora María Tellez and Ana Margarita Vijil were taken by force from their home on June 13, 2021. A few others that were in the home were also whisked away but then released. A large convoy of police in tactical gear barged into their home, ransacking and confiscating anything they deemed of some value although they didn't have a warrant nor could they elaborate on why they were being arrested.[70]

Ana Margarita Vijil (arrested on June 13th): Vijil, born in 1978, is a human rights defender and former president of MRS (now UNAMOS). In her mid-twenties she worked at the International Court of Justice in the Hague. She received a Fulbright Scholarship and graduated from the University of Arizona majoring in Political Science. Vijil was professor at the Universidad Politécnica de Managua.

Tamara Dávila (arrested on June 12th): Dávila and her five-year old daughter awoke in the middle of the night to the noise of Police tearing down the front door, who then, proceeded to ransack her home, confiscating the electronic equipment. She was taken to prison, leaving her daughter behind. Dávila is a forty-year old feminist and an executive member of UNAMOS. She is an experienced psychologist committed to the defense of human rights and gender equality.

Suyén Barahona (arrested on June 13th): On Sunday, June 13th, a huge police presence descended upon Barahona's home. She was taken prisoner without a lawyer and remained in isolation for months. Like Vijil, Barahona is also a Fulbright Scholar. She has a degree in International Relations and a Master's degree in Environmental Politics. She was a political science professor for eight years. She founded the project, "La Mujer Nica Como Emprendedora Social," that focuses on helping low-income women become entrepreneurs. She joined MRS, now UNAMOS in 2007 because she believed in the democratic principles, justice, equality, and respect for human rights. She looks to a brighter future for Nicaraguans, where no generation will ever have to live through another dictatorship. Barahona was elected president of the political party, Unión Democrática Renovadora (UNAMOS) in 2017.

Violeta Granero (arrested on June 8th): Granero, a sociologist by profession, is the leader of the Unidad Nacional Azul y Blanco political organization. *Maria Oviedo* (arrested on June 29th): Oviedo is the coordinator for the Comisión Permanente de Derechos Humanos (CPDH). Also, arrested and imprisoned were: *María Fernanda Flores; María Esperanza Sánchez García; Karla Escobar;* and *Julia Hernández Arévalo.*

***

The international community has overwhelmingly expressed outrage over the incarceration of the women and all other political prisoners. In a recent letter issued by the UN Human Rights Council, the Nicaragua Core Group makes a forthright plea, "We once again urge the Government of Nicaragua to immediately release all political detainees, refrain from reprisals and all acts of intimidation."[71] In a gesture of solidarity, representatives from fifty countries signed the letter. A similar statement was issued by the U.S. Secretary of State on September 14, 2021: "[President Ortega and Vice President Murillo] have closed all space for political competition and public discourse, cruelly jailing in recent months more than 30 opposition leaders, students, reporters, business leaders, human rights activists, and members of civil society."[72]

In Ortega's response, according to the article published in the newspaper, *Confidencial*, he maintains that his government seeks good relationships with all countries; and asks for their respect. He made an intriguing plea to the international community-- to continue their contributions (in donations) to combat poverty and develop the country. However, in previous public speeches, Ortega has insisted that the jailed political leaders are "criminals," who sought to depose the government and/or were complicit with imperial elements ("el imperialismo") to overthrow the government.[73]

Murillo's Tactics in Targeting Women That Oppose the Regime

Rosario Murillo is Ortega's best and formidable defense for the cruelty perpetrated against the women. The aforementioned women, Tellez, Vijil, Dávila, Barrios Chamorro, Barahona, Granero, Oviedo, Flores; Sánchez García; Escobar; Hernández Arévalo, are well-educated (two are Fulbright Scholars), have professional occupations, accomplished, intelligent; and some are wives and mothers. If Ortega were to call out each woman by name, accusing them of treason, conspiracy, money laundering, etc., he may risk losing some of his popularity amongst his female Sandinista supporters. Undoubtedly, the international feminist community would condemn him for his actions. Therefore, Murillo's role is crucial to Ortega's success in reaching both male and female political supporters. She interprets and enhances Ortega's messages, tailoring the content to match the discourse and audience. Supporters believe Murillo's passionate and persuasive rhetoric when she describes women as "bad mothers, traitors, liars, thieves, deceitful, evil, and dangerous." Murillo's daily speeches provide a simplified version of the news to an audience with limited access to information beyond their communities. Murillo emphasizes the importance of loyalty to "la patria," and portrays belief in "comandante" Daniel (Ortega) as equivalent to faith in God. Her actions and words cater to the deeply ingrained heteropatriarchal society in Nicaragua, reinforcing the kinds of gender-based violence that many women have longed fought against.

Silencing the voices of the opposition by cancelling the legal status of the non-profit organizations to which they belong is another tactic used by the Ortega Murillo regime. The National Assembly, heavily dominated by Ortega supporters, used their power to void the legal standing of NGOs.[74] Many of these have been critical of the government, not necessarily intended to confront the authorities but rather to denounce the serious problems and offer solutions. An example is the Centro de Estudios para la Gobernabilidad y Democracia (CEGODEM). Their leader, Fidel Moreira, gives a testimonial statement in the video located in the center's social media page, which describes the assaults, including murder of human rights defenders, and campesinos by paramilitary units operating with impunity. In a news report published in August, 2021, Deputy Brooklyn Rivera, gave testimony in objection to the closure of Acción Médica Cristiana which has aided the indigenous communities along the Caribbean Region in areas of health and emergency relief during natural disasters. He also opposed the shutter of the women's association, el *Colectivo de Mujeres de Matagalpa*, which has a lengthy trajectory of 31 years serving thousands of women and their families by creating Casas de Mujeres (women's shelters), libraries, constructing homes, to name a few of their efforts. Many of the canceled NGOs received international funds to carry out social, health, and educational projects.[75]

Three other women organizations, known for their feminist perspectives, and have served to defend women's rights and defenders, were ordered to close by the Ortega Murillo regime: *La Asociación de Mujeres de Jalapa contra la Violencia Oyanka*; *la Fundación entre Volcanes*; and *Fundación Xochiquetzal*. The National Assembly's president, Gustavo Porras, indicated in his statement published by nicaraguainvestiga.com that the NGOs' cancellations are as a result of the organizations' irregularities or noncompliance with accountability requirements on donor identification and the operational budget.[76] However, the IM-Defensoras article points to the belief that many feminists and human rights defenders perceive this action as part of the repression unleashed by the Sandinista government in the course of the presidential electoral process--to persecute, criminalize, and subject to imprisonment--dozens of people, including feminists, journalists, lawyers, and defenders of human rights, or simply to eliminate the opposition.[77]

The Case of Zoilamérica Narváez Murillo

At thirty-one years old, Zoilamérica, daughter of Rosario Murillo and (stepfather) Daniel Ortega, took the giant step toward recovery as a survivor of sexual abuse. For the previous decade, Narváez had undergone a transformative process to mitigate the emotional and psychological pain as a result of a twenty-year nightmare of sexual abuse perpetrated by her stepfather. As a final step toward her healing process, she petitioned the court to legally change her last name from Ortega to her late father's last name (Narváez), and stated the reason: that she had been sexually abused by her stepfather. However, for such an accusation to prove admissible in court she had to have evidence. In the spring of 1998, Narváez made public her painful admission that she had been sexually abused by Ortega since the age of eleven. She related her decision to do so in her *2002 declaration* a few days ahead of her testimony with the Inter-American Commission on Human Rights: "I was a prisoner of desperation and anguish at the time, but I've celebrated that day like a second birthday ever since. I celebrate it as the day I took off a mask and was able to break with a history that had scarred by life."[78]

Her denunciation sent shock waves throughout the country. The general public was in disbelief, and some felt offended that she even brought up such a private matter. But, the most ferocious attacks came from her mother and Ortega. Murillo and Ortega denied the accusations, although, in her testimony she recalls a private conversation with Ortega in which he admits to the abuse and blames his emotional problems on his seven-year prison term. These and other details are documented in Kenneth Morris' book.[79] Morris explains his analysis concerning the verity of Narváez' accusations: "… the evidence suggests that Narváez is telling the truth. No one has ever linked Narváez' accusations to any of Ortega's political opponents at home or abroad, and Narváez herself was a militant Sandinista at the time she leveled the charge. She has had nothing material or political to gain by accusing Ortega of sexually abusing her, and in fact had much to lose."[80] Narváez describes in detail the gross, criminal misconduct of Ortega toward her in the published, 1998 manuscript, *"Testimonio de Zoilamérica Narváez Murillo."*

When Narváez took her case to the Inter-Amercian Commission on Human Rights (IACHR) in 1999, Vilma Nuñez de Escorcia, founder of the Nicaraguan human rights center, CENIDH, was her legal representative. In the case document, Narváez contends that the State of Nicaragua had violated her right to a fair trial because the Court of Managua refused to suspend Ortega's congressional immunity.[81] (At the time Ortega was a member of the Parliament.) Thus, the court ruled in Ortega's favor without allowing witnesses or even a testimony from Narváez.

Later, when the case was re-activated, the IACHR did not make a ruling in Narváez' case because Ortega threatened to withdraw from the Organization of American States (OAS), of which the IACHR is an integral component. Having been re-elected in 2007, he used the power of his presidency to make this claim, and Narváez once again, was left defenseless.[82]

Although Narváez chose not to bring charges against her mother, it's clear from her testimony that Murillo had full knowledge of the sexual abuse, and instead of helping her daughter, she became an enabler. Murillo's sister had agreed to come forth as a witness in Narváez defense and testify what she saw and heard at their home in Costa Rica, before their move to Managua in 1978. Morris believes that Murillo knew about Ortega raping her daughter, but that when her sister confronted her about it, "Murillo dismissed her concerns."[83] Narváez asked her mother for help, but was rejected. Murillo must have known that Ortega was going into her bedroom at night because Narváez begged her mother to let her sleep with a sibling, as a way to protect herself, but she refused. Murillo chided Narváez for not wanting to sleep alone. When Narváez decided to go public with her accusations, Murillo was furious. Narváez harbored a resentment toward her mother for siding with the man that repeatedly assaulted her. Morris perceives the relationships between Murillo, Ortega, and Narváez from the perspective of a power pact. "Instead of helping the man she came to love overcome an obvious emotional problem, or the daughter who depended upon her for protection, she exploited the man's weaknesses by offering him her daughter. In exchange Murillo extracted real political power."[84]

Although Narváez' attempt to prove her case in court was not successful, her battle was not lost. Her video testimonies reveal her strong willingness to expose the truth regardless of the consequences.[85] Murillo and Ortega's futile attempts to hide their dark secret failed, and the more they ramped up their accusations against Narváez, the bigger their crime and conspiracy to cover it up. Narváez was steadfast in her determination to expose the horrid truth of sexual abuse in children. She came to recognize that, as a survivor, she possesses the powerful platform from which to advocate on behalf of child victims of sexual abuse, and demand the reconstruction and reform of the broken judicial system that favors the criminal and further persecutes the abused child.[86]

In the conclusion of her 2002 declaration (before she was forced to drop her case), Narváez makes the following statement: "Whatever happens in the international process at the IACHR, I cannot allow this case to be closed, because that would amount to closing the option of many other women to talk and to feel that justice is being done in their case. My struggle is no longer against Daniel Ortega, it is against the precedent that my case created through the complicit action of the executive branch, the legislative branch, the judicial branch and the country's whole political system.[87]

As Narváez' legal counsel, Vilma Nuñez was instrumental in navigating Narváez' case through a difficult and chaotic course. She prepared her defense despite Murillo's plea to refrain from representing her. Murillo's animosity against her became starkly evident after Nuñez was named the recipient of a prestigious award, *Woman of Courage*, from U.S. Ambassador to Nicaragua, Laura Farnsworth Dogu on March 7, 2017. Murillo tasked her female cabinet members with a letter to Ambassador Dogu, asserting their objections on the basis of Nuñez' "insults" toward the government. In learning about the letter, Nuñez was not surprised and indicated that Murillo's hostility toward her derived from the time she legally represented her daughter, Zoilamérica Narváez. Observers and critics (especially feminists) of the Ortega Murillo regime are synchronized in their analysis about the roles and functions of the large numbers of females in their government, which they believe are prohibited from working outside an anti-feminist agenda strictly controlled by Murillo. But the disparaging letter was only the beginning of Murillo's actions against Nuñez. In December, 2018, the *IM-Defensoras.org* reported that the Nicaraguan Human Rights Center (CENIDH) was cancelled by the National Assembly, in part by the Sandinista-dominated congress agenda to quash non-governmental opposition entities.[88] As founding member of CENIDH, Nuñez had been the target of personal attacks and threats; after the 2018 April Rebellion she worked with CENIDH to compile complaints of human rights violations against the State police forces. In February, 2021, the IACHR asked government officials to file a report that specifically responds to the "aggression and harassment faced by CENIDH workers," since the 2018 April Rebellion.[89] The Ortega Murillo government has yet to respond to the request for an investigation into the documented violations compiled by CENIDH, and has turned the state's repressive forces against the staff (human right defenders), some of whom had to self-exile for fear of their lives.

Concluding Remarks

Despite facing significant obstacles such as living under a dictatorship that punishes female activists and shutting down feminist organizations in an attempt to silence their dissenting voices, women have shown time and time again that they possess the strength, resilience, and determination to overcome adversity and create meaningful change. They have battled a force that threatens to weaken democratic institutions by politicizing their power and rewarding corruption. They've managed to deter the controlling and manipulating tactics of the media in exploiting the vulnerability of women in dire social and economic circumstances. The spirit of the Nicaraguan women survives even within the context of a paralyzing fear wrought by repressive forces that are becoming increasingly lethal.

The bond of sisterhood that exists today among women in Nicaragua, El Salvador, Honduras, and México was particularly evident during the periods of armed conflicts, such as in El Salvador, 1979-1991 and in Nicaragua, 1970s-mid-1980s, and beyond. Despite differences in origin and development, the armed conflicts shared by these women resulted in common problems, during and after the wars. For instance, the majority experienced similar discriminatory treatment as they sought to gain equal status with the men as combatants. After the war, they faced frustrating disappointments and were unable to achieve the substantive changes in favor of women at the highest levels of their "new" government. Through these experiences and others, the women developed a unique interpretation of the international women's movement in which they found their own powerful voice.

The United Nation committees responsible for overseeing the implementation of the Convention on the Elimination of All Forms of Discrimination against Women (CEDAW) have published reports which address the specific areas of issues related to the discriminatory practices against women. A careful perusal of these documents reveals patterns of similarities in regards to gender-based human rights in Nicaragua, Honduras, Guatemala, and El Salvador.[90]

Some of the common areas of human rights violations against women include: 1) increasing rates of femicides and the failure of the State to properly investigate, prosecute, and punish the perpetrators; 2) sexual and reproductive rights violations, resulting in an alarming increase of underage pregnancies; 3) increase in domestic violence and lack of appropriated funds to resolve cases, especially those that threaten the lives of the victims; 4) the absence of full protection for domestic violence victims where the courts favor the perpetrator or where laws such as Law 779 in Nicaragua, require the victim to confront the aggressor for purpose of mediation that results in the re-victimization of the victim; 5) increased violations against female human rights defenders, including the LGBTQ community members and indigenous women defending land rights and environmental resources—that have resulted in attacks, sexual violence, intimidation, and criminalization; 6) increase of sexual violence against women activists in general and specifically, the online violence against women; and 7) the increase in the deteriorating conditions in education and social services for girls and women.

Central American women---feminists, activists, advocates, and defenders of human rights—all form an indestructible link, especially evident in times of great need. They realize that their strength is in their collective force, and when they raise their voices in unison and deliver a heartfelt message on behalf of their *sisters in peril and resistance*, the international community listens. Such a clarion call is heard in the voices of three women in a brief video feature; all are members of the Iniciativa Mesoamericana-- Red Nacional de Derechos Humanos (IM-Defensoras/National Network Human Rights): Morena Herrerra, El Salvador; Gilda Rivera, Honduras; Yésica Sánchez, México; and Lydia Alpizar, México.[91] Their message clearly and accurately describes the conditions of repression in Nicaragua, and for some women, the constant fear of persecution.

They hunger for freedom, and although they are trapped in an anti-democratic, hostile state, they realize the liminality of their lives; today they struggle but their future is bright, and they will never give up.

Chapter Six

*'We are the Revolution:' The Nicaraguan Women's
Movement Taking Charge*

*"Love amongst women is revolutionary, it is resistance,
and it is giving yourself the opportunity to live each day
with a different perspective."*
*'Hormiguita,' Interviewed by
Aza Delgado Orduño, March 10, 2022*

Post-revolution Nicaragua in the 1980s ushered in an influx of ideas on how to reconstruct the "new" society. After four decades of the Somoza dictatorship (1937-1979), women emerged with a progressive feminist agenda and a determination to make fundamental and structural changes leading toward social, economic, and political equality. Their demands were justified, as over a third of the Sandinista revolutionary forces fighting as combatants and non-combatants were female.[2] Heroic actions by revolutionary Nicaraguan women are legendary, and some of their stories are included in archival documents of revolutions and civil wars throughout the Americas and Spain. In every case, the endgame was focused on improving not only their lives as women, but with consequential outcomes that would potentially affect the entire society. But, after a decade of struggle in the course of post-revolution negotiations, Nicaraguan feminists perceived their gains far less in their advances than anticipated or hoped for. The election of Violeta Barrios de Chamorro (1990-97), the first female, democratically-elected president after the revolution was particularly disheartening. She not only rejected an agenda favoring women's rights, but in a subtle display of hostility towards feminism, emphasized without objection the traditional, ideal roles of women as primarily wives and mothers. The election was also a loss politically for the FSLN revolutionary party.[3] Although it may have seemed like a serious and debilitating setback, for feminists living in an era of revolution and change their fight-after-the-

207

revolution became yet another challenge in their course of action. Notwithstanding the myriad of issues and problems that seemed impossible for the feminists to resolve, the successes in recent history far outweigh the failures, at least as determined in a 2010 publication by author and researcher, Karen Kampwirth, in her declaration that "Nicaragua has the most significant feminist movement in Central America..."[4]

However, in the current state of affairs, Nicaraguans are living under the repressive, authoritative government of Daniel Ortega and his wife and vice-president, Rosario Murillo. In a cruel and most unfortunate circumstance, the Ortega-Murillo regime has meticulously carved out a repressive government aimed at mostly the younger generation who seek democratic freedoms, but also, feminists for whom Daniel Ortega seems to have a personal vendetta against. Ortega's disdain toward feminists originated at the time (in 1998) that his stepdaughter, Zoilamérica, publicly accused him of sexually assaulting her during a period of about twenty years since she was eleven years old. An intense political campaign by feminists to hold Ortega accountable for his crime served to unnerve him, but he abused his power to wrangle his way out of the legal quagmire. Certainly, Murillo's protective shield was instrumental in her role as the grieving wife, even though she turned against her daughter, and denied even knowing about the abuse.

Since the April, 2018 Rebellion, the Orteguista regime, which holds overwhelming power and control throughout every branch of government, has mobilized a crackdown on social protests, systematically blocking any opposition movement. The extreme violence exercised by the various state police and parapolice has dealt a devastating blow to Nicaraguan democratic society. Over 300 people, most of whom were peaceful youthful protestors, were killed. Additionally, over a thousand people were injured and several hundred were detained, with many still incarcerated.

Featured in this chapter are women who are current leaders in the feminist movement in Nicaragua. Their expressions and acts of resistance demonstrate a dogged determination to reject the regime's repressive forces that attempt to deter them from advancing their social causes within a democratic governance. However, in order to actively participate in the analysis and problem-solving discussions of Nicaragua's current affairs, it is important to engage in a constructive dialog that leads to an understanding of the nature of the conflict and friction between and among the multitude of opinions and ideas.

Reconstructing the New Nicaragua

Perhaps, one of the best examples of the successful democratic initiatives undertaken by the Sandinistas in 1981 were the consultation efforts of the Ministry of Education. The Ministry's goal was to survey citizens that would collectively constitute a core representation of Nicaraguan society that would decide on the best education for everyone.[5] More than 50,000 participants responded from numerous organizations across the country, and the survey managers collected responses of over 50 open-ended questions on topics and issues related to the *New Education*. The focus on education reform was deliberately designed by the Sandinistas as an immediate priority after the Revolution. The illiteracy rate of over 50 percent in 1978 is an indicator of the gross negligence by which the Somoza regime failed to comply with its essential civic responsibilities.[6] The National Literacy Crusade was instrumental in increasing literacy rates at record speed: in just five months, results showed that the illiteracy rate had decreased to approximately 13 percent. Additionally, there were about 80,000 literacy crusade volunteers from a variety of backgrounds, many of whom had very little experience. The majority were high school and university students. It was an extraordinary event, not only because of the literacy development process but also for the manner by which people from diverse backgrounds came together for the first time in their lives. Many were convinced that the education that flourished in Nicaraguan society was only because of the revolution.[7]

Another instance on how Nicaraguans used democratic methods to achieve difficult results was in grass-roots, mass organizational planning and execution. During the 1978 final phase of the revolution, the masses played a critical role in finishing off the fighting. Recognizing this phenomenal success, the Sandinistas formulated a plan to promote the development of organizations for a broad array of projects. For example, the urban worker's organized against Somoza evolved into the Sandinista Workers' Confederation, the Civil Defense Committee was converted into the Sandinista Defense Committee, and the Association of Women Facing the National Problematic (AMPRONAC) became the Nicaraguan Women's Association Luisa Amanda Espinoza (AMNLAE).[8] Additionally, the newly-formed organizations were encouraged by the Sandinista leaders to become independent autonomous entities. They developed their own action plans and were allotted funds by which to administer their services to the community. Since these organizations played a vital role in achieving the Sandinista government's social agenda, they were granted specially-designed responsibilities as decision-makers.[9]

The women's organization, AMNLAE, continued as a provider for women's medical and psychological services, as well legal counseling. However, the Contra War (1980-1989) that had started shortly after the end of the revolution became increasingly costly. AMNLAE's close association with the FSLN meant that certain restrictions had to be followed. By the mid-1980s, women leaders in the major labor unions for rural workers began to achieve successful outcomes as they continuously strived for equality in the workplace. The women were members of the Women's Secretariats (*Secretarías de Mujer*) and by emphasizing the importance of women's roles in the war effort their demands were well-received by the FSLN. As a result, the Sandinistas approved the development of, among other proposals, "child care centers, corn mills, and wash basins."[10] However, once the Contra War concluded, the Women Secretariats were phased out. Even so, AMNLAE remained in close affiliation with the FSLN, continuing the organization's work as a social service provider but refusing to advocate in any manner for women's equal rights.

In 1987, feminists began their organizing efforts according to their vision of a post-revolution agenda. The founding of one the first autonomous feminist group, the Matagalpa Women's Collective (*Colectivo de Mujeres de Matagalpa*) was the first step in actualizing their plans to profoundly change

Nicaraguan's patriarchal society. The feminists' contacts with their counterparts in El Salvador, Mexico and other Latin American countries had strongly influenced their outlook on what they propose to accomplish.[11] Several similar autonomous feminist organizations emerged, and in the process of providing social services to women, feminists worked out legal and policy changes that addressed women's rights. The feminists were in the forefront during the development of the 1987 Constitution. As a result, several articles specific to the protection of women's rights were incorporated.[12] While the 1990 election of Violeta Barrios de Chamorro signaled a defeat for the Sandinista political party, the feminists had achieved a resounding victory for their own "revolution." More importantly, the feminists gradually acquired a huge following of women regardless of their views on feminism. The return of the FSLN political party with the election of Daniel Ortega in 2006 posed a different kind of challenge for the feminists. Their splinter from the FSLN-supported AMNLAE had caused a host of reactions from a politically-charged reality. Regardless of their successful exchanges in working with communities, making substantial improvements in the lives of women and their families, they realized that their livelihood as feminists would be difficult. Even though Daniel Ortega won the elections in 2006, 2011, 2016, and 2021, his victory in each electoral cycle had become increasingly problematic as he realized the opposition was growing. No doubt, the Nicaraguan uprising of 2018 created a serious fracture in Ortega's presidency. His reaction was not unlike a military general re-assessing his losses and re-calculating his strategies to assure his final victory. What appeared clear to even the passing observer was that *democracy* was placed on hold, perhaps, permanently.

Closures of Feminist Organizations

Ortega and Murillo's strategy for controlling the opposition included the closures of certain social and civic organizations that functioned independently of the government's purview. Over two hundred organizations have been forced to close their doors since the 2018 Rebellion, and their properties have been confiscated.[13] Many of these were established non-profit organizations that had served the community, especially women and their children, for several decades. The media sources reporting on these closures generally maintain that the reason behind the governmental order is the organizations' alleged acceptance of international funds to undermine the government or due to the lack of proper bookkeeping. However, the directors and board members flatly denied these allegations.

Sandra Ramos, a representative of the women's movement, *el Movimiento de Mujeres María Elena Cuadra* (MEC), describes the regime's actions to shutter their organization as *political violence*.[14] As Director of the non-profit organization for employed and unemployed women (*Asociación de Mujeres Trabajadoras y Desempleadas María Cuadra*), Ramos resolves that the government's punitive actions will not deter their work seeking the rights of women in the workplace. The organization has endured for 28 years, assisting women in their clamor for decent and fair working conditions in the industrial zones, and in assuring women legal protection in the court of law. On a social media video clip, Ramos explains that their organization's work has been continuously conflicted within the context of a society that is patriarchal and "machista," (sexist) and where women's political action is often disregarded and dismissed.[15] Ramos contends that the organization has established a solid structure of volunteers and supporters that will continue working and advocating, even if the government has cancelled their legal status.

Imprisoning Feminists

The Ortega-Murillo winning strategy for the presidential election in November 2021 was to incarcerate all potential candidates by the time the ballots were printed. It was an easy win for the duo, except that they were critically regarded as illegitimately elected, both nationally and internationally. But they were elected nevertheless, much to the chagrin of many Nicaraguans who anticipated a transitional change toward democracy. Among the more than 120 incarcerated political prisoners are women whose activism and feminism were particularly threatening to Ortega and Murillo. The women are completing a year of imprisonment, and some of them have been sentenced to around 8-12 years. The trial processes were reportedly a *sham*, clearly in violation of their rights according to the constitution and international law.[16] Incarceration was the only mechanism by which the Ortega Murillo could silence the women. Even so, their passionate pleas for acts of resistance still resonate among the populace, and Nicaraguans face enormous pressure to resolve the core of their crisis.[17]

In a June 6, 2021 interview with *Coyuntura*, just days before she was incarcerated, Tamara Dávila expresses confidence that the Ortega Murillo regime will *collapse* due to the escalating repression involving various segments of the population.[18] Her comments follow:

> *"It's unsustainable to live under these conditions, not only for those of us that are politically organized but for the population in general. There's a tremendous economic crisis in our country. Every day, more people are unemployed, businesses are closing, and there's a health crisis. With so much repression, and the economy stifling many families, an eruption is bound to happen. On April 17, 2018, the people didn't imagine what would happen the next day. The same thing can happen again."*

Dávila is a forty-year old feminist and an executive member of the political party, Union Democrática Renovadora (UNAMOS). She is a psychologist by profession, committed to the defense of human rights and gender equality. On the night that the Sandinista police tore down their front door, Dávila and her five-year old daughter awoke in terror and feared for their lives as their home was ransacked. The police confiscated their electronic equipment as well as a family album featuring her daughter growing up, which was later used as "evidence" against her during the sentencing procedure. She was taken to prison without the police allowing her to talk to her daughter.[19] Dávila commented in a podcast that although "machismo" is amplified by the dictator Daniel Ortega, who is a rapist (un violador), the fact is that women live within a societal structure that is profoundly "machista." Not only are women subjected to an extremely flawed dictatorship, she says, but we must also confront flagrant gender inequalities that exist throughout our society.[20]

Daniel Ortega Protected for His Crimes of Sexual Assault

When Zoilamérica Narváez, Daniel Ortega's stepdaughter, publicly denounced in 1998 that she had suffered sexual abuse perpetrated by then-presidential hopeful Daniel Ortega for two decades, people expressed a range of emotional sentiments. Ortega's supporters immediately responded with outright denials and accusations, while others remained silent and restrained. Feminists rallied around Zoilamérica's case and began to give voice to thousands of "silenced" women that had experienced sexual assault, particularly during the Contra War in the 1980s. Ortega's supporters, many of whom were regime militants, carried out an intense campaign aimed at discrediting Zoilamérica and hiding the truth. Zoilamérica explained that Ortega had insisted that she must refrain from revealing his acts of sexual indiscretion for the sake of the *Revolution*, which is why she had prolonged her pronouncement for so many years,.[21]

Sociologist, feminist and former member of the FSLN guerrilla, *María Teresa Blandón*, re-affirms Narváez' statement on how the system of militancy during the 1980s resulted in sexual assault cases where victims were too afraid or ashamed to seek justice. The ranking Sandinista militants gained preferential treatment, and the act of sexually assaulting young women was expected, especially among the officers. These acts of violence against women were "generalized, accepted, silenced, and concealed," according to Blandón. She asserts that besides that those that committed the assaults, there were others who were complicit and just as guilty. All of the sexual assault cases, recognized as violence against women, were considered of low priority in defense of the revolution. The prevalence of sexual violence and abuse suffered by women, especially the very young resulted in the "normalization" of this behavior.

Generally, the public had knowledge of the sexual assault problem during the war, but the government failed to systematize sexual assault cases and to conduct proper investigations. Instead, the government officials were likely to "dismiss" the problem ("borrón y cuenta nueva), in the same vein as recently observed when Ortega declared the 2018 Rebellion cases as "borrón y cuenta nueva."

Blandón's following declaration has similar sentiments as those spoken by Tamara Dávila:

> *"It's intolerable to think we have a president, a magistrate, or a member of parliament that is a rapist (violador), one that is a sexual predator; and if this continues to occur, it means that this society has not changed, and the level of tolerance for this violence still exists."[22]*

***

Luz Marina Torres, Coordinator of the Colectivo 8 de Marzo, explains that in 1987, during her work with members of the Asocación de Mujeres Nicaragüenses Luisa Amanda Espinoza (AMNLAE), she collected the testimonies of over 100 women serving in the military that had been sexually assaulted or abused. They refused to lodge official complaints against their perpetrators, citing fear of retaliation and shame. At the time of the violations, the women were told that the immediate attention to the revolution took precedence over the crimes committed against them.

Torres understands how victims of sexual assault experience long-term consequences, and yet, it's highly improbable to prove their cases in the court of law. Their "profound silence" brings to the foreground a broader reality that the revolution was disproportionately cruel to women.[23]

Even today, relatives of women murdered in the hands of their (ex)partners consistently voice their outrage over the failure of the courts to exercise their judicial order and punish the murderers. Each femicide, which is the killing of a woman because of her gender, has insurmountable consequences. However, in a broader historical context, social and economic circumstances have disadvantaged women and relegated them to an inferior position compared to men.[24]

Yoli was murdered on October of 2020 by her partner for whom she had sought a "breakup."[24] Yoli left behind an eight-year-old son, a grieving sister, and a mother in the hospital with a serious illness. Yoli's case brings into focus the flawed system of mediation, which she was required to participate in order to process a legal complaint against her partner. During the mediation process, she described to the officiating committee, *La Comisaría de Mujer y la Niñez de San Rafael del Sur*, her partner's relentless psychological violence against her, and asked for a legal separation. When asked by the committee whether she owned the house, she responded that she had used her earnings from selling fruits and vegetables to build the home, but the land belonged to her partner. The committee refused to resolve her complaint since her partner asked that *she* leave their house. Three months later, her partner went into the house and viciously stabbed her in the presence of her son. She died two days later. Her murderer (known as "el femicida") was eventually tried and sentenced to thirty years of prison term, although, the current status of his imprisonment is unknown.

Sentencing a convicted murderer by a judge is not a guarantee that the sentence will be served. For example, in the case of the man who murdered his partner, Felicia, in 2016, charged and convicted, was early-released after serving just four years of a 30-year sentence. After his prison release, he returned to his town and proceeded to psychologically torture the mother of the woman he had killed. The mother was not notified of his early release, nor was she given a reasonable explanation for it.

In the case of Yoli, several issues emerged as problematic in the handling of overall domestic violence. Women are at a disadvantage in abusive relationships because the men have the absolute, legal property rights, even when children are involved. Everything falls under the husband's name, and women are unable to acquire loans in their name unless, as in the case of Yoli, the loan was procured as a business microfinance debt.

Another issue revolves around the incompetence of both the policing units investigating domestic violence and the judicial court consisting of the regional women's commission, the Comisarías de las Mujeres, established by the government. Luz Marina Torres, (Director of the women's collective, Colectivo 8 de Marzo), explains that women who file a legal complaint with the women's commission (Comisaría) don't have the confidence that justice will be served on their behalf. Nor do they believe that they will be granted the protection and assurance that they and/or their children will not be harmed. The mediation process officiated by the Comisaría actually serves to further place the women at greater risk since the partners, who are present in these hearings, are usually given a "second" chance based on their "promise" to improve their behavior. Torres explains that time and time again these sorts of proceedings end in tragic circumstances, mostly violently, and sometimes the women are killed. The gross negligence and overall lack of competence on the part of the policing unit and members of the Comisaría in the handling of these cases is appalling. The women's organization such as *la colectiva* directed by Torres have the staff competence and experience to work on domestic violence issues. However, the Ortega Murillo regime has consistently disregarded her organization and others like it, effectively cutting off their strong advocacy efforts aimed at protecting women's human rights.[26]

***

In January, 2011, Perla had stepped off the bus after arriving at her municipality, called El Portón, not far from Managua, when in broad daylight, her husband lunged a dagger three times into her chest.[27] This act of violence would not be less significant than other femicides across the country, except that in this case, the community of their families and friends made a concerted effort to protect the *murderer*, helping him evade prosecutorial action. In the process, Perla's death was considered inconsequential as demonstrated by the community member's negative treatment toward her and the three daughters.

The case is particularly puzzling to members of *la colectiva* (la Colectiva 8 de Marzo), a woman's organization focused on domestic violence prevention and protection. The community of El Portón, both men and women, chose to protect the man who had killed his wife whom he had physically and psychologically abused throughout their 37-year marriage. In an act of defiance, some members of the community displayed egregious acts of hatred toward the police who wanted to arrest him, as well as animosity toward the women in *la colectiva* for attempting to help Perla.

Perla and her husband were married when she was 13 and he was twice her age. Aside from being a housewife and mother, Perla shared the farming workload with her husband, planting, harvesting, and tending to the cattle and other domestic animals. After thirty-seven years of marriage, and at the age of fifty, Perla decided to venture into a small business of raising cattle. She was able to secure the loan she needed but only with her husband's signature. However, when Perla attempted to engage in business interactions, her husband refused to acknowledge her ownership as per their previous agreement. This led to an argument, and her husband agreed to leave the house.

Her husband became enraged and his abusive behavior escalated. Perla felt afraid and powerless against his constant and vicious threats. Her only option was to ask *la colectiva* to help her attain a restraining order. This was a court procedure that required Perla and her husband to participate in "mediation," based on a law, Ley 779, that addresses "violence against women."[28] Perla presented her complaint during the hearing, but her husband's anger evolved into a physical altercation with the police, and he was ordered to remain in detention. He served two days in jail and was released. Having been forced to attend the mediation and then, serving jail time, Perla's husband amplified his furor and continued attacking her. Two days after his jail release, some of her husband's neighbors told him that Perla was seen traveling on a bus toward the nearby main town. They speculated that she may be going to *la colectiva* to file another complaint against him. She had in fact, gone shopping at the market. He waited at the bus stop for Perla's return, and stabbed her, eventually killing her.

The police went to El Portón to arrest her husband, now the suspect in her murder, but they were refused entry into the community; no one spoke to the police, much less complied with their orders. Perla's funeral wake was arranged by the women in *la colectiva*. Many community members expressed their bitterness toward the women in *la colectiva* and warned them to stay away from El Portón. However, the women of *la colectiva* proceeded to hold the funeral service as a way to demonstrate respect for Perla and her three daughters. Very few community members attended. Afterwards, the women decided to stay the night in El Portón, at a home where they had previously stayed as guests. That evening, Perla's husband went to the house and demanded to see the women. The owner managed to convince him to leave since enough violence had been committed.

Perla's three daughters were abandoned by their father and the local authorities denied them compensation for the violent murder of their mother. The former husband's family members took over the entire property, leaving the daughters without their home.

According to the women in *la colectiva,* the husband was never arrested; he lives in Managua and has been sighted with another woman, presumably his wife.

Questioning the Integrity of Institutions Complicates a Patriarchal Society

The case of Perla clearly illustrates the deeply entrenched sentiments against women, and how the laws function in favor of the husband, even in extreme violent circumstances that threaten the life of a woman. Perla's husband was a beloved member of the community; he was known as handsome (with green eyes) and charming, except when he had too much to drink. Despite being a problem drinker, he was perceived as an outstanding, peaceful citizen. His long-standing abusive behavior toward his wife was acknowledged by his immediate circle of friends and family, but it was not questioned. Even as a murderer, he maintained the affection and support of his inner circle. He falsely believed that killing Perla was justified, and his "machista" anger was buoyed by his family and friends. General mistrust toward the state and civic institutions was common among the social groups in the community, and defying the authorities and threatening the woman's organization (Colectiva 8 de Marzo), were acts of self-preservation. Any regard for the well-being of women in general is secondary to the values and beliefs espoused by the community as a whole.

The reasons why the women in El Portón refused to support Perla and her daughters during their time of crisis are not fully understood. While it is easy to assume the women's behaviors were consistent with the patriarchal social environment, there are still unanswered questions to draw conclusions in a generalized fashion.

In towns such as El Portón, feminists recognize their work as vital not only in educating the public about women's rights, but advocating for change at the highest ranks of governmental and civic institutions. Laws that protect women and defend their human rights are pivotal to building a responsive and responsible governance, but equally important are the adequate resources to develop programs of support and to build skills, knowledge, and competence among all those that work with the women. These concerns and others are commonly expressed by feminists that have first-hand experiences living under a repressive Ortega Murillo dictatorship.

Changes in the Workplace

In the absence of adequate pro-labor laws related to women in the workplace such as "sweatshops," maquiladoras, or manufacturing factories and plants, the international treaty, the *ILO Convention No. 190*, serves as a formidable defense against the work-related forms of violence and sexual harassment. Subjecting women to verbal abuse, inappropriate touching and groping, and harassment are commonplace, but even so, in a climate of repressive and harsh economic circumstances, many of these cases remain unresolved, or underreported.

***

Interviews with women in their workplace reveal the inside story, and a journalist with the digital news platform, *ondalocalni.com*, provides a descriptive context in her reporting to document the enormous challenges in the efforts to implement substantial change and improvements.[29] Director of MEC (*el Movimiento de Mujeres María Elena Cuadra*), Sandra Ramos, explains to the journalist that due to a pact devised by the private business sector and the government, *ILO 190* has yet to be ratified, presumably for reasons of preventing the destabilization of the work place order.[30] In the current repressive circumstances, many women refuse to formalize their own or others' complaints, citing fear and retaliation. Ramos reiterates that this makes her role as feminist and human rights defender extremely complicated.

Work place violence and sexual harassment are among many in the long list of human rights violations. Health issues are of great concern to women who slave over the grinding, long hours of labor that aggravate key areas of the body such as the shoulders, back, knees, hands, and wrists. After seven or eight years of heavy and intense labor, many women end up in the hospital with serious ailments that can only be corrected by abstaining from their jobs. Their options are limited to either continuing to work despite their disabilities or quitting and accepting a meager pension.

Nicaragua's labor law, "Ley General de Higiene y Seguridad del Trabajo," obligates the employer to adopt preventive measures to guarantee the rights of their workers. However, in general, employers have failed to comply with the law, evidenced by the affected women. Once the women are forced to drop out of the labor market, they are often denied adequate and fair compensation from both their employer and the national social security office. Due to a lack of coordination between the government, employers, and the labor unions in addressing the working conditions such as safety, security, and health, the women are left to fend for themselves, and no one is held accountable.

Women make up the majority in the industrial work force, which is approximately 52 percent of the total number of workers. Their monthly earnings of about $150 are less than the approximate amount deemed essential to feed a family of three or four, about $400. Apart from their full-time employment, the women, especially single mothers, assume other "informal" employments such as selling fruits and vegetables at the local market in order to provide for their children. Thus, women make up a large proportion of the informal sector of the work force.

The Survival Economy

In the northern department of Nueva Segovia, bordering with Honduras, women continue to work in low-skilled employment as they have for decades, and their earnings are barely enough to survive. Sociologist *Haydee Castillo* describes the women's work as self-employment in a "survival economy." Nueva Segovia's population relies largely on agricultural work, and women have very few opportunities to make advances in education and in acquiring specialized skills. Women are unable to develop a business plan because they lack literacy skills, explains Castillo, and whereas women in Managua have access to technology, learning English, and working with computers, the women in Nueva Segovia sell coffee, corn, fruits, and make bread to sell at the local markets, which is a form of *subsisting*.

Castillo believes that improving the lives of women begins with an education that is designed to develop a strong labor force. Women are at a disadvantage when their economic well-being depends on their cash flow from outside the home, but they must also take care of the home and their family.

***

Organizers and leaders of agricultural production cooperatives, *María del Rosario Alarcón Sánchez* with the, *Agropecuaria de Mujeres Productoras de Río Blanco* (a southern department bordering Costa Rica), and *Angela Rayo with the Cooperativa Multisectorial Angela Delgado, Chinandega* (a northern department bordering Honduras), responded to questions about their work during a recent digital podcast episode delivered by *ondalocalni.com*.[31] In their remarkable stories the women discussed how they began their organizations, the innumerable rewards and benefits derived

222

from their hard work, and the obstacles that stand in the way of achieving even greater goals.

For Alarcón, the reason for creating a cooperative emerged as a *survival* strategy at the end of the revolution in the late 1980s. Families were desperate to find a way to feed their families, and subsistence farming was no longer a viable solution during this critical period. The concept of creating a cooperative was familiar to the communities, but actually leading and organizing the "movement" was difficult. Alarcón's strategy was to organize the women, a practical approach considering that so many of the community male members were at war. Not every woman had experience working in the fields, planting, harvesting, and selling their products. But, the opportunity was too great to dismiss it, and Alarcón and the women worked diligently. They were highly successful in including more and more families in their collective, thus, assuring that the women could feed their families. Although their work was not as consistent and productive from year to year, nevertheless, the women maintained the cohesiveness within their organization.

Angela Rayo's idea for organizing a cooperative was similar to Alarcón's in that she recognized the need to create a space for *survival* in the aftermath of destruction, but in her case, it was due to the hurricanes. Rayo lives in an area that was heavily affected by natural disasters. She was participating in the group clean-up tasks when she realized that the people involved could benefit from a cooperative. It was a labor of hope and love that compelled her and other women to develop an organization where they could make their own decisions concerning what to grow and when, as well as to eliminate the use of toxic chemicals. The development of a successful collective opened up opportunities for the women to become better educated and to develop specific business skills.

Both women attest to the improvements in the quality of life for the participating women and the community as a whole. They argue that the women's collectives contribute widely to the overall economy at the national level. They envision a future where the cooperatives can continue to play a vital role in improving education for all children, opening more opportunities for women to actively engage in the labor market, and to adequately address the problem of increased migration amongst the youth. However, the women have battles to fight on a variety of fronts. One of the biggest challenges is procuring land to carry out the collective's production. In order to purchase land, the women must have access to credit, which they don't qualify for, and be able to pay off the loans with exorbitant high interest rates within a short period of time. Basically, the women believe that the private and government sectors are in a position to assist them, but their investment strategies are focused on big businesses with wealthy patrons.

Toward a 'Global' Feminist Movement

The feminist movement continues to intensify from the 1990s when women were increasingly concerned with establishing their organizational work as autonomous, removed from the Sandinista movement that had abandoned their position of support for women's equal rights. The women that began the movement were reluctant to articulate their identity as feminist, in fact, some rejected the term "feminism." The conservative faction in the Sandinista ranks was a powerful force against what the feminist wanted to accomplish. They were undeterred, however, and whereas their progress might have appeared waning in the face of the country's political turmoil, the feminists remained steadfast in their beliefs in the equality of women.[32] Today, veteran feminists stand firm in their dedication as first and foremost "feminists" and their work continues to influence other women, in Nicaragua, Central America, South America, and beyond.

What is different today, of course, is the extent to which technology has facilitated the development of the feminist movement. The social networks have extended throughout the Americas and in Europe, thus, widening the worldwide web, bringing together diversified voices and promoting a unified feminist agenda.[33]

Perhaps, one of the best-known feminist movement, Argentina's *Green Wave*, brought the world's attention to the 2018 march of over a million women, with green scarfs, demanding the legalization of abortion. In 2015, the Argentinians had organized a movement *#NiUnaMenos* (not one less), in reference to the skyrocketing femicide rates. México adopted their version of similar movement, *#NiUnaMas,* which served as a unified message that women demanded of their governments to take immediate action to eradicate crimes against women and girls.

The women in Colombia extended their feminist agenda, targeting the abortion bans in their country and helping others in a similar fight as well. It is the "shared struggle" of women around the world that results in a powerful, effective campaign that strengthens the global feminist movement.[34]

In Nicaragua, university students have taken a leadership role in the feminist movement. Amaya Coppens recounts how she and her classmates joined the peaceful social protests in 2018, protesting against the Ortega Murillo repression, injustices, and violence against women.[35] The consensus is that far too many young women fall prey as victims of sexual violence in their homes. Violators are rarely prosecuted, leaving women in revictimization that prolongs their suffering. The social media, then, becomes a way to deal with the injustices, according to María José Díaz Reyes. Publicly calling out the aggressors and violators for committing crimes against women is a way of treating the victims in a dignified way, letting them know that they are not alone.

Although the feminist movement embraces the critical causes that affect women in general, the need for change in Nicaragua has its particular nuances. María José Díaz Reyes discusses the localized themes that are critical to the feminist agenda: "leadership, power, the State, coalition, violence, human rights, technology, and collective memory."[36] As a leader in the feminist movement, Díaz Reyes acknowledges the diversity amongst its members, not only in the lived experiences but in the ideas, ideologies, opinions, concerns, even in their approaches to solving pressing problems. At the base of their collective narratives, Díaz Reyes explains, are the pleas for carrying out justice reparations for the overwhelming occurrence of the *machista* violence in its various manifestations. The agenda is inclusive of all women, regardless of their political affiliation.

Concluding Remarks

The challenges facing Nicaraguan feminists are immense, and with their freedoms indefinitely suspended, their future may appear bleak. However, they are emboldened by the overwhelming national and international support of feminists who are passionate about effecting change, despite the seemingly inexorable circumstances. Everyday resistance strengthens women's determination to break through the chains of gender-specific repression. They realize that their fight is revolutionary, and their efforts illuminate the power of sisterhood and the lessons that they can pass on to the rest of the world.[37]

***

Discussion and Reflection Questions

1. Share your thoughts concerning the United States foreign policy toward Nicaragua in the late 1800s and early twentieth century. What do you think was behind Nicaragua's plan to allow the United States into their country? What lessons can you extract from this historical period?

2. Discuss your views about Sandino's heroism. Why was he so popular throughout Latin America, especially after his death?

3. Describe the challenges of women during the Somoza era who aspired to a professional role in society?

4. Share your thoughts on whether Nora Astorga's actions in the killing of the National Guard general was justified?

5. What motivated the women, Dora María Tellez, Doris Tijerino, and Nora Astorga, to join the FSLN guerrilla? Share your opinions on whether you agreed or not with their decision.

6. Describe Rosario Murillo's powerful role as Vice President. Do you

believe that she was antifeminist? Discuss your ideas.

7. Do you think that the Ortega Murillo regime should be held accountable for the assassinations of over 300 people that were peacefully protesting during the 2018 Rebellion? If so, how? If not, what can be done to ensure that this kind of tragedy doesn't happen again?

8. Discuss the imprisonment of the political prisoners. Did Ortega Murillo accomplish what they intended to do so with the arrest and incarceration of these individuals? Should they be held accountable?

9. Are there other effective means by which the United and States and/or the international community can convince the Ortega Murillo regime to release the political prisoners?

10. Describe some of the democratic initiatives undertaken by the Sandinistas in the early 1980s. When did the democratic ideals began to change and how? What actions were the most corrosive by the Ortega Murillo regime in attacking democracy?

11. According to the research, women who were sexually assaulted or abused while serving in the FSLN guerrilla are reluctant to file formal complaints against their attackers due to the "profound silence." Describe what you think are the circumstance of women who are reluctant to seek justice for crimes committed against them.

12. In the case of Perla, what steps would you take to investigate the reasons why the community in which she lived shunned her and her children, and attempted to obstruct a police investigation into her murder.

13. In your opinion why do Nicaraguan women have such serious labor problems in the workplace. What do you think can facilitate the improvement of women's labor in the rural areas?

14. What future do you foresee for the younger generation of Nicaraguan women who are entering a world of technological advances and at the same time, live in a repressive, authoritative society?

Conclusion

History is the study of change, but the study of history itself is a transformative method of transcultural knowledge that engages in a dialogic reprise between the readers and the protagonists. The women featured in this study serve as protagonists who represent in general terms, the lived experiences of human beings during a period of intense crises. As women, they share narratives of survival, struggle, and reclamation. The initial questions that framed this study remain at the forefront, but the responses have become more complex and nuanced, reflecting a mature understanding of reality from disparate points of view. A "birds-eye view," which involves employing a contrasting analysis, is particularly applicable in this context. Transculturality challenges the reader to produce authentic interpretations, drawing on the assurance that the analysis of the text is based on the subjects' perceptions of reality and truth.

Given the recent series of tumultuous events in El Salvador, Guatemala, and Nicaragua, it is clear that the violent conflicts of the past persist in the present. However, it is also evident that the majority of citizens in all three countries reject any organized acts of violent aggressions. Currently, resistance is the prevailing mode of fighting against injustices, repression, and criminalization of human rights defenders, and women are in the forefront.

One of the most significant advancements in recent times is the emergence of innovative and distinctive feminisms that have garnered both praise and criticism worldwide. In Guatemala, feminist activism is rooted in a diverse range of identities, including indigenous and non-indigenous, and a combination or blend of both. Meanwhile, Nicaragua and El Salvador have established a remarkable foundation of professional feminists who are deeply committed to addressing social, economic, and political issues. Feminists from all three countries play crucial roles in the movements specific to the

Americas, such as #niunamenos and #niunamas. The feminists represent women from a wide range of backgrounds and social strata, with a particular focus on addressing gender-based structural violence. Rather than being revolutionary combatants, the front-line resistance fighters are made up of a diverse group of human rights defenders.

The Clandestine Resistance

Who are the women, the resistance fighters (las luchadoras)? According to the umbrella organization of human rights defenders, the Iniciativa Mesoamericana de Mujeres Defensoras de Derechos Humanos (IM-Defensoras), these women promote freedom, equality, and justice each day, and more than likely in difficult circumstances where fending off discriminatory practices and gender violence is a daily routine.[1] The network core serves to create and/or strengthen links between and among organizations that promote in their mission and in action the solidarity and protection for human rights defenders. Their on-line newsletter, el Boletín, is the essential communication tool to disseminate reports and "alert" messages that direct its membership to take immediate action. The networks create "safe" spaces for women, more so virtually rather than physically, to help other women defenders, which serves to spread their work and engage others in their activism.[2] Generally, they are invisible, unless, of course, their work propels them into the public eye, which may endanger their well-being as well as their families. They are mothers searching for their children, who purportedly have been murdered; teachers clamoring for a quality education accessible to all students; a factory worker demanding better working conditions and decent wages; a feminist/activist demanding equal rights for the LGTBI communities; community leaders in indigenous regions defending their ancestral rights to their territories; feminists insisting on abolishing the criminalization of abortion and in acquiring reproductive rights for all women; the journalists that expose corruption and abuse of power among politicians and in certain cases, how they are linked to criminal organizations. Initially, their protestations were lost in darkness, but since the rise of the resistance movement, a "cry in the dark" has been invariably replaced with a clamor for justice. Ensuring the safety and well-being of women defenders of paramount importance, and the IM_Defensoras organization takes deliberate steps to prioritize individual security as a central aspect of their work. For example, the human rights "defensoras" work in pairs or small groups and take extra precaution by maintaining a low profile by never revealing their identities, and they each follow a routine of self-help and support exercises.

Elvira Cuadra Lira, a sociologist who recently published a thorough, clear-cut report on violence against women in Nicaragua since the rebellion of 2018, comments on the emergence of a broad, formative resistance created by women who consider themselves as protagonists in their mission as agents of change.[3] Summarizing the comments from her research subjects and dedicating her publication to the incarcerated political prisoners in Nicaragua, Cuadra Lira believes that women are steadfast in their long-standing desire to fully participate in a democratic society as they choose.

Observing and monitoring human rights violations against women has long been the purview of organizations associated with the United Nations and related associations. However, the Central American countries have stepped up their efforts in the documentation processes. The IM-Defensoras organization has created a centralized registry of aggressions, constructed in conjunction with various networks in the region, including El Salvador, Nicaragua, Guatemala, Honduras, and Mexico. In their latest report, covering the period between January to August of 2022, the IM-Defensoras documented approximately 2,6215 aggressions against 504 defenders of human rights and 95 (human rights) organizations. Amongst these are the assassinations of two Mexican women who were searching for their disappeared loved ones ("buscadoras de personas desaparecidas"). The list of violations includes various acts of physical and verbal harassment, hostility, and threats against defenders, as well as instances of hostile surveillance and in some cases, even against their family members. Cuadro Liga adds other documented violations, such as political violence specifically directed toward women organizations, youthful protestors who are often violently beaten, women leaders that blatantly oppose the government - many of whom are feminists, women who publicly denounce human rights violations, journalists that expose a politician's malfeasance, defenders of political prisoners, and cyber-activists. Overall, the state military, paramilitary or policing actors in each country are responsible for carrying out the violence, although the governments share the blame for the repressive conditions that exacerbate the degree by which the pain and punitive measures are inflicted upon the victims. In Nicaragua, structural violence against women is systematic, as highlighted by Cuadra Liga's research. At the heart of the crisis is the state's egregious campaign to promote representations of women that reinforce a false image of *subordination* in a deeply patriarchal society. The violence, which has manifested in multiple forms, has been particularly exacerbated since the Covid-19 pandemic. This has had a huge impact on women in general and specifically, on a large population of women in single-parent households.

After the victorious Nicaraguan Revolution in 1979, a burgeoning feminist social movement gave rise to the collective belief that equality for women was a reality even in the face of a crushing patriarchal presence. That was a "promise" by the Sandinista directorate according to the overwhelming testimonies of women who fought in the FSLN frente. Instead, in the present conditions of a fractured society, the chaotic structural violence against feminists serves as a constant reminder of the complete reversal of that promise. Women who choose to continue the struggle for equality face the threat of "criminalization." If convicted, this can have enormous and impactful consequences not only for themselves but also for their families. The acts of struggle and resistance are perceived as treachery by the (Sandinista) regime, even when women risked their lives fighting in the revolution for these freedoms. The subject of the criminalization of women is the dominant theme in a report published by CEJIL (Center for Justice and International Law) and IM-Defensoras, title, "Perseguidos por defender y resistir: Criminalización de mujeres defensoras de derechos humanos en Honduras, México, y Nicaragua."[4] The author(s) explain that criminalization, as defined by the Comisión Interamericano de Derechos Humanos (CIDH) in 2015, refers to the manipulation of the state's extrajudicial power with the objectives to control, punish, and/or deter the work of human rights defenders. These types of cases involve arbitrary detentions based on unfounded or fabricated charges, and unnecessary prolonged judicial processes. Their practices of coercion, extortion, and threats push the boundaries of the legal system, yet no one challenges their actions. The perpetrators are state actors that can use (or abuse) their official positions to carry out these illegitimate processes with impunity. The human rights defenders caught in a web of corruption are given lengthy prison sentences under torturous conditions. Particularly targeted for unusually cruel and hard punishments are women in general, specifically feminists, of all ages but mostly young, and members of the indigenous and afro-descendent communities, as well as the LBGTI.[5]

In Guatemala, one of the well-known cases of criminalization is that of *María Magdalena Cuc Choc,* who on June 21, 2022, was convicted of aggravated usurpation (usurpación agravada) and sentenced to a two-year commutable prison term. Since her initial arrest in 2016, María Choc had disputed the charges against her, claiming that she didn't commit a crime when she served as an interpreter (Q'eqchi'-Spanish) for a Maya Q'eqchi' community facing a violent eviction by the mining company, Lisbal, S.A. in the department of Izabal. The Guatemalan penal system kept María Choc under a prolonged judicial process without substantial evidence and under a threat of a lengthy internment.[6] The state penal system continues to criminalize human rights defenders, and incidents of physical and verbal aggressions have recently increased in their severity and gross injustices. The IM-Defensoras organization points to the accumulation of 884 aggressions, including 39 assassinations during 2017-2018, each related to human rights defenders' protecting indigenous ancestral territories against extractive corporations. In some cases, entire communities experienced violent evictions of their homes.[7] The Guatemala government has allowed the escalation of criminalization cases against human rights defenders, rejecting the pleas from international organizations such as the Guatemalan Human Rights Commission (GHRC). In their latest investigative report, the *GHRC* concludes the following:

> *Through our visit, we observed abuses of power that reveal a coordinated government strategy to crush those who oppose the kleptocratic takeover of Guatemala. This strategy includes the criminalization, intimidation, harassment, surveillance, and defamation of defenders as well as serious violence.*[8]

A recently published Salvadoran investigative report, "Defendiendo derechos humanos en contextos de crisis," combines the work of eleven organizations that represent human rights defenders in both gender-related areas and journalism.[9] The report includes the analysis on data collected from two registries, the Salvadoran network, la Red Salvadoreña de Defensoras de Derechos Humanos, and the other consisting of two monitoring systems, Fundación de Estudios para la Aplicación del Derecho (FESPAD) and el Servicio Social Pasionista (SPASS). The gender-based organizations reported in their findings that from January to April of 2022, 246 aggressions occurred, and amongst media sources, 415 journalists experienced aggressions. While the aggressions targeted both men and women, the data show that the females were victimized in harsher terms. The aggressions against female human rights defenders were described as intimidations, assaults and threats, and victims of cyberbulling.[10] Compared to their male counterparts, the women's aggressions were contextualized within a misogynistic environment. The fact that these aggressions were recorded during the first half of 2022, brings into the discussion the impact of the Covid-19 pandemic and the chaotic human rights violations as a result of the Régimen de Excepción, which essentially allows the enforcement units to violate human rights as their prerogative. It's noteworthy to mention that documented reports list the principal perpetrators of human rights violations as state security units, including the military, as well as those emanating from the presidential offices.

Due to the clandestine nature of the resistance, one can only speculate the number of people involved, who they are, or how they manage to escape arrest and detention. But, we can discern from the published reports that a vast number of human rights defenders are feminists who believe that it's worth fighting for democracy, in whatever way they can. Their voices are clear in articulating what they believe is essential in a democratic society: a country where every citizen can duly exercise their freedoms and rights; where they can work with tranquility in spaces where their voices are heard; where their differences serve to strengthen their collective and not divide them; and where each person can walk freely without fear.[11]

In pursuit of free and independent elections is another constant clamor among human rights defenders, as declared in a statement of purpose by a Nicaraguan organization (urnasabiertas.com): "to describe and prevent the consolidation of authoritative regimes in future democracies."[12] Through their collaboration and participation in the solidarity networks, the women believe in the transformative journey of reconstructing new ways of learning, building, and *becoming* with the world.[13]

NOTES

Introduction (pp.1-13)

1. Pierre Bourdieu, *In Other Words: Essays Towards a Reflective Sociology* (Palo Alto, CA: Stanford University Press, 1990), 137.

2. Irmgard Emmelhainz, *Toxic Loves, Impossible Futures: Feminist Living as Resistance* (Nashville, TN: Vanderbilt University Press, 2022), 54.

3. According to the Migration Policy Institute, 2.1 million, first and second-generation Salvadorans, live in the United States. See "The Salvadoran Diaspora in the United States," migrationpolicy.org, June 2015, accessible at https://www.migrationpolicy.org/sites/default/files/publications/RAD-FullSet.pdf. The Pew Research Center estimates that 1.4 Guatemalans live in the U.S. See "Facts on Hispanics of Guatemalan Origin in the United States, 2017," accessible at https://www.pewresearch.org/hispanic/fact-sheet/u-s-hispanics-facts-on-guatemalan-origin-latinos/. See "Number of Displaced Nicaraguans in Costa Rica Doubles in Less Than a Year," on the fact that 150,000 Nicaraguans sought asylum in Costa Rica in an eight-month period (Aug. 2021 to March 2022), accessible at https://www.unhcr.org/en-us/news/briefing/2022/3/623d894c4/number-displaced-nicaraguans-costa-rica-doubles-year.html. The Pew Research Center estimates that 464,000 Nicaraguans live in the United States, however, huge numbers are continue to cross the border, as many as 72,000 in 2021, according to the Border Patrol, accessible at cbp.gov, U.S. Customs and Border Protection, accessible at https://www.cbp.gov/newsroom/stats/southwest-land-border-encounters.

4. See Stefan Levitsky and Lucan Way, "The New Competitive Authoritarianism," *Journal of Democracy, 31*(1), (2020): 1-15, Nancy Bermeo, "On Democratic Backsliding," *Journal of Democracy, 27*(1), (2016): 5-19, Thomas Carothers and Benjamin Press, "Understanding and Responding to Global Democratic Backsliding," *Journal of Democracy, 33*(1), (2022): 5-19.

5. Karen Kampwirth, *Women in Guerrilla Movements: Nicaragua, El*

Salvador, Chiapas, Cuba (University Park, PA: Pennsylvania State University Press, 2002).

6. John Foran, *Taking Power: On Origins of Third World Revolutions* (UK: Cambridge University Press, 2005).

7. Ilja Luciak, *After the Revolution: Gender and Democracy in El Salvador, Nicaragua, Guatemala* (Baltimore: Johns Hopkins University Press, 2001).

8. Ibid.

9. David Carey, *Oral history in Latin America: Unlocking the Spoken Archive* (NY: Routledge, 2017).

10. Martha Ackelsberg, *Free Women of Spain: Anarchism and the Struggle for the Emancipation of Women* (Oakland, CA: AK Press, 2005), 227.

11. The women's unit was named after Mariana Grajales Cuello, born in early 1800's, a mother of thirteen children, some of whom fought and died heroically in the Ten Years War (1868-1878). Grajales was known for her bravery and diligence as a field nurse in the battlefield. She was forced into exile in Jamaica but continued her work until her death in 1893. See Mary Alice Waters, ed., *Teté Puebla and the Mariana Grajales Women's Platoon in Cuba's Revolutionary War 1956-58* (NY: Pathfinder Press, 2003).

12. See Michelle Chase, *Revolution Within the Revolution: Women and Gender Politics in Cuba, 1952-1962* (Chapel Hill: The University of North Carolina, 2016).

13. See Irmgard Emmelhainz, *Toxic Loves, Impossible Futures: Feminist Living as Resistance,* 10-15. For an in-depth analysis on intersectionality from a legal, feminist perspective, see Kimberle Crenshaw, "Demarginalizing the Intersection of Race and Sex: A Black Feminist Critique of Antidiscrimination Doctrine, Feminist Theory, and Antiracist Politics," in *Feminist Legal Theory: Readings in Law and Gender*, eds. Katherine Bartlett and Rosanne Kennedy (NY: Routledge 2019), 57-58. For information about Latin American scholarship on historiography of female activism see Marysa Navarro, "Research on Latin American Women," *Signs,* 5(1), (1979): 111-120.

14. Catriona Macleod & Kevin Durrheim, "Foucauldian Feminism: The Implications of Governmentality," *Journal for the Theory of Social Behaviour, 32*(1), (2002): 41-60.

15. Catriona Macleod & Kevin Durrheim, "Foucauldian Feminism: The Implications of Governmentality." See also Michel Foucault, "The Subject and Power." *Critical inquiry, 8*(4), (1982): 777–795. http://www.jstor.org/stable/1343197

16. Amrita Basu, "Globalization of the Local/Localization of the Global Mapping Transnational Women's Movements, " in *Feminist Theory Reader: Local and Global Perspectives*, eds. Carole R. McCann, Seung-Kyung Kim, and Emek Ergun (NY: Routledge 2021), 38-44.

17. Jan Blommaert, *Ethnography, Superdiversity and Linguistic Landscapes: Chronicles of Complexity* (Bristol, UK: Multilingual Matters, Ltd. 2013), 195. See also, Steven Vertovec, "Super-diversity and Its Implications," *Ethnic and Racial Studies 30*(6), (2007): 1024-1054.

18. For reference and further discussion see book on the rhizomatic philosophical concept, i.e., multiple non-hierarchical entry and exit points: Gilles Deleuze and Felix Gauttari, *A Thousand Plateaus* (Minneapolis, MN: University of Minnesota Press, 1980).

19. Jan Blommaert, *Ethnography, Superdiversity and Linguistic landscapes: Chronicles of Complexity*, 217.

Chapter One (pp.14-69)

1. Jane S. Jaquette, "Women in Revolutionary Movements in Latin America," *Journal of Marriage and Family, Vol. 35*, No. 2 (1973): 344-354.

2. "From Madness to Hope: The Twelve-year War in El Salvador" ("De la locura a la esperanza: la guerra de doce años en El Salvador"), *Report of the Truth Commission for El Salvador* (New York: United Nations, 1993), https://www.usip.org/publications/1992/07/truth-commission-el-salvador.

3. For a comprehensive analysis, see Jeff Goodwin, *No Other Way Out: States and Revolutionary Movements, 1945-1991.* (UK: Cambridge, 2001).

4. Armed conflicts have erupted , for example, in the following countries: Chile, 1973; Argentina, 1966; Bolivia, 1969; Peru, 1968.

5. See for example, Cate Buchanan and Joaquín Chávez, *Negotiating Disarmament: Guns and Violence in El Salvador Peace Negotiations* (Geneva: Centre for Humanitarian Dialogue, 2008); and, also Raymond Bonner, *Weakness and Deceit: U.S. Policy and El Salvador* (NY: Times Books, 1984).

6. Joaquín Chávez, *Poets and Prophets of the Resistance: Intellectuals and the Origins of El Salvador's War* (UK: Oxford University Press, 2017).

7. Marti was born on May 5, 1893 and died on Feb. 1, 1932; Sandino was born on May 18, 1895 and died Feb 21,1934; both were assassinated.

8. Tommie Sue Montgomery, *Revolution in El Salvador: From Civil Strife to Civil Peace* (Boulder: Westview Press, 1995), 37.

9. See "Scar of Memory," Documentary (*Cicatriz de la memoria),* (San Salvador: Museo de la Palabra y de la Imágen). https://youtu.be/mLZTTxddCZg

10. Tommie Sue Montgomery, *Revolution in El Salvador,* 23-80.

11. Jeffrey Gould and Aldo Lauria-Santiago, *To Rise in Darkness: Revolution, Repression, and Memory in El Salvador 1920-1931* (Durham, NC: Duke University Press, 2008), 219.

12. See discussion on Rappaport's research in Jeffrey Gould and Aldo Lauria-Santiago, *To Rise in Darkness,* 258: (*What is unique about the Salvadoran experience is that the decisive cultural changes took place against the backdrop of the massacres of 1932*); and Tommie Sue Montgomery, *Revolution in El Salvador,* 37: (*Anyone in Indian dress or anyone running from the security forces was fair game*).

13. Alejandro Ramiro Chan, "The Resilience and Resistance of the Nahuat Pipil People of El Salvador." (Cultural Survival, May 8, 2020), accessible https://www.culturalsurvival.org/news/resilience-and-resistance-nahuat-pipil-peoples-el-salvador

14. See Raymond Bonner, *Weakness and Deceit,* 52. For example: 90 percent of the wealth of the country is held by about one half of one percent of the population. Thirty or 40 families own nearly everything in the country.

15. Joaquín Chávez, *Poets and Prophets of the Resistance,* 84.

16. See Dara Kerr, "Ghosts of El Salvador," (UC Berkeley Graduate School of Journalism), https://escholarship.org/uc/item/85f7b8zj. Also, "Memorias Bajo el Volcán," (San Salvador: Museo de la Palabra y de la Imágen), http://museo.com.sv/2012/07/la-cayetana-memorias-bajo-el-volcan/.

17. Joaquín Chávez, *Poets and Prophets of the Resistance,* 162.

18. Tommie Sue Montgomery, *Revolution in El Salvador*, 54.

19. See Raymond Bonner, *Weakness and Deceit.* In 1960 adult literacy was at 49 percent and 30 percent in rural areas; World Bank reported that only 8 percent of rural children, ages 13-15, were in school in 1970s.

20. See Richard C. Haggarty, *El Salvador: A Country Study* (Library of Congress, [November 1988]), 32-36, 235. The Anticommunist Wars of Elimination Liberation of Armed Forces (FALANGE) emerged in 1975. The exact number of death squads is unclear, but one group took the name of the former dictator/president, General Maximiliano Hernández Martínez Anticommunist Brigade. The General admired the fascist leaders of his era and sent his officers for training in Germany, Italy, and Spain. The consequences of this alliance could not have been more tragic: twenty years later when, between 1979 and 1983, the U.S. supported the Salvadoran military's brutal crackdown on mostly non-combatant civilians, and was largely responsible for the killing of 30,000 people,. The right-wing, death squad terrorism peaked during 1980-1982 when murders numbered about 700-800 a month.

21. See analysis in Tommie Sue Montgomery, *Revolution in El Salvador.* The most notable assassinations were Catholic priests Nicolás Rodríguez, Rutilio Grande, and Alfonso Navarro; Archbishop Oscar Romero was assassinated while celebrating Mass on March 24, 1980.

22. For example, see Mark Danner, *The Massacre at El Mozote* (NY: Vintage Books, 1994).

23. See Laura Pedraza Fariña, Spring Miller, and James L. Cavallaro, No Place to Hide: Gang, State, and Clandestine Violence in El Salvador (Cambridge: Harvard University Press, 2010).

24. Raymond Bonner, *Weakness and Deceit,* 171.

25. Joaquín Chávez, *Poets and Prophets of the Resistance*, 8.

26. Chávez, *Poets and Prophets of the Resistance,* 13.

27. Chávez, *Poets and Prophets of the Resistance*, 45.

28. Ibid.

29. Julia Denise Shayne, "Gendered Revolutionary Bridges: A Feminist Theory of Revolution," (Prepared for delivery at the 1998 meeting of the Latin American Studies Association, The Palmer House Hilton Hotel, Chicago, IL, September 24-26, 1998), 24.

30. Tommie Sue Montgomery, *Revolution in El Salvador,* 60.

31. Tommie Sue Montgomery, *Revolution in El Salvador*, 51-80.

32. Joaquín Chávez, *Poets and Prophets of the Resistance*, 55.

33. Tommie Sue Montgomery, *Revolution in El Salvador,* 64.

34. Joaquín Chávez, *Poets and Prophets of the Resistance*, 64.

35. Tommie Sue Montgomery, *Revolution in El Salvador,* 67.

36. Tommie Sue Montgomery, *Revolution in El Salvador*, 67.

37. Joaquín Chávez, *Poets and Prophets of the Resistance*, 80.

38. Chávez, *Poets and Prophets of the Resistance*, 163-194.

39. Alberto Martín Alvarez and Eudald Cortina Orero, "The Genesis and Internal Dynamics of El Salvador's People's Revolutionary Army, 1970-1976." *Journal of Latin American Studies, (*November 2014), https://www.cambridge.org/core/journals/journal-of-latin-american-studies/article/genesis-and-internal-dynamics-of-el-salvadors-peoples-revolutionary-army-19701976/5115E4A593CC21E6FCE84A7B75800A4B. Lil Milagro Ramírez' poems are accessible at this site: "Twelve Poems by Female Fighters." (Guernica, 2020), https://www.guernicamag.com/twelve-poems-by-female-fighters/

40. Tommie Sue Montgomery, *Revolution in El Salvador*, 83.

41. Tommie Sue Montgomery, *Revolution in El Salvador*, 83.

42. Tommie Sue Montgomery, *Revolution in El Salvador, 85*

43. Tommie Sue Montgomery, *Revolution in El Salvador*, 84.

44. Joaquín Chávez, *Poets and Prophets of the Resistance* 61.

45. Joaquín Chávez, *Poets and Prophets of the Resistance*, 138.

46. Joaquín Chávez, *Poets and Prophets of the Resistance*, 139.

47. Joaquín Chávez, *Poets and Prophets of the Resistance.* 142.

48. Joaquín Chávez, *Poets and Prophets of the Resistance*, 148.

49. Mélida Anaya Montes was murdered on April 6, 1979 in Managua, Nicaragua. The "war economy" impact on education included the following: between 1980 and 1984, 4,500 teachers left El Salvador; over 1,200 primary schools were shuttered; illiteracy rate grew to 65 percent and in some rural areas – 90 percent. For additional facts see Tommie Sue Montgomery, *Revolution in El Salvador,* 190.

50. Tommie Sue Montgomery, *Revolution in El Salvador, 82.*

51. Tommie Sue Montgomery, *Revolution in El Salvador*, 97-99.

52. In the United Nations document, "From Madness to Hope: Report on the Commission on the Truth for El Salvador," Major Roberto D'Aubuisson ordered the assassination of Archbishop Oscar Romero. The report is accessible at https://www.usip.org/sites/default/files/file/ElSalvador-Report.pdf

53. In 1984, Sergeant Colindres Alemán and the four guardsmen were charged, convicted and sentenced to 30 years in prison; later, Col. Vides Casanova was charged for his involvement.

54. Raymond Bonner, *Weakness and Deceit,* 634.

55. "From Madness to Hope," report of the Commission on the Truth for El Salvador (2001) details the following: 22,000 human rights violation complaints; 60 percent extrajudicial killings; 25 percent disappearances; 20 percent tortured. 85 percent of all deaths and disappearances attributed to the government forces of El Salvador and 5 percent attributed to the FMLN. Accessible report, https://www.usip.org/sites/default/files/file/ElSalvador-Report.pdf

56. Joaquín Chávez, *Poets and Prophets of the Resistance*, 257, N44.

57. Bryan Manewal and David Stark, "Religion in the Trenches: Liberation Theology and Evangelical Protestantism as Tools of Social Control in the Guatemalan Civil War (1960-1996)." *McNair Scholars Journal* (2007), 53.

58. Raymond Bonner, *Weakness and Deceit,* 598.

59. Ibid, 545.

60. See Cate Buchanan and Joaquín Chávez, *Negotiating Disarmament.* Approximately six billion USD were spent by the United States on the Salvadoran Civil War.

61. It was known as "Operación Rescate" and the Atlacatl Battalion, the elite, highly trained and equipped by the United States with machine-gun helicopters and heavy artillery, stormed into the area, destroying everything in its path.

62. Tommie Sue Montgomery, *Revolution in El Salvador, 149.*

63. Raymond Bonner, *Weakness and Deceit,* 478.

64. Raymond Bonner, *Weakness and Deceit,* 480.

65. Ilja Luciak, *After the Revolution: Gender and Democracy in El Salvador, Nicaragua, and Guatemala.* (Baltimore: Johns Hopkins University Press, 2001), 11-13.

65. For discussion on this topic, see Lisa Baldez, *Why Women Protest: Women's Movements in Chile* (UK: Cambridge University Press, 2004).

66. Norma Vásquez, Cristina Ibañez, Clara Murguialdy, *Mujeres-Montaña: Vivencias de guerrilleras y colaboradoras de FMLN.* (San Salvador: Centro Cultural de España en El Salvador, 2020), https://issuu.com/publicacionesaecid/docs/pdf_isuu_mujeres_monta_a .

67. Karen Kampwirth, *Women in Guerrilla Movements: Nicaragua, El Salvador, Chiapas, Cuba.* (University Park, PA: Pennsylvania State University Press, 2002).

68. Joaquín Chávez, *Poets and Prophets of the Resistance,* 63.

69. Kampwirth notes that 25.5 percent of her respondents were students.

70. Joaquín Chávez, *Poets and Prophets of the Resistance,* 68.

71. Tommie Sue Montgomery, *Revolution in El Salvador,* 125.

72. Tommie Sue Montgomery, *Revolution in El Salvador,* 121.

73. Raymond Bonner, *Weakness and Deceit,* 561.

74. Tommie Sue Montgomery, *Revolution in El Salvador,* 120-121.

75. See photo album (caution: some graphic images), Guazapa, https://www.alamy.com/stock-photo/guazapa.html

76. Ilja Luciak, *After the Revolution, 70-72.*

77. Karen Kampwirth, *Women in Guerrilla Movements, 59-81.*

78. Kampwirth includes Aguinada's real name because she is a public figure, having run for office and elected to Congress in 1994, representing the FMLN.

79. Karen Kampwirth, *Women in Guerrilla Movements, 137-155.*

80. For more information and discussion on how women were discriminated against see Ilja Luciak, *After the Revolution,* 15; and Leigh Binford, "Hegemony in the Interior of Salvadoran Revolution: The ERP in Northern Morazán." *Journal of Latin American Anthropology (1999)*: 24-27.

81. Karen Kampwirth, *Women in Guerrilla Movements, 78-79.*

82. Lynn Stephen, *Women and Social Movements in Latin America: Power From Below* (Austin, TX: University of Texas Press, 1997), 67-84.

83. Sonia Alvarez, Elisabeth Jay Friedman, Ericka Beckman, Maylei Blackwell, Norma Stoltz Chinchilla, Nathalie Lebon, Marysa Navarro, and Marcela Ríos Tobar, "Encountering Latin American and Caribbean Feminisms." (*Signs: Journal of Women in Culture and Society*, 2002).

84. Las Dignas, "Una Década Construyendo Feminismo." (El Salvador: Las Dignas, 2000). Accessible at https://www.lasdignas.org.sv.

85. Lynn Stephen, *Women and Social Movements in Latin America*, 72.

86. Lynn Stephen, ed., *Hear My Testimony: María Teresa Tula, Human Rights Activist of El Salvador*. (Boston: South End Press, 1994), 210.

87. See Las Dignas for information on their work and sources of international funding, https://www.lasdignas.org.sv.

88. Las Dignas, "Una Década Construyendo Feminism," Accessible at https://www.lasdignas.org.sv.

89. Elisabeth Jean Wood, *Insurgent Collective Action and Civil War in El Salvador* (UK: Cambridge University Press, 2003), 260.

90. United Nations Beijing Platform for Action of 1994-95 can be accessed, https://www.un.org/womenwatch/daw/beijing/platform/.

91. The UN Convention on the Elimination of All Forms of Discrimination against Women (CEDAW) can be accessed at https://tbinternet.ohchr.org/_layouts/15/treatybodyexternal/Download.aspx?symbolno=CEDAW%2fC%2fSLV%2fCO%2f8-9&Lang=en.

92. See nbcnews.com article, "A Woman Lost Her Pregnancy But Was Jailed For Abortion. She Later Died," https://www.nbcnews.com/news/latino/woman-lost-pregnancy-was-jailed-abortion-later-died-rcna440.

1. Ilja Luciak, *After the Revolution: Gender and Democracy in El Salvador, Nicaragua, and Guatemala* (Baltimore: Johns Hopkins University Press, 2001), 39-49.

2. "Una década construyendo feminismo: Las Dignas" (El Salvador: Las Dignas, 2000), 60-64. Document acccessible at https://www.lasdignas.org.sv/una-decada-construyendo-feminismo-dignas-2000/.

3. Ibid.

4. Norma Vásquez, Cristina Ibañez, Clara Murguialdy, *Mujeres-Montaña: Vivencias de Guerrilleras y Colaboradoras de FMLN* (San Salvador: Centro Cultural de España en El Salvador, 2020). NOTE: In their analysis, 60,000 women participated in the war; out of the 13,000 men and women mobilized in the guerrillas, 30 percent were women. The number of women reportedly killed in the war is a staggering 5,293. Document accessible at https://issuu.com/publicacionesaecid/docs/pdf_isuu_mujeres_monta_a.

5. Beth Verhey, "The Demobilization and Reintegration of Child Soldiers: El Salvador Case Study" (World Bank, 2001). Verhey acknowledges gratitude to José Simeón Cañas Universidad Centroamericana, UCA, specifically José Miquel Cruz, Rubi Esmeralda Arana and María Santacruz Giralt. Also, UNICEF El Salvador, Ximena de la Barra and Jean Gough, and Rädda Barnen, and Jon Skurdal; and ACISAM, Ernestina Chávez, Ilene Cohn, Father Jon Cortina, Suleyna Durán, Marcelo Fabre, Homies Unidos and Andrew Russell.

6. Alan Marcelo Henríquez Chávez, "De la Locura a Las Esperanza Truncada: Memorias de Desarme, Desmovilización, y Reinserción de Excombatientes en El Salvador Posconflicto." Tesis, Maestro en historia moderna y contemporánea (México: Instituto Mora, 2018). Document accessible at https://mx.boell.org/sites/default/files/tesis_alan_marcelo_henriquez_chavez.pdf. The author conducted the interviews in 2017 and 2018.

7. "Interview with Srta. Ana Guadalupe Martínez by Jean Krasno," dag.un.org, United Nations Dag Hammarskjold Library, June 21, 1997, accessible at http://dag.un.org/handle/11176/89669.

8. Ana Guadalupe Martínez, *Las cárceles clandestinas* (El Salvador: UCA Editores, 1992).

9. Luciak, *After the Revolution, 30.*

10. Esther Portillo-Gonzales, "FMLN Reflections, 20 Years Later: An Interview with Nidia Díaz," *NACLA Report on the Americas, Vol.45*(1), (2012), 55-57. Díaz published, *Nunca estuve sola* (Colección Testigos de la historia) Spanish Edition. (El Salvador: UCA Editores, 1988). The English version is titled, *I Was Never Alone.*

11. Marta Harneker, "Los Retos de la Mujer Dirigente," (Cuba: Ediciones MEPLA, 1994). Document accessible at https://www.rebelion.org/docs/95820.pdf. Lorena Peña is the author of *Relatos de Mi Vida* (NY: Ocean Press, 2009).

12. Mélida Anaya Montes, *Ana María Combatiente de la Vida* (NY: Ocean Sur, editorial latinoamericana, (2013).

13. Febe Elizabeth Vásquez, "Fenastras en la Calle," YouTube interview with Velásquez, accessible at https://youtu.be/mfKFksly5PM. This 1989 interview was recorded shortly before her death.

14. "The Story of Alicia Emelina Panameno de García (1945-2010)," interview by embraceingelsalvador.org, Afflicted with Hope, in English and Spanish, October 15, 2012, accessible at https://www.embracingelsalvador.org/alicia-de-garcia/#/-1/.

15. The Bruno Kreisky Foundation for Human Rights awarded the 1984 prize to Marianella García Villas; Bruno Kreisky was a successful socialist Austrian Chancellor.

16. Joaquín Chávez, *Poets and Prophets of the Resistance: Intellectuals and the Origins of El Salvador's War* (UK: Oxford University Press, 2017), 166.

17. "Lil Milagro Ramírez," a brief biography by guernicamag.com, Guernica, accessible at https://www.guernicamag.com/author/lil-milagro-ramirez/.

18. "From Madness to Hope: The Twelve-year War in El Salvador" (De la locura a la esperanza: la guerra de doce años en El Salvador). Report

of the Truth Commission for El Salvador. New York: United Nations,
1993, https://www.usip.org/publications/1992/07/truth-commission-el-
salvador. Lagadec and García Arandigoyen cases are found in the following
section: *IV. Cases and Patterns of Violence, B., 2., h and i.*

19. Ibid.

Chapter Three (pp.92-140)

1. Ana Silvia Monzón, "Entre Líneas: Participación Política de las
Mujeres en la Década 1944-54," (Tesina del Diplomado en Especialización
en Estudios de Género, Fundación Guatemala/Universidad Rafael
Landívar, Guatemala, 1998).

2.Ana Silvia Monzón, *Las Mujeres, los Feminismos y los Movimientos
Sociales en Guatemala: Relaciones, Articulaciones y Desencuentros,*
(Facultad Latinoamericana de Ciencias Sociales FLACSO-Sede Académico
Guatemala, 2021). Accessible at
https://www.puees.unam.mx/curso2021/materiales/Sesion13/Monzon_Las
MujeresLosFeminismosYLosMovimientosSociales.pdf.

3. See Michael D. Coe and Stephen Houston, *The Maya.* (NY:
Thames & Hudson, 2015).

4. Christopher H. Lutz and W. George Lovell, "Core and Periphery in
Colonial Guatemala," in *Guatemalan Indians and the State: 1940 to 1998,*
ed. Carol A. Smith (Austin: University of Texas Press, 1990), 35-51.

5. CEH (Comisión para el Esclarecimiento Histórico). *Guatemala
Memoria del Silencio* (Guatemala Memory of Silence). *Conclusions and
Recommendations.* (Guatemala City: United Nations Office for Project
Service, 1999). Accessible at https://www.aaas.org/sites/default/files/s3fs-
public/mos_en.pdf?adobe_mc=MCMID%3D31219200981284036790026633326666170976%7CMCORGID%3D242B6472541199F70A4C98A6%2540AdobeOrg%7CTS%3D1640551966

6. REMHI, *El informe del proyecto interdiocesano de recuperación
de la memoria histórico Guatemala: nunca más* (a summary, *un resumen*),
(Oficina de Derechos Humanos del Arzobispado de Guatemala, 1998), 113-
114. This document is accessible at
http://www.odhag.org.gt/publicaciones/remhi-guatemala-nunca-mas/.

7. Carol A. Smith, ed., *Guatemalan Indians and the State: 1540 to 1988*. (Austin: University of Texas Press, 1990).

8. Carol A. Smith, ed., *Guatemalan Indians and the State*, 169.

9. Ana Silvia Monzón, "Entre Líneas," 30-33.

10. Guzmán won with 65 percent of the 400,000 votes; women's right to vote was granted if proven to be literate in 1945; indigenous women were disqualified since the majority lacked literacy skills in Spanish. Eventually, all women were granted the right to vote in 1965.

11. Ana Silvia Monzón, "Entre Líneas," 43.

12. Ana Silvia Monzón, "Entre Líneas," 36.

13. Ana Silvia Monzón, "Entre Líneas," 68.

14. Ana Silvia Monzón, "Entre Líneas," 39.

15. Stephen Schlesinger and Stephen Kinzer, *Bitter Fruit: the Untold Story of the American Coup in Guatemala*. (NY: Doubleday Publishing, 1983).

16. Schlesinger and Kinzer, *Bitter Fruit*, 131-140.

17. Jim Handy, "The Corporate Community, Campesino Organizations, and Agrarian Reform: 1950-1954," Carol A. Smith, ed., *Guatemalan Indians and the State: 1540 to 1988*. (Austin: University of Texas Press, 1990), 163-182.

18. Schlesinger and Kinzer, *Bitter Fruit*, 216-225.

19. Schlesinger and Kinzer, *Bitter Fruit*, 224.

20. Castillo Armas was assassinated in 1957 by a lone gunman who afterward committed suicide; Secretary Dulles had to reduce his workload due to health problems; he died in 1959. His brother, Allen W. Dulles was a controversial director of the CIA until 1961. In his book *The Brothers: John Foster Dulles, Allen Dulles, and Their Secret War* (NY: McMillan Publishers, 2013), author Stephen Kinzer, writes a biographical portrayal of the duo and their role in the international stage of diplomacy and power. David Talbot's book, *The Devil's Chessboard: Allen Dulles, the CIA, and the Rise of the America's Secret Government* (NY: Harper Collins, 2015), allows the reader to take a closer look behind the incredibly powerful CIA director and the assassination of JFK.

21. Jim Handy, "The Corporate Community, Campesino Organizations, and Agrarian Reform," 173-176.

22. Jim Handy, "The Corporate Community, Campesino Organizations, and Agrarian Reform," 180.

23. David Stoll, *Between Two Armies in the Ixil Towns of Guatemala.* Columbia, NY: University Press, 1993).

24. Stoll, *Between Two Armies in the Ixil Towns of Guatemala*, 2-59.

25. Stoll, *Between Two Armies in the Ixil Towns of Guatemala*, 71-74.

26. Ana Silvia Monzón, "Entre Líneas," 58.

27. Stephen Schlesinger and Stephen Kinzer, *Bitter fruit: the Untold Story of the American Coup in Guatemala.* (NY: Doubleday Publishing, 1983). Additional references for this section include Greg Grandin, *The blood of Guatemala: A history of race and nation.* (Durham: Duke University Press, 2000); John H. Coatsworth, *Central America and the United States: The Clients and the Colossus.* NY: Twayne Publishers, 1994).

28. Schlesinger and Kinzer, *Bitter Fruit*, 245.

29. Schlesinger and Kinzer, *Bitter Fruit*, 113-117. Note that Bay of Pigs operation was launched out of Puerto Cabezas.

30. Schlesinger and Kinzer, *Bitter Fruit*, 184.

31. Schlesinger and Kinzer, *Bitter Fruit*, 240-242.

32. Ibid.

33. Dirk Kruijt, *Guerrillas: War and Peace in Central America.* (London: Zed Books, 2008), 81-86.

34. Schlesinger and Kinzer, *Bitter Fruit,* 244-246.

35. Stoll, *Between Two Armies in the Ixil Towns of Guatemala,* 108.

36. Schlesinger and Kinzer, *Bitter Fruit,* 246.

37. Schlesinger and Kinzer, *Bitter Fruit,* 247.

38. Schlesinger and Kinzer, *Bitter Fruit,* 247.

39. Schlesinger and Kinzer, *Bitter Fruit,* 248.

40. Schlesinger and Kinzer, *Bitter Fruit,* 248-249.

41. Mario Payeras, *Days of the Jungle: The Testimony of a Guatemalan Guerrillero.* (NY: Monthly Review Press, 1983).

42. Schlesinger and Kinzer, *Bitter Fruit,* 249-250.

43. David Stoll, *Between Two Armies in the Ixil Towns of Guatemala,* 96.

44. Schlesinger and Kinzer, *Bitter Fruit,* 249-251.

45. David Stoll, *Between Two Armies in the Ixil Towns of Guatemala,* 93-128

46. See also Jennifer Schirmer, *The Guatemala Military Project: A Violence in Democracy.* (Philadelphia: Pennsylvania University Press, 1998).

47. See John H. Coatsworth, *Central America and the United States: The Clients and the Colossus.* NY: Twayne Publishers, 1994).

48. Mario Payeras, *Days of the Jungle: The Testimony of a Guatemalan Guerrillero.* (NY: Monthly Review Press, 1983). See also Ricardo Falla, *Masacres de la Selva: Ixcán, Guatemala, 1975-1982.* (Guatemala: Editorial Universitaria, 1992).

49. David Stoll, *Between Two Armies in the Ixil Towns of Guatemala,* 65-67.

50. Stoll, *Between Two Armies in the Ixil Towns of Guatemala,* 74-75.

51. Stoll, *Between Two Armies in the Ixil Towns of Guatemala,* 14-24.

52. Stoll, *Between Two Armies in the Ixil Towns of Guatemala,* 96-99.

53. Ibid. 104-105

54. Stoll, *Between Two Armies in the Ixil Towns of Guatemala,* 110.

55. Stoll, *Between Two Armies in the Ixil Towns of Guatemala,* 107-113.

56. This document is accesible at https://www.usip.org/publications/1997/02/truth-commission-guatemala.

57. This document is accesible at https://www.ohchr.org/en/instruments-mechanisms/instruments/convention-prevention-and-punishment-crime-genocide.

58. This document is accesible at http://www.derechoshumanos.net/lesahumanidad/informes/guatemala/informeREMHI-Tomo1.htm.

59. These documents are accesible at https://pazysolidaridad.ccoo.es/cms/cli/000001/o/67/671df2619b4dd9a9f9f64fff3b4083e5000001.pdf.

60. CEH, 40.

61. *Operation Sofía* is accessible at
https://pazysolidaridad.ccoo.es/cms/cli/000001/o/67/671df2619b4dd9a9f9f
64fff3b4083e5000001.pdf; also see CEH, 25-26.

62. CEH, 38-41.

63. CEH, 41.

64. REMHI, 306.

65. CEH, 30-31.

66. CEH, 7.

66. REMHI, 99-101.

67. David Stoll, *Between Two Armies in the Ixil Towns of Guatemala,* 14-24.

68. Beatriz Mantz, *Paradise in ashes: A Guatemalan journey of courage, terror, and hope.* (Berkeley: University of California Press, 2005), 183-224.

69. CEH, 19.

70. See Prensa Libre's article on the futives, September 20, 2016, https://www.prensalibre.com/guatemala/justicia/interpol-busca-a-87-profugos/.

71. See informational article, accessible at https://www.ijmonitor.org/efrain-rios-montt-and-mauricio-rodriguez-sanchez-background/.

72. See article, "Victims Testify in Genocide Retrial of Ríos Montt and Rodríguez Sánchez, accessible at https://www.ijmonitor.org/2017/12/victims-testify-in-genocide-retrial-of-rios-montt-and-rodriguez-sanchez/. See *5oo Years: Life in Resistance* film information, accessible at https://500years.skylight.is/en/synopsis/.

73. Bishop Juan José Gerardi Conedra, accessible at https://www.ghrc-usa.org/our-work/important-cases/assassination-of-bishop-gerardi/.

74. Francisco Goldman, *The Art of Political Murder: Who Killed the Bishop?* (NY: Grove Press, 2007).

75. Jennifer K. Harbury, *Searching for Everardo: A Story of Love, War, and the CIA in Guatemala.* (NY: Warner Books, Inc, 1997).

76. *Acuerdo de Paz Firme y Duradero (Peace Accords),* accessible at https://www.usip.org/publications/1998/11/peace-agreements-guatemala.

77. *International Human Rights Declarations*, accessible at https://www.un.org/esa/socdev/unpfii/documents/DRIPS_en.pdf.

78. *International Labour Organization Convention 169*, accessible at https://www.ilo.org/dyn/normlex/en/f?p=NORMLEXPUB:12100:0::N O::P12100_ILO_CODE:C169

79. CEH, 23 and 35; REMHI, 111-127.

80. See Doña Teresa's story in Chapter 4. *Reindicación* refers to recovery based on what was violently taken away end.

81. Ana Silvia Monzón, *Las Mujeres, los Feminismos y los Movimientos Sociales en Guatemala: Relaciones, Articulaciones y Desencuentros,* (Facultad Latinoamericana de Ciencias Sociales FLACSO-Sede Académico Guatemala, 2021), 24. Accessible at https://www.puees.unam.mx/curso2021/materiales/Sesion13/Monzon_Las MujeresLosFeminismosYLosMovimientosSociales.pdf. See also, *Entre Mujeres: La identidad étnica, factor de tension en el movimiento de mujeres en Guatemala, 1990-2000.* Accessible at https://repositorio.flacsoandes.edu.ec/handle/10469/1854 (http://hdl.handle.net/10469/1854).

82. "Baqtun" refers to the calendrical cycle in the ancient Maya Long Count Calendar; the "new" Baqtun started on December 21, 2012.

83. Ana Silvia Monzón, *Las Mujeres*, 29.

84. Alberto Manguel, *The City of Words*. (Toronto, ON: House of Anansi Press Inc., 2007), 3.

Chapter Four (pp.141-163)

1. Zacualpa is in the department of El Quiché, Guatemala, about 100 kilometers northwest of Guatemala City. This excerpt is based on an interview and is accessible in YouTube, *Doña Teresa*, at https://youtu.be/0cax5MMvBBg.

2. The official investigative reports concurred that during the Internal Armed Conflict, from 1960 to 1996, at least 440 rural massacres (some reports estimate 669 massacres) took the lives of 200,000 people; 83.3 percent were Mayans; the department of Quiché had 45.5 percent of the total violence and had the most casualties; the perpetrators consisted of 93

percent state forces (Army, Civil Patrols, Commissioners). Additionally, 45,000 people, mostly civilians, have been reported "disappeared" and over a million inhabitants, mostly Maya, were forced to flee their homes. See CEH: Report for Historical Clarification, 1999, the English language *summary* version, accessible at https://www.aaas.org/sites/default/files/s3fs-public/mos_en.pdf?adobe_mc=MCMID%3D31219200981284036790026633326666170976%7CMCORGID%3D242B6472541199F70A4C98A6%2540AdobeOrg%7CTS%3D1640551966.

3. The *Comisión para el Esclarecimiento Histórico (CEH)* is a comprehensive report that chronicles the Armed Conflict from its beginnings in 1960s to the 1996 Peace Accords; the investigations yielded detailed information regarding human rights violations, deaths, massacres, forced disappearances, physical destruction, etc. A trove of evidence was acquired from direct testimonies of survivors and witnesses. See the CEH, the English language *summary*, 39.

4. CEH, 23.

5. Information about the torture tactics used by the military is posted on the webpage, Zacualpa Parish of Espiritu Santo, accessible at http://faithandlabor.blogspot.com/2014/06/the-parish-of-espiritu-santo-in.html.

6. See *Main Page* of REMHI, *El informe del proyecto interdiocesano de recuperación de la memoria histórico Guatemala: nunca más* (a summary, *un resumen*), (Oficina de Derechos Humanos del Arzobispado de Guatemala, 1998), 113-114. This document is accessible at http://www.odhag.org.gt/publicaciones/remhi-guatemala-nunca-mas/.

7. See *TOMO 1*, 91. This document is one of four volumes, accessible at http://www.odhag.org.gt/publicaciones/remhi-guatemala-nunca-mas/.

8. CEH, 41.

9. CEH, 40.

10. Luz Méndez Gutiérrez and Amanda Carrera Guerra, *Mujeres indígenas: clamor por la justicia: violencia sexual, conflicto armado y despojo violento de tierras*. (Guatemala: ECAP and UNAMG, 2014), 78.

11. Luz Méndez Gutiérrez and Amanda Carrera Guerra, *Mujeres indígenas: clamor por la justicia: violencia sexual, conflicto armado y despojo violento de tierras.* (Guatemala: ECAP and UNAMG, 2014).

12. Amandine Fulchirone, (and her team: Olga Alicia Paz, Angélica Lopez, María José Pérez, Patricia Castañeda, & Luisa Cabrera), ***Tejidos que lleva el alma: memoria de las mujeres mayas sobrevivientes de violación sexual durante el conflicto armado,*** (Guatemala: ECAP and UNAMG, 2011), accessible at https://unam.academia.edu/AmandineFulchiron.

13. For additional information, see *Summary of Caal v. HudBay (Lawsuit regarding the rapes at the community of Lote Ocho),* accessible at http://www.chocversushudbay.com/about/#Summary%20of%20Caal

14. Similar violent evictions that occurred in the Lote Ocho, Q'eqchi' community had been repeated throughout the Internal Armed Conflict. The military was responsible for hundreds of massacres and killed and injured thousands of innocent people, mostly among the indigenous population, and thousands of women were sexually assaulted. In the Izabal/Alta Verapaz region, nine percent of the 1980-1983 genocide victims were Maya, or at least 18,000. This information is recorded in both the *CEH* and the *REMHI* reports.

15. The film, *Defensora,* is produced by 6Kidsproduction, Girl Edge Films and the Right Actions Organization. Included are interviews with the three plaintiffs. The film is accessible at https://youtu.be/G-1qQoUEeO8.

16. Luz Méndez Gutiérrez and Amanda Carrera Guerra, *Mujeres indígenas: clamor por la justicia.*

17. In the 2017, the CEDAW report includes the following statement that underscores the government's lack of attention to this matter: "**(22.)** The Committee is concerned, however, about the significant delay in the implementation of the Agreement on a firm and lasting peace, especially with regard to reparations for the crimes perpetrated against women during the internal conflict and the pledges relating to the advancement of women." See Guatemala's response in the document, "List of issues and questions in relation to the combined eighth and ninth periodic reports of Guatemala," accessible at https://documents-dds-

ny.un.org/doc/UNDOC/GEN/N17/204/19/PDF/N1720419.pdf?OpenEleme
nt.

18. See Actoras de Cambio website, "Actores de cambio o la historia de un sueño hecho realidad," (*Agents of change or the history of a dream made real*), accessible at https://www.actorasdecambio.org.gt.

19. See *Entremundos* website for historical information on Mamá Maquín, accessible at https://www.entremundos.org/revista/environment/megaprojects-en/mama-maquin-the-brave-defender-qeqchi-murdered-for-defending-panzos/?lang=en; information on the Unión Nacional de Mujeres Guatemaltecas, https://unamg.org; and Equipo de Estudios Comunitarios y Atención Psicosocial, https://ecapguatemala.org.gt.

20. The publications listed as "Publicaciones propias" include nine women narratives and a collection of documents that serve as guides and manuals on the development of the Consorcio project. See *Actoras de Cambio*. For specific information about their methodology see "Metodología de formación sanación con mujeres sobrevivientes de violencia sexual y de la guerra en Guatemala" on their website: https://www.actorasdecambio.org.gt.

21. "La candela es la luz," is Doña Julia's story. Actoras de Cambio, https://www.actorasdecambio.org.gt/wp-content/uploads/2020/11/historia-vida-Julia.pdf.

22. "La candela es la luz."

23. Ibid.

24. Doña Dorotea's story, "La piedra, el maíz y la canasta," is accessible at https://www.actorasdecambio.org.gt/wp-content/uploads/2020/11/historia-vida-Carlota.pdf.

25. Richard Wilson. *Maya resurgence in Guatemala.: Q'eqchi' experiences*. (Norman, OK: University of Oklahoma,1995), 85.

26. Over a million people and mostly from indigenous communities, were displaced due to the Internal Armed Conflict; the process of return or relocation took place between 1993-95. See the *CEH* for additional information.

27. Amandine Fulchirone, ***Tejidos que lleva el alma***, accessible at https://unam.academia.edu/AmandineFulchiron, 349.

29. Doña Carolina's story is "Estoy Viva," in Actoras de Cambio, accessible at https://www.actorasdecambio.org.gt/wp-content/uploads/2020/11/historia-vida-Carolina.pdf.

30. Amandine Fulchirone, *Tejidos que lleva el alma*, accessible at https://unam.academia.edu/AmandineFulchiron, 327-329.

31. "Reparación Transformadora: El Caso Sepur Zarco," documentary film is accessible at https://youtu.be/wtjnUfvUDXE.

32. The Alliance to End Silence and Impunity included the following organizations: UN Women, https://www.unwomen.org/en/about-us; Mujeres Transformando el Mundo, https://mujerestransformandoelmundo.org; el Equipo de Estudios Comunitarios y Atención Psicosocial, https://ecapguatemala.org.gt; and la Unión Nacional de Mujeres Guatemaltecas, https://unamg.org.

33. Information about litigated cases stemming from the Internal Armed Conflict is available at the Guatemala Human Rights Commission website, https://www.ghrc-usa.org/our-work/important-cases/.

34. See the *UN Women* article, October 2017, about the Sepur Zarco case. Also, watch the You Tube video featuring Judge Yasmin Barrios discuss the two trials that she has presided over: the Rios-Montt genocide trial and the Sepur Zarco case, accessible at https://www.youtube.com/watch?v=9Vf4--Y00h4. Details about the Rios-Montt genocide trial are accessible at https://www.justiceinitiative.org/publications/judging-dictator-trial-guatemala-s-rios-montt.

35. For information about the trial filed by the Maya Achi women, see Jo-Marie Burt and Paulo Estrada, "In Guatemala, Ex-Paramilitaries Face Trial for Wartime Rape of Indigenous Women." (North American Congress on Latin America (NACLA), January 11, 2020, https://nacla.org/news/2022/01/11/guatemala-maya-achi-rape

36. See Immunity Watch article, "Executive Summary: Monitoring Report of Resolution 1325 in Guatemala 2016-2019," accessible at https://cad5e396-f48c-4e90-80f5-27ccad29f65e.filesusr.com/ugd/f3f989_9b1425e5a38c4725bcebc5add5fe2ddc.pdf

37. See "El caso Sepur Zarco: las mujeres guatemaltecas que

exigieron justicia en una nación destrozada por la guerra," (*The Sepur Zarco Case: the Guatemalan women that demanded justice in a country destroyed by the war*), accessible at ONU Mujeres, https://www.unwomen.org/es/news/stories/2018/10/feature-sepur-zarco-case.

38. See interview, "I am Generation Equality" by ONU Mujeres, featuring one of the Sepur Zarco *abuelas*, Demecia Yat, accessible at https://www.unwomen.org/en/news/stories/2019/10/i-am-generation-equality-demecia-yat.

39. Luz Méndez Gutiérrez was selected as the 2004 Woman Peacemaker, an award by the Joan B. Kroc Institute for Peace and Justice, accessible at https://www.sandiego.edu/peace/institute-for-peace-justice/initiatives/women-peace-security/women-peacemakers/biography.php?id=46. Also, see video of the Luz Méndez interview by Nobel Women's Initiative where she discusses her work with the Peace Accords process, accessible at https://youtu.be/GJcuQTY1xuY.

40. See Rachel Sieder's article, "Reframing Citizenship: Indigenous Rights, Local Power and the Peace Process in Guatemala," which is part of a manuscript, *Negotiating Rights: The Guatemalan Peace Process*, 1997, accessible at https://rc-services-assets.s3.eu-west-1.amazonaws.com/s3fs-public/Accord%2002_6Reframing%20citizenship_1997_ENG.pdf.

41. Luz Méndez Gutiérrez and Amanda Carrera Guerra, *Mujeres indígenas: clamor por la justicia, 65.*

42. *David Stoll, Between Two Armies in the Ixil Towns of Guatemala. (NY: Columbia University Press, 1993), 108.*

43. See the *Walls of Hope*, an international art and human rights project: "TZUULTAQ'A Earth and Valley, High and Low, Woman and Man Good and Evil, the opposites that hold the Universe," accessible at http://www.wallsofhope.org/en/tag/polochic/.

44. Guatemala News and Information Bureau, "Guatemala: Peasant Massacre." (North American Congress on Latin America (NACLA), September 25, 2007), https://nacla.org/article/guatemala-peasant-massacre.

45. Luz Méndez Gutiérrez and Amanda Carrera Guerra, *Mujeres indígenas: clamor por la justicia, 28.* Eighty-four percent of land is owned

by men; 16 percent by women; the mining of nickel increased 164.4 percent annually between 2002 and 2012.

46. Arturo Arias, "Changing Indian identity: Guatemala's violent transition to modernity." In C. Smith (Ed)., *Guatemalan Indians and the state, 1540 to 1988*. (Austin: University of Texas Press, 1990), 230-257. The Committee for Campesino Unity (CUC) led the preparations for the May 1, 1978 demonstrations, which were hugely successful, and large, unexpected numbers of protestors participated.

47. In 1972, the guerrilla organization, Ejército Guerrilla de los Pobres – the Guerrilla Army of the Poor (EGP) settled in the northern part of Quiché, close to the Maya pueblo Ixil (Nebaj, Chajul, and Cotzal) and the Christian base communities. In the Spring of 1976, the military began its repressive operations upon the request of Sebastian Guzman, a ladino landowner who had the names of men "presumably" collaborating with the guerrilla (the "blacklist"). Three thousand army troops were stationed in the region. The repression resulted in the deaths and injuries of thousands of civilians, later deemed as a genocidal event.

48. Arturo Arias, "Changing Indian identity," 230-257.

49. Beatriz Manz, *Paradise in ashes: A Guatemalan journey of courage, terror, and hope. (*Berkeley, CA: University of California Press, 2005).

50. Beatriz Manz, *Paradise in ashes*, 200-203. Rosalía Hernández succumbed to cancer and died at the age of 36.

51. CONAVIGUA, the National Association of Guatemalan Widows is accessible at https://memoriavirtualguatemala.org/?page_id=2011. See "Los huesos son buenos testigos, aunque hablan en voz baja, nunca mienten y nunca olvidan," accessible in FAFG: Fundación de Antropología Forense de Guatemala website, https://fafg.org. Over 3500 human remains have been identified from the Internal Armed Conflict; over 8200 have been recovered but not identified. See also, Centro de Analisis Forense y Ciencias Aplicadas, investigación antropológica forense, accessible at http://www.cafca.gt.

52. See interview article with Rosalina Tuyuc Velásquez, "From Where I Stand: 'Forgiveness is still very far from our reality,' (UN Women, October 19, 2020),

https://www.unwomen.org/en/news/stories/2020/10/from-where-i-stand-rosalina-tuyuc-velasquez.

Chapter Five (pp.164-206)

1. Thomas W. Walker, ed., *Nicaragua Without Illusions: Regime Transition and Structural Adjustment in the 1990s.* (Wilmington, DE: Scholarly Resources, 1997).

2. Carlos Vilas, *The Sandinista Revolution: National Liberation and Social Transformation in Central America.* (NY: Monthly Review Press, 1986).

3. Jaime Incer Barquero, Carlos Alemán Ocampo, and Jorge Eduardo Arellano, *Colón y la costa Caribe de Centroamérica.* (Managua: Fundación Vida Colección Cultural de Centro America, 2002). Although most of the remaining dominant indigenous languages (Chorotega, Nahuat, Xiu, Cacaopera) have become extinct, according to linguists, a large portion of the population self-identifies as indigenous ("indio").

4. See Bernard Nietschmann, *"Chapter Seven: Protecting Indigenous Coral Reefs and Sea Territories, Miskito Coast, Raan, Nicaragua,"* in Stanley Stevens, ed., *Conservation Through Survival,* (Washington, DC: Island Press, 1995), 357-415.

5. *Country Reports.* 2022. Published by countryreports.org. Accessible at https://www.countryreports.org/country/Nicaragua/economy.htm.

6. Zelaya's presidency is also known as the Liberal Revolution, reminiscent of Guatemala's Liberal Reform period of President Justo Rufino Barrios in 1871. For a profile of President Zelaya see Thomas W. Walker, *Nicaragua: Living in the Shadow of the Eagle.* (Cambridge, MA: Westview Press, 2003), 15.

7. Thomas W. Walker, *Nicaragua: Living in the Shadow of the Eagle.* In 1926, President Coolidge ordered U.S. troops to the Caribbean town of Puerto Cabezas and in 1927, 5,000 U.S. Marines were deployed along with 16 warships. After the Battle of Chinandega and the signing of the Peace Treaty in Espina Negra, President Coolidge, followed by President Hoover, signed an order that upon removal of the U.S. armed forces, the Nicaraguan

National Guard will serve as its replacement under the command of U.S. generals.

8. In Stephen Kinzer, *Blood of Brothers: Life and War in Nicaragua.* (Cambridge, Mass.: Harvard University Press, 1991), 27.

9. Kinzer, *Blood of Brothers*, 26-35.

10. Walker, *Nicaragua*, 25-31.

11. David Francois, *Nicaragua 1961-1990: Volume 1, the downfall of the Somoza Dictatorship.* (Warwick, UK: Helion & Company Limited, 2018).

12. Walker, *Nicaragua*, 26.

13. Daniel Chávez, *Nicaragua and the Politics of Utopia.* Nashville: Vanderbilt University Press, 2015), 18.

14. Kinzer, *Blood of Brothers,* 33.

15. Sergio Ramírez, *Adiós Muchachos: A Memoir of the Sandinista Revolution.* (Translated by Stacey Alba D. Skar). (Durham: Duke University Press, 2012), 32.

16. Victoria Gonzalez-Rivera, *Before the Revolution: Women's Rights and Right-Wing Politics in Nicaragua, 1821-1979.* (University Park, PA: The Pennsylvania State University, 2011).

17. Victoria Gonzalez-Rivera, *Before the Revolution,* 138. The Ala Femenina boasted a membership of 6,000 women.

18. Victoria Gonzalez-Rivera, *Before the Revolution,* 244-245.

19. Victoria Gonzalez-Rivera, *Before the Revolution,* 251 and 256.

20. Victoria Gonzalez-Rivera, *Before the Revolution,* 262.

21. Ibid., 240-241.

22. Margaret Randall, *Sandino's Daughters: Testimonies of Nicaraguan Women in Struggle.* (New Brunswick, NJ: Rutgers University Press, 1995), 116-128.

23. Nora Astorga died at the age of 39. In an article by NYTimes, General Pérez Vega was revealed as a former CIA asset. See article in NY Times archives:
http://timesmachine.nytimes.com/timesmachine/1988/02/24/715088.html

24. See article on biography of Nora Astorga: *Envío:*
https://www.envio.org.ni/articulo/3134

25. Kristine Byron, *"Doris Tijerino: Revolution, Writing, and*

Resistance in Nicaragua," in *NWSA Journal, V.8*(3), 2006, 104-121.

26. Rape is a form of gendered violence and within the context of an armed conflict, female prisoners are subject to the most heinous, inhumane cruelty.

27. See David Francois, *Nicaragua 1961-1991.* The Nicaraguan "Revolution" was a 20-year struggle from 1960 to 1979. The dictator, Anastasio Somoza Debayle left the country for Miami, with the help of the United States, on July 16, 1979, leaving behind a ruthless, brutal repression, and on July 19, 1979 the Sandinistas took a victory lap in Managua with all fronts represented: the Northern, Southern, Central, Eastern, Western, Southeastern, and lastly, the "elite" Southern Front.

28. Randall, *Sandino's Daughters,* 40-54.

29. Ibid., 54.

30. Margaret Randall, *Sandino's Daughters.*

31. Ibid., 57.

32. Ibid., 80.

33. Randall, *Sandino's Daughters*, 92.

34. Carlos Dada, "Nicaragua: The End of Poetry." ElFaro.net, December 11, 2020. The article is accessible at https://elfaro.net/en/202012/internacionales/25073/Nicaragua-—-The-End-of-Poetry.htm?st-full_text=all&tpl=11.

35. Information about Rosario Murillo Zembrana accessible at https://pennyspoetry.fandom.com/wiki/Rosario_Murillo.

36. Ortega's brother, Humberto, served in the FSLN as a ranking military officer and his brother Camilo, was killed in 1978 during a battle with the National Guard.

37. John Beverley and Marc Zimmerman, *Literature and Politics in the Central American Revolution.* (Austin: University of Texas Press, 1990), 64-65.

38. Beverley and Zimmerman, *Literature and Politics*, 65.

39. Pedro Joaquin Chamorro was considered an important man that would help others in dire need. For example, he paid for the funeral services of Luisa Amanda Espinosa, upon her family's request after she was killed by the National Guard on April 3, 1970. See Randall, *Sandino's Daughters*, 29.

40. David Francois, *Nicaragua 1961-1991,* 133-134.

41. Beverley and Zimmerman, *Literature and Politics*, 89.

42. La Prensa newspaper/organization was ordered to shut down by the Ortega Murillo regime, see "La Prensa notifica despidos a sus trabajadores tras 33 días de allanamiento policial," October 22, 2021, accessible at https://www.fuentesconfiables.com/post/la-prensa-notifica-despidos-a-sus-trabajadores-tras-33-d%C3%ADas-de-allanamiento-policial, and the explanation of the losses suffered from this politically motivated order in "Hemeroteca de la prensa, un fabuloso registro de la historia de Nicaragua en manos de Ortega," August 13, 2021, accessible at https://www.fuentesconfiables.com/post/la-prensa-notifica-despidos-a-sus-trabajadores-tras-33-d%C3%ADas-de-allanamiento-policial.

43. See *Rosario Murillo Zembrana* accessible at https://pennyspoetry.fandom.com/wiki/Rosario_Murillo.

44. Ortega was elected president for the first time in 1985 then, was defeated in 1990.

45. Murillo did not serve in combat although her involvement with the Sandinistas in the mid-1970s led to a brief jail sentence.

46. *Solentiname* is the largest island on the 38-island archipelago in Lake Nicaragua. Cardenal founded the Our Lady of Solentiname, a lay monastery that includes a farmer's collective, an artist center and a clinic. See Ernesto Cardenal, *The Gospel in Solentiname.* (Maryknoll, NY: Orbis Books,1976).

47. Known as the *Literacy Campaign* in the countryside – 60,000 to 80,000 volunteer literacy workers, 1980-81. See Beverley and Zimmerman, *Literature and Politics*, 95-97. Also, Sergio Ramírez, *Adiós Muchachos,* and Carlos Vilas, *The Sandinista Revolution: National Liberation and Social Transformation in Central America.* Berkeley, CA: Monthly Review Press Center for the Study of the Americas, 1986), 214.

48. *Pedagogy of the Oppressed* by Paulo Freire (NY: Bloomsbury Publishing Inc.) was published in Portuguese in 1968 and then, in English in 1970. The proposed pedagogy in the book focuses on the irrevocable relationship between teacher, student, and society.

49. Costa Rican Mayra Jimenez was the coordinator and teacher of the Solentiname Writing Project. See Mayra Jimenez, *Fogata en la Oscuridad:*

Los Talleres de Poesía en la Alfabetización. (Managua: Editorial Nueva Nicaragua, 1985).

50. See Debra Sabia, *Contradiction and Conflict: The Popular Church in Nicaragua.* (Tuscaloosa, AL: The University of Alabama Press, 1997).

51. See the *Barricada* article and photos, accessible at https://diariobarricada.com/comandante-daniel-condecora-a-la-heroina-amada-pineda/.

52. See *"Presos politicos libres bajo autoamnistía orteguista,"* accessible at https://www.confidencial.com.ni/nacion/todos-los-presos-politicos-libres-bajo-autoamnistia-orteguista/.

53. See "IACHR Expresses Concern Over the Passing of the Amnesty Law in Nicaragua," June 12, 2019, accessible at https://www.oas.org/en/iachr/media_center/PReleases/2019/145.asp.

54. See Noelia Celina Gutiérrez, *"The Price Paid by Nicaraguan Women Opposing the Ortega Government,"* August 1, 2019, accessible at Diplomatic Courier, https://www.diplomaticourier.com/posts/the-price-paid-by-nicaraguan-women-opposing-the-ortega-government.

55. See Amnesty International, "Nicaragua: The Government of Daniel Ortega Violates its Commitment to Release All Detainees," June 19, 2019, accessible at https://www.amnesty.org/en/latest/news/2019/06/el-gobierno-de-ortega-incumple-al-no-liberar-a-todas-las-personas-detenidas/.

56. "April Mothers' Association: No Peace for Us Until There's Justice," confidencial.com.ni, December 10, 2019, accessible at https://www.amnesty.org/en/latest/news/2019/06/el-gobierno-de-ortega-incumple-al-no-liberar-a-todas-las-personas-detenidas/.

57. Ama y No Olvida Museo de la Memoria Contra la Impunidad, accessible at https://www.museodelamemorianicaragua.org/sobre-el-museo/.

58. The AMA *virtual* museum is accessible at https://www.museodelamemorianicaragua.org.

59. The new release, "Police Surround Mothers of April 2018 Victims, Harass Them, and Decommission Commemorative Books of Their Murdered Sons," *Iniciativa Mesoamericana de Mujeres Defensoras,* April 21, 2021, is accessible at https://im-defensoras.org/2021/04/whrd-

alert-nicaragua-police-surround-mothers-of-april-2018-victims-harass-them-and-decommission-commemorative-books-of-their-murdered-sons/.

60. "Detention and Assault of Women Human Rights Defenders From the Asociación Madres of Abril," *Front Line Defenders,* April 21, 2021, is accessible at https://www.frontlinedefenders.org/en/case/detention-and-assault-women-human-rights-defenders-asociación-madres-de-abril-ama.

61. "Nicaragua: Las Madres Que Buscan a Sus Hijos Ecarcelados Tras Protestar Contra el Gobierno," *BBC World Service,* August 15, 2018, YouTube video accessible at https://youtu.be/U2QJQg-e23c.

62. "Human Rights Violations and Abuses in the Context o Protests in Nicaragua, April – August 2018" *United Nations Human Rights Office of the High Commissioner*, is accessible at https://www.ohchr.org/sites/default/files/Documents/Countries/NI/HumanRightsViolationsNicaraguaApr_Aug2018_EN.pdf. "Situation of Human Rights in Nicaragua Report of the United Nations High Commissioner for Human Rights," *United Nations*, February 19, 2021, accessible at https://reliefweb.int/report/nicaragua/situation-human-rights-nicaragua-report-united-nations-high-commissioner-human-0.

63. Nuñez points out in the same article that the Secretary of the Organization of American States (OEA), Luis Almagro, declared in a statement that Nicaragua was a "failed state." The article, "Ni Somoza, la destrucción judicial del gobierno Ortega-Murillo," nicaraguainvestiga.com, January 14, 2021, is accessible at https://nicaraguainvestiga.com/memoria/52944-juicios-politicos-nicaragua-2021-opositores/.

64. The article, "Murillo clama justicia contra la corrupción y la huaca golpista," nicaraguinvestiga.com, June 7, 2021, is accessible at https://nicaraguainvestiga.com/nacion/52838-murillo-clama-justicia-contra-la-corrupcion-y-la-huaca-golpista/.

65. Nuñez profile can be retrieved at https://web.archive.org/web/20180508054202/https://www.laprensa.com.ni/2017/03/19/suplemento/la-prensa-domingo/2200577-los-motivos-de-vilma-nunez. Since this article is archived in web.archive.org, the download may take a little longer than usual. On some days the web.archive.org may be out for maintenance purposes, so you may need to try another day.

66. See Elizabeth Dore, and Maxine Molyneux, eds., *Hidden histories of Gender and the State in Latin America*. Durham, NC: Duke University Press, 2000).

67. *"La piñata,"* refers to how Somoza's possessions (e.g., land, homes, business properties) were purported to be expropriated by the Sandinista government but instead, these were distributed to individuals by Ortega and Murillo regime as a payment method, especially for personal gain. The YouTube video report is accessible at https://youtu.be/Df5Re2Spwds.

68. See an investigative report on the wealth accumulation of the Ortega and Murillo children, accessible at https://nicaraguainvestiga.com/reportajes/56872-huaca-estatal-hijos-daniel-ortega-ocho-millones-cordobas-licitaciones/. The YouTube video reporting on the ownership of businesses of the Ortega/Murillo family is accessible at https://youtu.be/xiLeQDUcJOU.

69. "Los Rehenes Electorales de Daniel Ortega y Rosario Murillo," confidencial.com.ni, July 8, 2021, an article that reports on the political prisoners is accessible at https://www.confidencial.com.ni/especiales/los-rehenes-electorales-de-daniel-ortega-y-rosario-murillo/.

70. *Envío* digital is accessible at https://www.envio.org.ni/index.en.

71. The "Joint Statement Presented by the Nicaragua Core Group," U.S. Mission to International Organizations in Geneva, September 14, 2021, is accessible at https://geneva.usmission.gov/2021/09/14/joint-statement-on-nicaragua/.

72. The "press statement" issued by Secretary of State Anthony Blinken, on September 14, 2021, is accessible at https://ni.usembassy.gov/nicaraguan-independence-day/. Also, see the latest statements from the U.S. Mission to the Organization of American States (OAS), https://usoas.usmission.gov/oas-resolution-condemns-ortega-regime-in-nicaragua-2/

73. "50 países piden ante la ONU la liberación de los presos politicos en Nicaragua," confidencial.com.ni, September 16, 2021, is accessible at https://www.confidencial.com.ni/nacion/50-paises-piden-ante-la-onu-la-liberacion-de-los-presos-politicos-en-nicaragua/.

74. "Asamblea Nacional cancela personería jurídica a 15 ONGs,"

nicaraguainvestiga.com, August 26, 2021, is accessible at https://nicaraguainvestiga.com/politica/58468-asamblea-cancela-personeria-juridica-ongs/. As of April, 2022, the regime has cancelled over 200 ONGs.

75. "Ortega Cierra Otras 15 ONG en Nicaragua; Suman 55," local10.com, August 26, 2021; accessible at https://www.local10.com/espanol/2021/08/26/ortega-cierra-otras-15-ong-en-nicaragua-suman-55/. The website for the organization, *Colectivo de Mujeres Matagalpa*, is accessible as of April, 2022 at https://www.cmmmatagalpaorg.net.

76. "Asamblea Nacional cancela personería jurídica a 15 ONGs," nicaraguainvestiga.com, August 26, 2021, is accessible at https://nicaraguainvestiga.com/politica/58468-asamblea-cancela-personeria-juridica-ongs/.

77. "Asociación Colectivo de Mujeres de Matagalpa, la Asociación de Mujeres de Jalapa contra la Violencia Oyanka y la Fundación entre Volcanes," Im-Defensoras.org, August 27, 2021, reports on the women organizations shuttered by the Ortega Murillo regime. The article is accessible at https://im-defensoras.org/2021/08/alerta-defensoras-nicaragua-gobierno-nicaraguense-cancela-la-personeria-juridica-de-otras-tres-organizaciones-feministas/. Please note that La Corriente Programa Feminista was cancelled by the regime in April, 2022. Their website is accessible at https://lacorrientenicaragua.org.

78. "Case 12,230: Zoilamérica Narváez vs. the Nicaraguan State," envio.org.ni, envío información sobre Nicaragua y Centroamérica, March 2002, accessible at https://www.envio.org.ni/articulo/1567.

79. Kenneth Morris, *Unfinished Revolution: David Ortega and Nicaragua's Struggle for Liberation*. (Chicago: Lawrence Hill Books, 2010).

80. Morris, *Unfinished Revolution*, 136.

81. "Report No. 118/01 Case 12,230, Zoilamérica Narváez Murillo," Inter-American Commission on Human Rights, Organization of American States, October 15, 2001, accessible at http://cidh.org/annualrep/2001eng/Nicaragua12230.htm.

82. Morris, *Unfinished Revolution*, 136.

83. Ibid., 137.

84. Ibid., 139.

85. "Lo más escalofriante del testimonio de Zoilamérica," nicaraguainvestiga.com, October 30, 2018, accessible at https://nicaraguainvestiga.com/memoria/2495-lo-mas-escalofriante-del-testimonio-de-zoilamerica/.

86. The Institute of Legal Medicine 2018 report concludes the following 2017 data: 1,679 girls from ages 0-12 and 1,643 girls ages 13-17 were sexually abused. The report is accessible at https://nicaraguainvestiga.com/reportajes/8927-cinco-ninas-son-abusadas-sexualmente-cada-dia-en-nicaragua/. See also, "Abuso sexual: Un mal silenciado en la guerra de los 80," a YouTube documentary video by nicaraguainvestiga.com, *Nicaragua Investiga,* September 17, 2020, about the sexual abuse of Sandinista female combatants during the Revolution, accessible at https://youtu.be/tKOCXApjjVw.

87. "Report No. 118/01 Case 12,230, Zoilamérica Narváez Murillo," accessible at http://cidh.org/annualrep/2001eng/Nicaragua12230.htm.

88. "Gobierno Cancela Personería Jurídica de Organizaciones de Derechos Humanos," im-defensoras.org, Iniciativa Mesoamericana de Mujeres Defensoras de Derechos Humanos, December 12, 2018, accessible at https://im-defensoras.org/2018/12/alertaurgente-nicaragua-gobierno-cancela-personeria-juridica-de-organizaciones-de-derechos-humanos/.

89. "IACHR asks the State of Nicaragua to comment on the CENIDH case," cejil.org, the Center for Justice and International Law, February 10, 2021, accessible at https://cejil.org/en/press-releases/iachr-asks-the-state-of-nicaragua-to-comment-on-the-cenidh-case/.

90. "UN Committee on the Elimination of Discrimination against Women: Nicaragua," accessible at https://www.refworld.org/docid/45f90db12.html; "Report of the Special Rapporteur on Violence against Women, its Causes and Consequences, Honduras," accessible at https://evaw-global-database.unwomen.org/-/media/files/un%20women/vaw/country%20report/america/honduras/honduras%20srvaw.pdf?vs=3000; CEDAW-Guatemala, accessible at https://tbinternet.ohchr.org/_layouts/15/treatybodyexternal/Download.aspx?

symbolno=CEDAW%2fC%2fGTM%2fCO%2f8-9&Lang=en; CEDAW-El Salvador accessible at https://tbinternet.ohchr.org/_layouts/15/treatybodyexternal/SessionDetails1.aspx?SessionID=1071&Lang=en.

91. "The Nicaraguan government harasses, imprisons and exiles women struggling for a better country," YouTube video documentary, August 30, 2021, accessible at https://youtu.be/PiHv3dlrxlY.

Chapter Six (pp.207-227)

1. Epigraph: "Love amongst women is revolutionary," says Mexican feminist." See *Global Voices*, accessible at https://globalvoices.org/2022/03/10/love-amongst-women-is-revolutionary-says-mexican-feminist/?utm_source=Global+Voices&utm_campaign=47d54758eb-Daily_Digest_COPY_01&utm_medium=email&utm_term=0_633e82444a-47d54758eb-290674993&ct=t(Daily_Digest_COPY_01).

2. Kampwirth, Karen, *Women and Guerilla Movements: Nicaragua, El Salvador, Chiapas, Cuba.* (University Park, PA: Pennsylvania State University Press, 2002), 137-155.

3 Sergio Ramírez, *Adiós Muchachos: A Memoir of the Sandinista Revolution.* (Translated by Stacey Alba D. Skar). (Durham: Duke University Press, 2012), 199-205.

4. Karen Kampwirth, "Gender Politics in Nicaragua: Feminism, Antifeminism, and the Return of Daniel Ortega," in *Women's Activism in Latin America and the Caribbean: Engendering Social Justice, Democratizing Citizenship*, eds. Elizabeth Maier and Nathalie Lebon (New Brunswick, NJ: Rutgers University Press, 2010), 111.

5. Carlos Vilas, *The Sandinista Revolution: National Liberation and Social Transformation in Central America.* (NY: Monthly Review Press, 1986), 219.

6. Ibid., 214.

7. Ibid., 224.

8. Ibid., 148.

9. Thomas W. Walker, ed., *Nicaragua Without Illusions: Regime Transition and Structural Adjustment in the 1990s.* (Wilmington, DE: Scholarly Resources, 1997), 10.

10. Karen Kampwirth, "Gender Politics in Nicaragua: Feminism, Antifeminism, and the Return of Daniel Ortega," 113.

11. Ibid.

12. Ibid., 114

13. For information on the NGOs that have thus far been canceled by the Ortega Murillo regime, i.e., when they were cancelled, the name of the entity, and corresponding acronym, see article in confidencial.com, "Las fundaciones y asociaciones afectadas promovían los derechos humanos, la democracia, la salud, la educación, el desarrollo social y económico," March 1, 2022, accessible at https://www.confidencial.com.ni/nacion/guillotina-contra-oeneges-mas-de-110-personerias-juridicas-canceladas-por-daniel-ortega/. The Ortega Murilla regime closed seven private universities and seven international universities; see article, "HE in crisis—What role for the global academic community?" accessible at https://www.universityworldnews.com/post.php?story=2022090608434870

14. "Sandra Ramos: Es una embestida política, pero el María Elena Cuadra no son cuatro paredes," news article in artículo66.com, February 15, 2022, accessible at https://www.articulo66.com/2022/02/15/movimiento-maria-elena-cuadra-nicaragua-cierre-ong-regimen-daniel-ortega/. Also, see the article in English, "Government shuts down two more feminist organizations: FUNDEMUNI and the María Elena Cuadra Women's Movement," by the Iniciativa Mesoamericana de Mujeres Defensoras de Derechos Humanos, im-defensoras.org, February 16, 2022, accessible at http://im-defensoras.org/2022/02/whrd-alert-nicaragua-government-shuts-down-two-more-feminist-organizations-fundemuni-and-the-maria-elena-cuadra-womens-movement/.

15. Twitter post by @OndaLocal, February 15, 2022, ondalocal.com, accessible at https://twitter.com/OndaLocal/status/1493729063147646979.

16. As an example of the trial proceedings, see report, "Briefing Note on the Trial of Juan Sebastián Chamorro and Félix Maradiaga," February-

March 2022, in English and Spanish, accessible at https://www.perseus-strategies.com/wp-content/uploads/2022/03/trial-summary-report-03.03.22_VERSION-FINAL_eng_esp-1.pdf, and the YouTube video via Jared Genser, an international lawyer, via his Twitter: @JaredGenser, accessible at https://youtu.be/q_NJlj2598E. See also confidencial,com.ni, March 5, 2022, article, "Cómo selecciona el régimen a los fiscales que acusan a los preso políticos," on how prosecutors are selected to preside in the trials of political prisoners, selected through a process initiated by the Attorney General Ana Julia Guido Ochoa who was sanctioned by the U.S. in 2020 for the formation of a judicial entity to work with the National Police on fabricating charges against political prisoners and their families. Article accessible at https://www.confidencial.com.ni/politica/como-selecciona-el-regimen-a-los-fiscales-que-acusan-a-los-presos-politicos/.

17. The previous chapter includes brief descriptions on the following women: ***Dora María Tellez, Ana Margarita Vijil, Suyén Barahona***, and ***Violeta Granero, Maria Oviedo, María Fernanda Flores, María Esperanza Sánchez García, Karla Escobar***, and ***Julia Hernández Arévalo.***

18. "Tamara Dávila: Esto va a volver a estallar. Es insostenible vivir en estas condiciones," coyuntura.co, COYUNTURA, June 6, 2021, accessible at https://www.coyuntura.co/post/tamara-dávila-esto-va-a-volver-a-estallar-es-insostenible-vivir-en-estas-condiciones.

19. See "Mensaje de Tamara Dávila," message by Tamara Dávila posted on Twitter by @MaryChelis, on February 24, 2022, accessible at https://twitter.com/MaryChelis/status/1496832163785936898.

20. "Mujeres de Nicaragua luchan por la igualdad y la no violencia," Duyerling Ríos, on ondalocalni.com, Onda Local, March 6, 2020, podcast accessible at https://ondalocalni.com/galeria/audios/reportajes/551-mujeres-nicaragua-igualdad-violencia/.

21. See information about Zoilamérica's declarations in Chapter Five.

22. "Abuso sexual, un mal silenciado en la guerra de los 80," Indiana Cajina, nicaraguainvestiga.com, Nicaragua Investiga, April 24, 2020, accessible at https://nicaraguainvestiga.com/memoria/29136-el-abuso-sexual-un-mal-silenciado-en-la-guerra-de-los-80/.

23. Ibid.

24. See Dore, E. (2000). Property households and public regulations of domestic life. In Dore, E., & Molyneux, M. (Eds.). (2000). *Hidden histories of gender and the state in Latin America*. Durham, NC: Duke University Press.

25. Story originally published in: https://mujereseimpunidadnic.com/cuando-la-violencia-machista-mata-tambien-a-la-mediacion Please note that this page may no longer be accessible.

26. The Comisarías de Mujeres was originally established in 1993 to specifically focus on violence against women, then were completely shuttered in 2016. In early 2020, Murillo ordered the re-openings of similar organizations without the specialty care needed to work with women who have experienced violence in their homes.

27. "El femicida de El Portón," Duyerling Ríos, ondalocalni.com, Onda Local, November 25, 2020, podcast accessible at https://ondalocalni.com/galeria/audios/podcast/622-femicidios-nicaragua-violencia-machista/.

28. (Ley 779) Ley Integral Contra la Violencia hacia las Mujeres was passed by the National Assembly in 2012; a year later the Supreme Court added the reforms that included the process of mediation.

29. "¿A qué se enfrentan las nicaragüenses en el mundo laboral?" Duyerling Ríos, ondalocalni.com, Onda Local, November 2020, https://ondalocal.com.ni/multimedia/30-mujeres-desigualdad-laboral-nicaragua/.

30. See information on *ILO 190*, accessible at https://www.ilo.org/global/topics/violence-harassment/lang--en/index.htm

31. "Mujeres cooperativistas apuestan por el empoderamiento económico," ondalocalni.com, Ondalocal.com, February 19, 2022, accessible at https://ondalocalni.com/galeria/audios/podcast/799-mujeres-cooperativistas-apuestan-empoderamiento-economico/

32. "Los derechos de las mujeres, qué lugar ocupan en las agendas políticas," October 23, 2020, a podcast episode by ondalocalin.com that summarizes some of the key issues confronting women, including the ratification of CEDAW (Committee on the Elimination of Discrimination

Against Women), accessible
at https://ondalocal.com.ni/galeria/audios/reportajes/613-derechos-mujeres-nicaragua-agendas-politicas/.

33. "How the Green Wave Movement Did the Unthinkable in Latin America," by Ximena Casas, nytimes.com, The New York Times, November 1, 2021, accessible
at https://www.nytimes.com/2021/11/01/opinion/abortion-latin-america.html.

34. "The Key Argument on Abortion That Changed Everything in Colombia," by Catalina Martínez Coral, nytimes, The New York Times, March, 14, 2022, accessible
at https://www.nytimes.com/2022/03/14/opinion/latin-america-colombia-abortion.html?campaign_id=39&emc=edit_ty_20220314&instance_id=557 40&nl=opinion-today®i_id=35815915&segment_id=85517&te=1&user_id=a2a47b53a 1398e2b788287d4c1e0a8f8.

35. "Nicas rompen el silencio ante la violencia machista," by Duyerling Ríos, ondalocalni.com, Onda Local, April 22, 2020, accessible at https://ondalocal.com.ni/noticias/908-mujeres-rompen-silencio-ante-violencia-machista/. Please note that Amaya Coppens was recipient of the International Woman of Courage Award in 2020. Information accessible at https://ni.usembassy.gov/2020-international-women-of-courage-award-recipients-announced/.

36. "Feministas nicaragüenses en la sociedad denominada Azul y Blanco," by María José Díaz Reyes, ondalocalni.com, Onda Local, June 23, 2020, accessible at https://ondalocal.com.ni/opinion/151-rupturas-feministas-nicaraguenses-sociedad-azul-blanco/.

37. Their acts of resistance are reminiscent of Bourdieu's notion of reflexivity, the "conscious, rational use of power to resist all various forms of subordination." See Bridget Fowler, Review of *Bourdieu's Turn to La Domination Masculine*, by Pierre Bourdieu. *Contemporary Sociology 28*, no. 4 (1999): 478–82, accessible at https://doi.org/10.2307/2655352.

Conclusion (pp.228-234)

1. The Iniciativa Mesoamericana de Mujeres Defensoras de Derechos Humanos (IM-Defensoras), a non-profit organization founded in 2010, has the purpose of providing a comprehensive response to the violence against female human rights defenders in the (Mesoamerican) region that includes El Salvador, Guatemala, Honduras, Mexico, and Nicaragua.

2. For more information, see https://im-defensoras.org/trayectoria/.

3. Elvira Cuadra Lira, "Quebrar el cuerpo, quebrar el alma: La reconfiguración de las violencias hacia las mujeres en Nicaragua," Centro Trandisciplinarios de Centroamerica, 2022. According to the documentation, 40 percent of women, ages 15-49 has suffered some form of violence, including femicides. Report accessible at https://www.cetcam.org/wp-content/uploads/2022/10/CETCAM-INVESTIGACION-191022.pdf and YouTube, https://youtu.be/TYb7yxxtwFs.

4. "Perseguidos por defender y resistir: Criminalización de mujeres defensoras de derechos humanos en Honduras, México, y Nicaragua" CEJIL and Iniciativa Mesoamericana de Mujeres Defensoras de Derechos Humanos, 2022. CEJIL (also known as el Sístema Interamericano de Derechos Humanos) was founded thirty years ago by the Organización de los Estados Americanos (OEA) and consists of the Comisión Interamericano de Derechos Humanos (CIDH) and la Corte Interamericana de Derechos Humanos (Corte IDH). The publication is accessible at https://im-defensoras.org/wp-content/uploads/2022/11/IMD-Perseguidas-Ni-4rd-Final-1.pdf.

5. "Perseguidos por defender y resistir: Criminalización de mujeres defensoras de derechos humanos en Honduras, México, y Nicaragua," 19.

6. "Condenan a 2 años de cárcel comutables a la defensora maya Q'eqchi María Choc" Iniciativa Mesoamericana de Mujeres Defensoras de Derechos Humanos, 2022. Article is accessible at https://im-defensoras.org/2022/06/alerta-defensoras-guatemala-condenan-a-2-anos-de-carcel-conmutables-a-la-defensora-maya-qeqchi-maria-choc/.

7. Lara Dopazao Ruibal, "María Cuc Choc: El corazón en alto" Iniciativa Mesoamericana de Mujeres Defensoras de Derechos Humanos,

2021. The article is accessible at https://im-defensoras.org/wp-content/uploads/2021/04/Maria-Cuc-Choc-el-corazon-en-alto_online.pdf.

8. "Wounds Reoponed: Impacts of Democratic Backsliding on Human Rights in Guatemala: 2022 Emergency Human Rights Delegation Report" Guatemala Human Rights Commission, 27.

9. "Defendiendo derechos humanos en contextos de crisis: Analisis de caos de agresiones contra personas defensoras y periodistas 2021-2022" Mesa Por el Derecho a Defender Derechos, 2022. The Executive Summary is accessible at https://im-defensoras.org/2022/09/mesa-por-el-derecho-a-defender-derechos-presenta-informe-sobre-agresiones-contra-personas-defensoras-y-periodistas-2021-2022-en-el-salvador/.

10. See article, "En El Salvador, la violencia digital es violencia estatal," Iniciativa Mesoamericana de Mujeres Defensoras de Derechos Humanos, 2022, accessible at https://im-defensoras.org/2022/10/pronunciamiento-en-el-salvador-la-violencia-digital-es-violencia-de-estado/.

11. "Defendiendo derechos humanos en contextos de crisis." 12. "Aquí se obedece: Analisis del poder local," urnasabiertas.com, https://urnasabiertas.com/wp-content/uploads/2022/10/Analisis-del-poder-local-Informe-4.pdf. See the English language report, https://urnasabiertas.com/wp-content/uploads/2021/10/Resumen-Ejecutivo-ESP-ING.pdf.

13. "Perseguidos por defender y resistir: Criminalización de mujeres defensoras de derechos humanos en Honduras, México, y Nicaragua."

AUTHOR'S BIO

Irma N. Guadarrama holds a Ph.D. from the College of Education at the University of Texas at Austin, specializing in Language and Culture, Interdisciplinary Studies with an emphasis in Bilingual and ESL Education. She also earned a Master of Arts in Bicultural Bilingual Teacher Education from the University of Texas at San Antonio and a Bachelor of Science in Elementary Education and Reading from Texas Christian University in Ft. Worth, Texas.

With over 45 years of experience working with children and their families from diverse backgrounds, I have dedicated my career to advocating for their educational needs. My undergraduate training in urban community-based education has shaped my educational philosophy, which combines classroom goals with those of community activism. At the Master's and doctoral levels, I focused on interdisciplinary fields of study, including social, cultural, linguistic, economic, and political aspects of education. As a tenured professor at the University of Houston, I developed a field-based, anthropological program in Yucatán, providing university students with opportunities for service learning experiences within the Maya community. Additionally, I conducted ethnographic research in Oaxaca and Guatemala, working with indigenous populations and volunteering with a women's group to develop a school for elementary children in a Quiché community.

Author's website: www.bilingualfrontera.com

www.ingramcontent.com/pod-product-compliance
Lightning Source LLC
Chambersburg PA
CBHW061622250726
48659CB00004B/1051